PENNSYLVANIA ELECTIONS

Revised Edition

John J. Kennedy

University Press of America,® Inc.
Lanham · Boulder · New York · Toronto · Plymouth, UK

Copyright © 2014 by
University Press of America,® Inc.
4501 Forbes Boulevard
Suite 200
Lanham, Maryland 20706
UPA Acquisitions Department (301) 459-3366

10 Thornbury Road
Plymouth PL6 7PP
United Kingdom

Library of Congress Control Number: 2014943552
ISBN: 978-0-7618-6442-4 (paperback : alk. paper)
eISBN: 978-0-7618-6443-1

FOR CLARE AND SHANNON,
WHO CONTINUALLY AMAZE ME

TABLE OF CONTENTS

LIST OF FIGURES

LIST OF TABLES

PREFACE

My earliest memory of Pennsylvania politics came as a young boy growing up in Catasauqua, a small town just outside of Allentown. I still recall a large billboard posted on Second and Race Streets, in big blue lettering proclaiming, "CASEY, A MAN ON YOUR SIDE—FOR A CHANGE." I'm not sure anymore whether it was for his campaign in either 1966 or 1970, but I do remember thinking at the time that it sure sounded nice. I still do.

Years later, after my interest in politics became more pronounced, I was drawn to elections at the national level, specifically the United States Senate. I had a number of theories on the question of candidate recruitment that would come to serve as the basis for my doctoral dissertation. However, when the time came it wasn't at the national level that I ended up researching, it was Pennsylvania, and this subsequently led to the publication of my first book entitled, *The Contemporary Pennsylvania Legislature* (1999). I found that studying politics within the state of Pennsylvania provided a significant relevancy historically while also possessing a tradition of colorful politicians that are unrivaled anywhere else.

The following project is the manifestation of a vision I first realized when I was back in graduate school well over a two decades ago. My goal was to undertake a systematic and thorough analysis of elections in Pennsylvania, focusing on voting trends across the state, while also developing a narrative of the people and places which have shaped those results. The first edition of this book, *Pennsylvania Elections, Statewide Contests from 1950-2004*, was the culmination of this effort. It is my hope that by combining the elements of political history, and political geography, and quantitative political science, this book will both pique the interest of those interested in the state's politics today, while also serving as a reference source for future scholars. This edition updates the statewide elections which have taken place in the intervening years, in total 106 individual statewide races are analyzed and election data compiled within each of the state's 67 counties reported.

While plowing through this archival information, a number of memories from my own youth were recalled. Names such as Leonard Staisey, Ernest Kline, Herb Denenberg and Bud Haabestad were just a few of those that had slipped away a long time ago only to be revived in my mind once again. The various scandals that rocked the state during the 1970s were certainly another memory as well. Even the old Sunday morning public affairs program featuring the state's two U.S. Senators, Joe Clark and Hugh Scott discussing and debating the issues of the day could be vaguely recalled. It was pleasure to go back and relive these events and others from my youths. I only hope the reader finds as much enjoyment in reading what follows as I certainly did in writing it.

It's also unfortunate to report the loss of several historic figures in Pennsylvania that are discussed within that have passed since the first edition of this book was published ten years ago. This includes the state's longest serving United States Senator Arlen Specter. Also, former Governors George Leader, Bill Scranton, and Ray Shafer have left us. Lieutenant Governor Ernest Kline, State Treasurer and Lieutenant Governor Katherine Baker Knoll as well. In addition, a few individuals who didn't win the statewide prize must also be mentioned. This includes former the Mayor of Pittsburgh and also nominee for Governor and United States Senate Pete Flaherty, former Congressman and candidate for the United States Senate Bob Edgar, State Senator and nominee for Attorney General Michael O'Pake, and State Senator and candidate for Lieutenant Governor, Harold Mowery. I apologize if I've overlooked anyone, certainly no slight was intended.

I want to thank my publisher, University Press of America, and especially Nicolette Amstutz, for the guidance that she provided through completion of this project. I also want to offer my sincerest appreciation to everyone in the West Chester University community who has been so supportive of all my endeavors throughout the years. In particular, I want to extend my gratitude to the chair of the Political Science Department, Dr. Frauke Schnell. Additionally, I want to acknowledge our administrative assistant Tara Easterling, for generously helping me along the way, particularly in formatting the tables. I also want to thank Dr. Kristen Crossney and Anthony Thomas from the Geography Department who did a great job with the putting together the state maps. And to all the students I've taught at West Chester University, particularly those in my Pennsylvania Politics classes who've been so enthusiastic to learn about our state's great political history. It's been a pleasure to be your instructor.

Foremost, I want to thank my family for their continued support and encouragement. First, to my mom, Helen Kennedy, whose love and energy are limitless, and to my dad, Robert Kennedy, whose memory is always present. To Kelli, my wife and always best friend, I'm so fortunate to be able to spend my life with you. Finally, to Clare and Shannon, our sweet, smart, athletic, and beautiful daughters of Pennsylvania, whose laughter and love brings me joy and happiness each day.

John J. Kennedy
June, 2014

AUTHOR'S NOTES
ON DATA COLLECTION

A few items about the presentation of this book should be mentioned. First, because the Democrats were the majority party in the state for most of the past 64 years, all of the data in the tables are presented from the Democratic Party perspective. This is done purely for the sake of clarity—and for no other reason. It is far easier to analyze long-term data when using the same base point.

Additionally, third parties and other minor parties are totally eliminated from the tabulations. All the election information presented in the tables is based on the share of the two-party vote, not on the total percentages. However, because of Pennsylvania's tradition of strong political parties (and being a closed-primary state), a relatively small number of voters are registered as anything but Republicans or Democrats. Also, in only a few instances have third-party candidates played an important role in a statewide election (and those are mentioned in the narrative). Once again, however, the desire to present what is an abundant amount of information in the clearest way possible ultimately prevailed. Finally, names of the victorious candidates are listed first in all of the subheadings throughout the book.

The election results were drawn from appropriate issues of *The Pennsylvania Manual*, with one exception. The 1964 Schuylkill County results needed to be delivered by that county's Bureau of Elections, as they were not listed in the Manual. Apart from this book, I also depended upon archival information drawn from a number of the state's newspapers, in particular, *The Philadelphia Inquirer, The Pittsburgh Post-Gazette, The Allentown Morning Call, The Harrisburg Patriot, the Wilkes-Barre Times Leader,* and *The York Dispatch.*

CHAPTER ONE

THE POLITICAL GEOGRAPHY OF PENNSYLVANIA

The roughly one hundred years of Pennsylvania politics from the time the Civil War ended in 1865 until 1950, the year this project begins, can be summarized by two main points. One, strong party organizations dominated the political system. Whether these organizations were operating in the public eye, as represented by elected office holders or were instead individuals who pulled the strings of power in back-room parlors, party bosses such as Simon Cameron, Matthew Quay, and Boies Penrose (each of whom did both) dominated Pennsylvania. Two, it wasn't political parties in general that were in control; it was more specifically the Republican Party that had total hegemony over the government of Pennsylvania.

Democrats were on the defensive, and their Republican opponents would seldom hesitate to wave the bloody shirt of the Civil War if the need arose. Pennsylvania, the state whose soil was trod upon by a Confederate Army that reached its high-water mark on the battlefield at Gettysburg, located in Adams County, was receptive to the charge linking the Democrats to the old south. Additionally, the various forces that propelled the state's economy also favored the Republican Party. The GOP was closely aligned with all of the major economic powers in the state: manufacturing, railroads, and oil. Those forces combined to produce a political system that state historian Wayland F. Dunaway described in 1948 as, other than Maine and Vermont, the most consistently Republican state in the union.

The scant Democratic support that did exist was generally isolated to certain hardscrabble pockets in the southwestern and northeastern parts of the state. In the presidential election of 1928, Democratic candidate Al Smith carried just 3 of the state's 67 counties (Elk, Lackawanna, and Luzerne). Four years later, on the precipice of the New Deal, Democrats held a majority of registered voters in just 6 counties (Berks, Columbia, Fulton, Greene, Monroe, and Northampton), and could claim just 22 percent of the state's registered voters. In that 1932 election, which triggered a remaking of much of the nation's political map, Pennsylvania held firm. It was one of only five states—and the only one outside New England—that supported President Herbert Hoover over Franklin D. Roosevelt. The Republican incumbent carried 40 counties in all, including Philadelphia, en route to a 5-point victory. While the popularity of Roosevelt's administration would soon propel the Democrats to majority status throughout much of the nation, Pennsylvania would remain stubbornly committed to the GOP.

However, the New Deal coalition that FDR had assembled elsewhere would soon begin to meld here, and by 1936 the second most populous county, Allegheny, would tip to the Democrats. Just four years earlier, the Republicans had held a 375,000-person edge among that county's registered voters. The largest city in the state was a tougher sell, however. Philadelphia, home to thousands on the Republican Party payroll resisted, although city voters began supporting Democratic presidential candidates as early as 1936. It wasn't until voters became sufficiently disgusted enough with the type of corruption oftentimes fostered by unchecked power, that the Republican machine at mid-century finally lost its grip. Democrat Joe Clark's mayoral victory in 1951 turned around the fortunes of the two major parties in Philadelphia almost overnight. By 1958, the Democrats had increased their share of the registered vote total to 56 percent, up from the 30 percent they had held just eight years earlier.

For the next several decades, this pattern for the state had been pretty much solidified. Philadelphia and southwestern Pennsylvania (centered in Pittsburgh) would serve as the base of the Democratic Party, although they are often at odds with one another over ideology (Philadelphia being generally more liberal) and basic turf issues. Conversely, the Philadelphia suburbs and the vast central "T" of the state, an area that contains 47 counties would be staunchly Republican. The industrial northeast, like the southwest, historically possessed a strong labor base and leaned Democratic. As in the southwest, however, many northeastern voters are more socially conservative than those in the Philadelphia area, thus making voting behavior less predictable.

In recent years there have been some changes which have placed the state on the verge of a new partisan realignment. Not much has changed in Philadelphia and with a local GOP organization on what could only be described as life-support; the fact is that the city has become even more Democratic in recent years. The same can be said of central Pennsylvania, with the Republicans still in control. The northeast has shifted slightly and become a little more Democratic overall than it once was, but the difference is relatively minor, and in some areas in the region the GOP has improved its position.

However, the most significant development relating to politics in Pennsylvania over the past quarter century has been the movement in the suburbs of Philadelphia to an area that now marginally favors the Democrats. Once the bedrock of the state GOP (certainly financially), the shift across these four counties has amplified the Democratic registration advantage in the state and is the major reason why they've carried six straight presidential elections. On the other hand, Republicans are increasingly becoming successful in the southwest, chipping away at Democratic support within the heart of their traditional base. While the erosion has been less pronounced and the population effected is not yet sufficient to counter their losses in the southeast, it does provide the Republicans with some optimism for a future resurgence.

As Figure 1.1 illustrates, the Republicans dominated Pennsylvania's political map in 1950. They had a majority of registered voters in 53 counties across the Commonwealth—and 59 percent of registered voters. Once Philadelphia fell to the Democrats in 1951, however, the state's landscape began to change practically overnight. A decade later, when John F. Kennedy headed their ticket and became the first Democrat since FDR to carry the state, Democrats had even taken a slight advantage. Also, the number of counties where the Republicans had the majority had dipped to 47, although that still constituted 70 percent of the 67-county total.

Fig 1-1. Pennsylvania Counties by Majority Party 1950

The GOP momentarily regained the edge in registered voters by the late 1960s, but by the start of the next decade the Democrats had regained control, and since then they have yet to relinquish it. In fact, during the 1970s, the Democrats achieved a high of 58 percent of registered voters statewide. The number of Republican-controlled counties at that time had also declined—to just 38. Although that was still the majority of counties, the Democrats had gained control of such former GOP bastions as Bucks County in the southeast (although this was brief) and a number of unlikely central Pennsylvania counties, such as Cameron, Centre, Clarion, and Montour.

The Republicans began to chip away at the Democratic edge throughout the 1980s, and by 1990 the Democratic lead was down to 54–46 percent—where it would basically remain until 2006. However, two years later, a combination of forces including the sweeping changes in the southeast and the presidential primary battle between Barack Obama and Hillary Clinton propelled the Democrats to that 58 percent mark again—a figure that remains to this day. As Figure 1.2 shows, by 2012, the Democrats had also chipped away at the GOP county edge, picking up several along the way, so that has now been reduced to a 41/26 Republicans advantage. Clearly, the once-long-suffering Democratic Party has securely settled into its status as the majority party in the state.

Fig 1-2. Pennsylvania Counties by Majority Party 2012

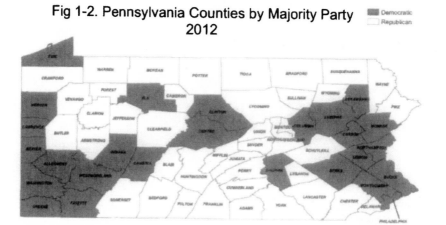

However, even though the Democrats have been the majority party for 26 of the 32 election cycles covered in this book (and for all of the past 22), their registration advantage hasn't always translated to actually winning elections. In top-tier races, which include Presidential, United States Senate, and Pennsylvania Gubernatorial contests, the Republicans have won (or in the case of presidential races, carried the state) in 32 of the 55 elections held, a 58 percent success rate (Table 1.1). The Democrats recent domination in second-tier contests has enabled them to take a slight 28-23 overall in those matches. These include the three offices (State Treasurer, Auditor General, and Attorney General) that are currently elected by the voters and the two others that haven't been since 1970 (Lieutenant Governor and Internal Affairs). Overall, the Republicans hold a very slim 55-51 advantage among all contests held since 1950, a 52 percent rate. So although the Democrats have been the majority party with regard to party registration for most of the period covered by this project, the actual electoral environment is actually very competitive between the two parties.

Table 1.1 Parties' Victories in State by Decade

	50-59		60-69		70-79		80-89	
	D	R	D	R	D	R	D	R
Top Tiered Party Victories	3	6	4	4	3	5	1	8
Second Tiered Party Victories	4	6	7	3	4	0	3	6
Totals	7	12	11	7	7	5	4	14

	90-99		00-09		10-12		Totals	
	D	R	D	R	D	R	D	R
Top Tiered Party Victories	4	5	6	2	2	2	23	32
Second-Tiered Party Victories	2	4	6	4	3	0	28	23
Totals	6	9	12	6	5	2	51	55

Another relevant point to consider about Pennsylvania, and one that affects not just statewide politics but also its national stature, relates to the state's population. In 1952, the first presidential election held during the period of this study, Republican Dwight D. Eisenhower captured Pennsylvania and the 32 electoral votes (the same number as California!) that went with it. By 2012, however, Barack Obama's victory netted the Democratic ticket only 20 electors (now 35 less than California), a 38 percent decline over the past 60-years.

Whereas Pennsylvania had a population of 10.49 million in 1950, the 2010 total was just 12.70 million, a gain of only 17 percent. In contrast, the population of the United States as a whole has changed from 151.3 million to 308.7 million, a 51 percent increase. Over the past sixty years, 23 counties across the Commonwealth have lost population. The biggest loser has been Cambria, with a 37 percent decline, followed by both Philadelphia and Schuylkill at 26 percent. While there are a few counties in the northeast or central Pennsylvania struggling to maintain their population base, the region hardest hit has been the southwest. Here, seven of the nine counties classified within the southwestern part of the state by this study have lost population. The political implications of this downward trend are enormous and will be examined in later chapters.

The counties that have experienced the largest population gains tend to be located in three specific areas of the state, the first being the four suburban counties that surround Philadelphia: Bucks, Chester, Delaware, and Montgomery. Another is a group of counties in south-central Pennsylvania, Adams, Cumberland, Franklin, Lancaster, and York, largely due to the in-migration of people from northern Maryland. The third area of the state with a growing population has also benefited from the relocation of out-of-state residents. Monroe, Pike, Wayne, and Wyoming counties, located in the far northeast corner of the state, have welcomed many new inhabitants who have arrived primarily from New York State. In fact, Pike County's 82 percent population increase is the largest recorded in the state since 1950. Nevertheless, despite these pockets of growth, a stagnant population base has plagued the Commonwealth overall, particularly when compared to states located in the Sunbelt. As proof, Pennsylvania's share of the nation's population stood at just 4.36 percent in 2010 compared with 6.94 percent back in 1950.

The rest of this chapter focuses on each of Pennsylvania's five political regions, as detailed in Figure 1.3. It begins with a discussion of southeastern Pennsylvania, which contains two of those regions, Philadelphia and its four suburban counties. The interrelatedness of those five counties dictates that they must be viewed as a whole. Another region sits at the opposite end of the Commonwealth: the nine counties of the southwest, anchored by Allegheny. Another region comprises the six counties of northeastern Pennsylvania, which often has served as an accurate barometer of the state's overall vote. Finally, the chapter concludes with an overview of central Pennsylvania, what is referred to in this book as the central "T"—47 counties in all, many of which are both overwhelmingly rural and Republican.

Fig 1-3. Pennsylvania Political Regions

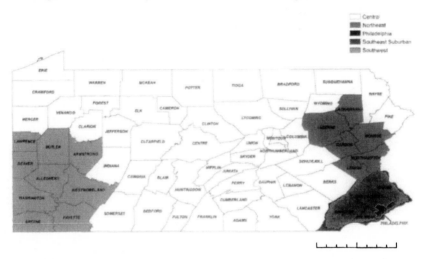

SOUTHEASTERN PENNSYLVANIA

When discussing the politics of southeastern Pennsylvania, one must begin by addressing voter migration. Although there is migration of the sort previously mentioned—the preponderance of people relocating to sunnier climates in the southern or western United States—there is another type of migration that is particularly relevant to Pennsylvania's internal politics. This involves individuals fleeing large cities and moving to their surrounding suburbs. Just as the national shift toward the Sunbelt has important political implications, suburban flight has had its consequences as well. Cities all across the nation have watched their populations erode over the past sixty years, largely because of their residents' relocating to suburban subdivisions. And just as political clout has shifted nationally from north to south, within the states themselves it has likewise headed from large cities to their expanding suburban communities.

Several decades ago, in the early years of this national migration, two competing theories were offered to explain why the Republican Party could be expected to eventually dominate the newly burgeoning suburbs. One theory, *conversion*, suggested that as central city Democrats moved out to Republican-dominated suburbs, many would ultimately shift their allegiances to the GOP in order to minimize partisan cross-pressures. Furthermore, many of them would become more conscious of the impact of government once they were required to pay the property taxes needed to support it. That would minimize the appeal of some government-run programs. Those Democrats would therefore find themselves influenced—by both their new status and their new neighbors—to become more conservative.

Another theory of suburban voter migration, propagated a few years later, became known as *transplantation*. Although the theory has two varieties, their differences appear subtle and unlikely to make a significant impact in the long run. One view of transplantation suggests that the new suburbanites were primarily Republican partisans even before they moved. Rather than being converted Democrats, they were simply transplanted Republicans. The alternative form of the transplantation theory offers that it was upwardly mobile Democrats who were moving to suburbia in the first place; and being upwardly mobile, they were ripe to be picked off by the GOP. Essentially, because the change in attitudes occurred before the moved, they could also be characterized as transplanted Republicans rather than as converted Democrats. In other words, they were already Republicans but didn't know it yet.

If conversion had indeed materialized, its ramifications would have spelled serious political trouble for the Democratic Party throughout the nation, as even party loyalists switched to suit their new suburban lifestyle. Conversely, if transplantation had been the rule, its impact would have been far less deleterious to the Democrats. The reason is that the newly registered Republicans had probably been voting Republican anyway. The net effect would have been that within a region there would largely have been a maintaining of the political status quo.

In recent years, however, a new development has emerged, and it seems to best describe the current state of the city/suburban political dichotomy. Specifically, what if, despite their move to the suburbs, those voters took their voting habits with them and maintained their Democratic identification? That would do more than simply maintain the status quo—it would produce a net gain for the Democrats in the region. In fact, in recent years, this is what appears to have occurred, as the once overwhelmingly Republican suburbs now face much stronger political competition, and in some cases been overtaken as the Democrats have made much better gains among these new voters. In addition, the central city, Philadelphia, continues to become even more one-sidedly Democratic, partly fueled by the political leanings of people who are moving into the city. Without question, this scenario produces quite a departure from what many predicted a half century ago.

What is clear, however, is that Philadelphia's political clout has been severely weakened over the years. A city that in the 1950s had as many as six U. S. Congressional seats can now claim only two in which the majority of the districts resident reside within the city. Not surprisingly, Philadelphia has also suffered a severe deterioration of its political leverage in southeastern Pennsylvania. As Table 1.2 shows, in 1950, 67 percent of registered voters in the five-county southeastern Pennsylvania region lived in Philadelphia County (the city and county boundaries coincide). Delaware County was the second highest, with 14 percent, and Montgomery was third, with 11 percent. The remaining two counties, the lightly populated Bucks and Chester counties, each had only 4 percent of the region's population. The 1950s marked Philadelphia's high point. From then on, Philadelphia experienced a slow, consistent decline in its share of the region's population.

Table 1.2 Registration Percentage of Southeast Region by County

	1950	1952	1954	1956	1958	1960	1962	1964
Philadelphia	67%	65%	63%	61%	59%	57%	56%	56%
Bucks	4%	4%	5%	6%	7%	8%	8%	8%
Chester	4%	4%	4%	5%	5%	5%	5%	5%
Delaware	14%	15%	15%	16%	16%	16%	16%	16%
Montgomery	11%	12%	12%	13%	13%	14%	15%	15%
Suburban Totals	**33%**	**35%**	**37%**	**39%**	**41%**	**43%**	**44%**	**44%**

	1966	1968	1970	1972	1974	1976	1978	1980
Philadelphia	55%	53%	52%	51%	50%	51%	51%	52%
Bucks	8%	9%	9%	10%	10%	10%	10%	12%
Chester	6%	6%	6%	6%	7%	7%	7%	7%
Delaware	16%	16%	17%	17%	17%	17%	16%	16%
Montgomery	15%	16%	16%	16%	17%	16%	16%	17%
Suburban Totals	**45%**	**47%**	**48%**	**49%**	**50%**	**49%**	**49%**	**48%**

	1982	1984	1986	1988	1990	1992	1994	1996
Philadelphia	49%	51%	47%	49%	46%	44%	42%	42%
Bucks	12%	12%	13%	12%	13%	14%	14%	14%
Chester	7%	7%	8%	8%	9%	9%	10%	10%
Delaware	16%	15%	16%	15%	15%	16%	16%	15%
Montgomery	16%	15%	16%	16%	17%	17%	18%	19%
Suburban Total	**51%**	**49%**	**53%**	**51%**	**54%**	**56%**	**58%**	**58%**

	1998	2000	2002	2004	2006	2008	2010	2012
Philadelphia	41%	41%	41%	40%	40%	40%	39%	40%
Bucks	14%	15%	15%	16%	15%	15%	15%	15%
Chester	10%	11%	11%	11%	11%	11%	11%	11%
Delaware	15%	15%	15%	14%	15%	14%	14%	14%
Montgomery	19%	19%	19%	20%	20%	20%	20%	19%
Suburban Totals	**59%**	**59%**	**59%**	**60%**	**60%**	**60%**	**61%**	**60%**

By 1960, Philadelphia's share of the region's population would drop to 57 percent, with each of the four surrounding counties experiencing a slight gain. The 1950s are especially important, because they marked not only the beginning of Philadelphia's decline but also the peak growth decade for three of the four suburban counties (Chester County did not experience its peak growth decade until the 1960s). Overall, Montgomery County enjoyed the strongest growth, placing it in a position to rival Delaware as the suburbs' most populous county.

Southeastern Pennsylvania reached another milestone a little more than two decades later. In 1982, for the first time, more registered voters lived in the four suburban counties than in the city, this while Philadelphia's share of the region's registered voters dropped to 49 percent. Although the city had gained voters two years later, that quickly reversed, and by 1986 the suburbs could claim 53 percent of the region's voters. It is highly unlikely that this trend will change in the foreseeable future.

By 2010, Philadelphia's share of the southeastern Pennsylvania vote had slipped to just 39 percent. It should be noted, however, that in recent years the hemorrhaging appears to have abated. In fact, the decade which began in 2000 is the first since the 1940s that the city witnessed an actually increase in its overall raw numbers. This enabled it to even tick back up a point in its overall share of the region's registered voters. This is certainly welcome news for city officials and supporters (and also Democrats) as they try to maintain their political clout.

Of the suburban counties, Montgomery has become the largest vote producer, with 19 percent of the region's registered voters. In contrast, Delaware County has the distinction of being the only suburban county to see its share of the vote stagnate during the past half century. In 1986, it reached a high of 16 percent, and after leveling off for a period of years, has now begun to lose pace with the other suburbs, containing just 14 percent of the region's registered voters today. The other two counties, Bucks and Chester, which totaled just 4 percent of the registered voters in 1950, have both shown steady increases. Bucks County, which now contains 15 percent of the region's voters, has even passed Delaware County for second place among the suburban counties. Chester County, whose development lagged behind the other three counties for years, can now claim 11 percent. In fact, Chester County had the fastest growth in recent years. Containing a large reservoir of land just waiting to be developed, Chester County (the largest of the five southeastern counties in actual land area) appears ready to become an even greater force in the region's political system.

Today it is hard to believe that Philadelphia was ever anything but a Democratic city. In 1950, however, the GOP was supreme, not only in the city and its four suburbs but also across almost the entire Commonwealth. The linchpin to Republican control was its continued domination of Philadelphia. While similar cities, such as Cleveland, Detroit and St. Louis, eventually followed Franklin D. Roosevelt into the Democratic Party, Philadelphia partisans remained loyal to the GOP. Although FDR had carried the city as far back as 1936, registration and voting behavior in more localized contests did not immediately follow. The time lag between voting behavior and partisan realignment is not unusual. In recent decades, a similar phenomenon has occurred in the once overwhelmingly Democratic South. The tendency is for voters to first cross party lines when selecting a president and then, over a period of years, begin moving down to statewide elections, then to congressional elections, and ultimately to local elections. Only at that point are many voters finally willing to change their formal party allegiance.

But in Pennsylvania, with its history of boss rule and political patronage, the risks of changing one's party identification could be quite high, even to the point of jeopardizing one's job. As Table 1.3 illustrates, as late as 1950, the Democratic Party could claim only 30 percent of the registered two-party vote. (Again, in this and other tables, third parties and independents do not appear. The two-party vote share is simply the total of the Democratic and Republican numbers divided by the Democratic figure.) Democratic Party fortunes were even bleaker in the suburbs. The best example of Democratic futility was Delaware County, where the state's most powerful Republican political machine held Democratic registration to just 10 percent, an astonishingly low number.

Table 1.3 Democratic Share of Two-Party Registration Totals, Southeastern Pennsylvania

	1950	1952	1954	1956	1958	1960	1962	1964
Philadelphia	30%	36%	38%	49%	54%	59%	62%	63%
Bucks	28%	28%	31%	39%	42%	44%	45%	45%
Chester	22%	21%	21%	25%	26%	27%	28%	28%
Delaware	10%	13%	13%	17%	19%	21%	22%	23%
Montgomery	19%	19%	18%	21%	23%	25%	26%	27%
Suburban Totals	**17%**	**18%**	**18%**	**23%**	**25%**	**27%**	**28%**	**29%**
Southeast Totals	**26%**	**30%**	**31%**	**38%**	**42%**	**45%**	**47%**	**48%**
State Totals	**41%**	**41%**	**41%**	**46%**	**48%**	**50%**	**52%**	**51%**

	1966	1968	1970	1972	1974	1976	1978	1980
Philadelphia	62%	61%	60%	65%	68%	76%	79%	78%
Bucks	45%	43%	43%	46%	48%	51%	51%	48%
Chester	28%	27%	26%	29%	30%	32%	33%	30%
Delaware	23%	21%	21%	25%	25%	28%	28%	28%
Montgomery	27%	26%	26%	30%	31%	33%	34%	33%
Suburban Totals	**29%**	**28%**	**28%**	**31%**	**32%**	**35%**	**36%**	**34%**
Southeast Totals	**47%**	**45%**	**44%**	**49%**	**50%**	**56%**	**58%**	**54%**
State Totals	**51%**	**49%**	**50%**	**53%**	**54%**	**57%**	**58%**	**56%**

	1982	1984	1986	1988	1990	1992	1994	1996
Philadelphia	78%	82%	80%	75%	73%	75%	76%	77%
Bucks	46%	46%	46%	44%	43%	43%	42%	42%
Chester	32%	31%	31%	29%	29%	31%	31%	32%
Delaware	28%	28%	28%	27%	26%	27%	28%	29%
Montgomery	33%	33%	33%	32%	31%	33%	34%	35%
Suburban Totals	**34%**	**34%**	**34%**	**33%**	**32%**	**34%**	**34%**	**35%**
Southeast Totals	**55%**	**58%**	**56%**	**53%**	**51%**	**52%**	**51%**	**53%**
State Totals	**56%**	**58%**	**56%**	**55%**	**54%**	**54%**	**54%**	**53%**

	1998	2000	2002	2004	2006	2008	2010	2012
Philadelphia	78%	79%	80%	82%	83%	86%	86%	87%
Bucks	42%	43%	44%	45%	46%	52%	52%	51%
Chester	32%	33%	34%	37%	37%	45%	46%	46%
Delaware	30%	32%	34%	38%	39%	47%	48%	50%
Montgomery	37%	39%	42%	44%	46%	52%	53%	54%
Suburban Totals	**36%**	**37%**	**39%**	**42%**	**43%**	**50%**	**50%**	**51%**
Southeast Totals	**53%**	**55%**	**56%**	**58%**	**59%**	**64%**	**64%**	**65%**
State Totals	**53%**	**53%**	**54%**	**54%**	**54%**	**58%**	**58%**	**58%**

After years of resisting the New Deal realignment, Philadelphia finally did fall to the Democrats. After Democrat George Leader broke the Republican lock on the governor's mansion in 1954, the expected realignment materialized, as voters no longer needed to fear political reprisals for changing their party allegiances. As Frank Sorauf remarked in his book *Party and Representation*, "only since 1950 have the Democrats of Pennsylvania shaken off some of the traditional party appeals and begun to create the coalition of social and economic interests that Franklin Roosevelt built nationally in the 1930s." And, once a Democratic trend (or any party trend) begins in a patronage-laden state such as Pennsylvania, political success breeds success. The incentive of nearly 50,000 political plum jobs attracts party registrants with a political "multiplier" effect."

By the end of Leader's term in 1958, the Democrats already had a majority of the registered voters in Philadelphia. Additionally, the Democratic Party's share of the vote increased in each of the suburban counties, particularly Bucks, where Democrats went from 28 percent to 42 percent in just eight years. By the time Leader's Democratic successor, Governor David Lawrence, left office in 1962, the change in party registration figures was even more dramatic. The Democrats share of the vote in Philadelphia had climbed to 62 percent, while Democrats' percentage throughout the region had expanded to 47 percent. That constitutes a 107 percent increase in little more than a decade. Buoyed by the presidential candidacy of John F. Kennedy in 1960, Democrats became the majority party statewide. Except for a brief period in the late 1960s, it is a claim they have yet to relinquish.

Party registration figures in southeastern Pennsylvania eventually stabilized, with the Republican Party holding a slight advantage. Then, another rupture—a presidential scandal in Washington known as Watergate—further shattered the GOP. In 1976, Democrats for the first time had a majority of registered voters in Bucks County (though it was temporary). Democratic gains in the other counties, although less impressive, were nevertheless consistent. By 1978, until recently the Democrats' high-water mark, they had 79 percent of the registered voters in Philadelphia and 58 percent in the southeast region.

Registration figures have for the most part stabilized over the course of the next several decades. By 2006, 83 percent of voters in Philadelphia County were registered Democrats, and the party also enjoyed a modest increase in Chester, in addition to more noticeable increases in Delaware and Montgomery. The only bad news for Democrats during this period was in Bucks, where the party had experienced a steady erosion of support. Overall, in the southeast, the Democrats could claim 67 percent of the two party registration totals.

Then the floodgates opened. A combination of factors, such as the in-migration issue previously discussed, as well as other demographic changes, the Barack Obama/Hillary Clinton primary battle, and even a damaging GOP internecine fight in Montgomery County between two rival factions, elevated the Democrats to highs in the suburbs that would have been previously deemed unthinkable. By the fall of 2008, the Democrats had jumped to 72 percent of the southeast and captured a majority in both Bucks and Montgomery, while closing the gap significantly in Chester and Delaware. In Philadelphia, the Democratic share of the two party registration totals increased to an incredible 86 percent. All of this allowed the Democrats to increase their overall advantage statewide by four points in just a two year period.

Republicans who had hoped the shift was temporary and would reverse itself have been disappointed in the years since. In fact, the numbers now appear to have stabilized in Philadelphia, Bucks and Chester, while Montgomery, were they now hold 54 percent, has continued to trend even more to the Democrats. The next domino which appears ready to fall is Delaware County. At the time of this writing, the two parties are now essentially tied, an increase for the Democrats of 16 percentage points from where they stood only a decade ago. All told, the Democrats have increased their party's share of registration in the region from a low of 26 percent in 1950 to 73 percent today, a change that can only be described as a thorough realignment across southeastern Pennsylvania.

The dramatic change which has taken place in the southeast is made clear when analyzing voting throughout the region over the past six decades. Democratic candidates have outperformed Republicans 69-37 in the 106 statewide elections held since 1950. What's particularly revealing is that after the two parties were evenly matched from 1950 to 1980; Republican candidates carried the five counties in 13 of the 18 elections held in the 1980s. Helped along by strong presidential and senatorial candidates, the GOP prevailed in eight of the nine top-tiered contests. Since then, however, it has been a virtual clean sweep for the Democrats. In the 1990s, their statewide candidates defeated their Republican rivals in 12 of the 15 races, and they have carried the southeast region in each of the 24 contests held since 2000. There is no question, that this change in the voting habits of southeastern Pennsylvanians is the most important development in statewide politics in decades. It will certainly have long-lasting implication for both parties if it continues at this pace.

SOUTHWESTERN PENNSYLVANIA

The traditional political base for the Democratic Party through more than a half century, southwestern Pennsylvania had, until recently, the largest concentration of registered Democrats in the state. The nine-county area, centered by Allegheny County and by Pittsburgh, the state's second largest city, is home to many of the blue-collar voters who have identified themselves as Democrats since the New Deal. Nevertheless, it has also been a prime source of many of their biggest electoral disappointments. Additionally, while southeastern Pennsylvanians have been trending more Democratic in recent years, their counterparts in the southwest have been heading in the opposite direction.

In the 1930s, Pittsburgh and its surrounding areas followed a political trend established in many other cities, shifting allegiances from the Republican Party to the Democratic Party as part of Franklin D. Roosevelt's New Deal coalition. (This contrasted with the state's largest city, Philadelphia, where the trend was delayed until the 1950s.) The blue-collar towns of the southwest provided a fertile ground for Democratic efforts to harvest votes. FDR carried the region in 1932 by more than 120,000 votes, even though Republican President Herbert Hoover carried Philadelphia and Pennsylvania.

Another difference between the state's two largest cities is that while Democrats dominate Philadelphia, the city was until recently surrounded by Republican-friendly voters in the suburbs. Democratic Pittsburgh, located within Allegheny County, contends with some wealthier suburban areas that vote Republican, but was more politically compatible with those encircling it. In fact, just outside Allegheny County are counties such as Washington, Greene, and Fayette, which have an even older and stronger Democratic Party tradition than Pittsburgh does itself.

Although all this may suggest an electoral boon for the Democrats in the southwest, such has not always been the case, especially recently. In key statewide elections of the past half-century, many of the Democrats' most bitter disappointments fall squarely on the backs of voters whom one would expect to be their strongest supporters, these southwestern voters.

Beginning in 1950, two-party registration totals tallied every two years illustrate how important southwestern Pennsylvania is to the Democratic Party in Pennsylvania (Table 1.4). That year, the starting point of this study, Democrats were at a huge disadvantage statewide—with only 41 percent of the voters—but they had 57 percent of registered voters in the southwest. By the time the Democrats finally reached a slight majority statewide in 1960, they had already climbed to 61 percent in the region. In the 1980s, while the GOP rolled to victory after victory in national elections, the Democrats improved their position in this region, achieving a high of 71 percent of registered voters in 1986. However, in recent years, the GOP has made some inroads, pulling the Democrats down to 65 percent by 2004, were it has remained the same ever since.

**Table 1.4 Democratic Share of Two-Party Registration Totals,
Southwestern Pennsylvania**

	1950	1952	1954	1956	1958	1960	1962	1964
Allegheny	59%	57%	57%	60%	61%	62%	64%	64%
Armstrong	38%	37%	38%	43%	44%	44%	46%	44%
Beaver	42%	41%	42%	48%	52%	54%	57%	59%
Butler	34%	34%	34%	36%	37%	39%	41%	42%
Fayette	63%	63%	64%	68%	70%	71%	73%	70%
Greene	72%	72%	73%	75%	76%	77%	78%	76%
Lawrence	32%	33%	33%	38%	41%	44%	47%	46%
Washington	64%	63%	64%	66%	67%	68%	70%	68%
Westmoreland	53%	62%	63%	65%	66%	67%	68%	67%
Southwest Totals	**57%**	**56%**	**56%**	**59%**	**60%**	**61%**	**61%**	**60%**
State Totals	**41%**	**41%**	**41%**	**46%**	**48%**	**50%**	**52%**	**51%**

	1966	1968	1970	1972	1974	1976	1978	1980
Allegheny	64%	64%	64%	66%	67%	68%	69%	69%
Armstrong	44%	43%	42%	45%	48%	49%	49%	49%
Beaver	60%	60%	61%	63%	64%	66%	68%	68%
Butler	43%	42%	43%	46%	46%	50%	51%	50%
Fayette	69%	68%	69%	72%	74%	77%	77%	77%
Greene	76%	75%	75%	76%	77%	79%	79%	77%
Lawrence	46%	45%	45%	49%	51%	55%	56%	56%
Washington	69%	68%	69%	69%	70%	72%	73%	72%
Westmoreland	68%	67%	67%	68%	68%	70%	71%	70%
Southwest Totals	**61%**	**62%**	**63%**	**65%**	**66%**	**68%**	**68%**	**68%**
State Totals	**51%**	**49%**	**50%**	**53%**	**54%**	**57%**	**58%**	**56%**

	1982	1984	1986	1988	1990	1992	1994	1996
Allegheny	70%	72%	72%	71%	71%	71%	71%	69%

Armstrong	50%	53%	53%	53%	54%	55%	55%	53%
Beaver	70%	71%	72%	71%	71%	71%	71%	70%
Butler	51%	52%	51%	49%	48%	49%	48%	46%
Fayette	78%	79%	79%	79%	80%	80%	80%	78%
Greene	78%	80%	80%	80%	80%	80%	80%	77%
Lawrence	57%	61%	61%	60%	60%	63%	62%	62%
Washington	72%	73%	74%	72%	72%	72%	72%	70%
Westmoreland	71%	71%	68%	71%	70%	70%	70%	67%
Southwest Totals	**69%**	**70%**	**71%**	**70%**	**70%**	**70%**	**69%**	**68%**
State Totals	**56%**	**58%**	**56%**	**55%**	**54%**	**54%**	**54%**	**53%**

	1998	**2000**	**2002**	**2004**	**2006**	**2008**	**2010**	**2012**
Allegheny	69%	69%	68%	68%	68%	70%	70%	69%
Armstrong	53%	52%	51%	50%	49%	50%	48%	46%
Beaver	69%	69%	68%	66%	65%	66%	65%	64%
Butler	46%	45%	44%	42%	42%	44%	43%	41%
Fayette	78%	77%	76%	74%	74%	74%	73%	72%
Greene	76%	75%	74%	72%	72%	72%	71%	69%
Lawrence	62%	61%	61%	60%	60%	61%	60%	59%
Washington	69%	68%	67%	65%	64%	64%	63%	61%
Westmoreland	66%	65%	64%	62%	61%	61%	60%	58%
Southwest Totals	**67%**	**66%**	**66%**	**65%**	**64%**	**66%**	**65%**	**64%**
State Totals	**53%**	**53%**	**54%**	**54%**	**54%**	**58%**	**58%**	**58%**

However, when examining the numbers at the individual county level, the data can be even more revealing. It is only in the southwest, for instance, that the Democrats recent surge in registration failed to materialize. Contrary, in the last decade, (outside of Allegheny, were the Democrats have held firm), the Republicans have chipped away at their rival's advantage by over four percentage points on average in the remaining counties.

While Democrats have carried the region in 86 of the 106 elections that are part of this study, the shift of party loyalty has begun to manifest in actual election outcomes. For instance, in each of the presidential elections held since 1950, the Democrats outperformed Republicans in the southwest in each of them compared to their statewide numbers. However, in the last two they have not. Though President Obama narrowly carried the region, he ran three points behind his statewide totals in 2008 and one point behind the same in 2012. While the overall shift has not been near enough to balance out the changing voting patterns in the southeast, the potential exists for the GOP over the long haul to compensate for their decline in the southeast if they can continue to improve their level of support here. As an example, the state of West Virginia, which has much in common with western Pennsylvania, was also once among the most Democratic states in the nation (Michael Dukakis even carried it in 1988), but has now been won by the GOP in the last four presidential contests.

One might posit that as the Democrats become even more dominant at the other end of the state, it may, in fact, be necessary, if Pennsylvania is going to maintain any sort of competitive equilibrium.

NORTHEASTERN PENNSYLVANIA

With slightly more than 12 percent of the state's registered voters, northeastern Pennsylvania is by far the smallest of the Pennsylvania's five geographic regions carved out in this study. This is one reason why only a few statewide candidates have managed to come out of this area of the state. Of the 212 candidates for statewide office between 1950 and 2012, only 21 have hailed from this region, and only seven of them had a last name other than *Scranton* or *Casey* (Table 1.5). Also, of those 21, all but 4 were from Lackawanna County, with two from Northampton, and one each from Lehigh and Luzerne. The competitive swing county of Lehigh, centrally located in the third largest metro area in the state, had failed to provide even one candidate on a general-election ballot since 1950, until Pat Toomey's successful senate bid in 2010.

Table 1.5 Pennsylvania Statewide Candidates 1950-2012

Year	Office	Democratic Candidate	County	Republican Candidate	County
1950	Senate	Francis Myers	Philadelphia	James Duff	Allegheny
	Governor	Richardson Dilworth	Philadelphia	John Fine	Luzerne
	Lt. Gov.	Michael Musmanno	Allegheny	Lloyd Wood	Montgomery
	Int. Affairs	Frank Ruth	Berks	William Livengood	Somerset
1952	Senate	Guy Kurtz Bard	Lancaster	Edward Martin	Greene
	Treasurer	George Leader	York	Weldon Heyburn	Delaware
	Aud. Gen.	Genevieve Blatt	Allegheny	Charles Barber	Erie
1954	Governor	George Leader	York	Lloyd Wood	Montgomery
	Lt. Gov.	Roy Furman	Greene	Frank Truscott	Philadelphia
	Int. Affairs	Genevieve Blatt	Allegheny	Gaynelle Dixon	Butler
1956	Senate	Joseph Clark	Philadelphia	James Duff	Allegheny
	Treasurer	James Knox	Allegheny	Robert Kent	Crawford
	Aud. Gen.	Francis Smith	Philadelphia	Charles Smith	Philadelphia
1958	Senate	George Leader	York	Hugh Scott	Philadelphia
	Governor	David Lawrence	Allegheny	Arthur McGonigle	Berks
	Lt. Gov.	John Morgan Davis	Philadelphia	John Walker	Allegheny
	Int. Affairs	Genevieve Blatt	Allegheny	Andrew Gleason	Cambria
1960	Treasurer	Grace Sloan	Clarion	Charles Smith	Philadelphia
	Auditor Gen.	Thomas Minehart	Montgomery	Robert Kent	Crawford
1962	Senate	Joseph Clark	Philadelphia	James Van Zandt	Blair
	Governor	Richardson Dilworth	Philadelphia	William Scranton	Lackawanna
	Lt. Gov.	Stephen McCann	Greene	Ray Shafer	Crawford
	Int. Affairs	Genevieve Blatt	Allegheny	Audrey Kelly	Susquehanna
1964	Senate	Genevieve Blatt	Allegheny	Hugh Scott	Philadelphia
	Treasurer	Thomas Minehart	Montgomery	Robert Fleming	Allegheny
	Aud. Gen.	Grace Sloan	Clarion	W. Stuart Helm	Armstrong
1966	Governor	Milton Shapp	Philadelphia	Ray Shafer	Crawford
	Lt. Gov.	Leonard Staisey	Allegheny	Ray Broderick	Philadelphia
	Int. Affairs	Genevieve Blatt	Allegheny	John Tabor	Allegheny

Year	Office	Candidate	County	Candidate	County
1968	Senate	Joseph Clark	Philadelphia	Richard Schweiker	Montgomery
	Treasurer	Grace Sloan	Clarion	Frank Pasquerilla	Cambria
	Aud. Gen	Robert P. Casey	Lackawanna	Warner Depuy	Pike
1970	Senate	William Sesler	Erie	Hugh Scott	Philadelphia
	Governor	Milton Shapp	Philadelphia	Ray Broderick	Philadelphia
	Lt. Gov.	Ernest Kline	Beaver	Ralph Scalera	Beaver
1972	Treasurer	Grace Sloan	Clarion	Glenn Williams	Dauphin
	Aud. Gen.	Robert P. Casey	Lackawanna	Franklin McCorkel	Lancaster
1974	Senator	Pete Flaherty	Allegheny	Richard Schweiker	Montgomery
	Governor	Milton Shapp	Philadelphia	Drew Lewis	Montgomery
	Lt. Gov.	Ernest Kline	Beaver	Kenneth Lee	Sullivan
1976	Senate	William Green	Philadelphia	John Heinz	Allegheny
	Treasurer	Robert E. Casey	Cambria	Patricia Crawford	Chester
	Aud. Gen.	Al Benedict	Erie	Patrick Gleason	Cambria
1978	Governor	Pete Flaherty	Allegheny	Dick Thornburgh	Allegheny
	Lt. Gov.	Robert Casey	Allegheny	William Scranton III	Scranton
1980	Senate	Pete Flaherty	Allegheny	Arlen Specter	Philadelphia
	Treasurer	Robert. E. Casey	Cambria	Budd Dwyer	Crawford
	Aud. Gen.	Al Benedict	Erie	James Knepper	Allegheny
	Att. Gen.	Michael O'Pake	Berks	LeRoy Zimmerman	Dauphin
1982	Senate	Cyril Wecht	Allegheny	John Heinz	Allegheny
	Governor	Allen Ertel	Lycoming	Dick Thornburg	Allegheny
	Lt. Gov.	James Lloyd	Philadelphia	William Scranton III	Scranton
1984	Treasurer	Al Benedict	Erie	Budd Dwyer	Crawford
	Aud. Gen.	Don Bailey	Westmoreland	Susan Shanaman	Lebanon
	Att. Gen.	Allen Ertel	Lycoming	LeRoy Zimmerman	Dauphin
1986	Senate	Bob Edgar	Delaware	Arlen Specter	Philadelphia
	Gov.	Robert P. Casey	Lackawanna	William Scranton III	Lackawanna
	Lt. Gov.	Mark Singel	Cambria	Mike Fisher	Allegheny
1988	Senate	Joe Vignola	Philadelphia	John Heinz	Allegheny
	Treasurer	Catherine B. Knoll	Allegheny	Philip English	Erie
	Aud. Gen.	Don Bailey	Westmoreland	Barbara Hafer	Allegheny
	Att. Gen.	Edward Mezvinsky	Montgomery	Ernie Preate	Lackawanna
1990	Governor	Robert P. Casey	Lackawanna	Barbara Hafer	Allegheny
	Lt. Gov.	Mark Singel	Cambria	Harold Mowery	Cumberland
1991	Senate	Harris Wofford	Montgomery	Dick Thornburgh	Allegheny
1992	Senate	Lynn Yeakel	Montgomery	Arlen Specter	Philadelphia
	Treasurer	Catherine B. Knoll	Allegheny	Lowman Henry	Westmoreland
	Aud. Gen.	Craig Lewis	Bucks	Barbara Hafer	Allegheny
	Att. Gen.	Joe Kohn	Chester	Ernie Preate	Lackawanna
1994	Senate	Harris Wofford	Montgomery	Rick Santorum	Allegheny
	Governor	Mark Singel	Cambria	Tom Ridge	Erie
	Lt. Gov.	Tom Foley	Montgomery	Mark Schweiker	Bucks
1996	Treasurer	Mina Baker Knoll	Allegheny	Barbara Hafer	Allegheny
	Aud. Gen.	Bob Casey Jr.	Lackawanna	Bob Nyce	Northampton
	Att. Gen.	Joe Kohn	Philadelphia	Mike Fisher	Allegheny
1998	Senate	Bill Lloyd	Somerset	Arlen Specter	Philadelphia
	Governor	Ivan Itkin	Allegheny	Tom Ridge	Erie
	Lt. Gov.	Marjorie M. Mezvinsky	Montgomery	Mark Schweiker	Bucks
2000	Senate	Ron Klink	Allegheny	Rick Santorum	Allegheny
	Treasurer	Catherine B. Knoll	Allegheny	Barbara Hafer	Allegheny
	Aud. Gen.	Bob Casey Jr.	Lackawanna	Katie True	Lancaster
	Att. Gen.	Jim Eisenhower	Philadelphia	Mike Fisher	Allegheny
2002	Governor	Ed Rendell	Philadelphia	Mike Fisher	Allegheny
	Lt. Gov.	Catherine B. Knoll	Allegheny	Jane Earll	Erie
2004	Senate	Joe Hoeffel	Montgomery	Arlen Specter	Philadelphia
	Treasurer	Bob Casey Jr.	Lackawanna	Jean Craige Pepper	Erie
	Aud. Gen.	Jack Wagner	Allegheny	Joe Peters	Lackawanna
	Att. Gen.	Jim Eisenhower	Philadelphia	Tom Corbett	Allegheny
2006	Senate	Bob Casey Jr.	Lackawanna	Rich Santorum	Allegheny
	Governor	Ed Rendell	Philadelphia	Lynn Swann	Allegheny
	Lt. Gov.	Catherine B. Knoll	Allegheny	Jim Matthews	Montgomery
2008	Treasurer	Rob McCord	Montgomery	Tom Ellis	Montgomery

	Aud. Gen. Att. Gen.	Jack Wagner John Morganelli	Allegheny Northhampton	Chet Beiler Tom Corbett	Lancaster Allegheny
2010	Senate Governor Lt. Gov.	Joe Sestak Dan Onorato Scott Conklin	Delaware Allegheny Centre	Pat Toomey Tom Corbett Jim Cawley	Lehigh Allegheny Bucks
2012	Senate Treasurer Aud. Gen. Att. Gen.	Bob Casey Jr. Rob McCord Eugene DePasquale Kathleen Kane	Lackawanna Montgomery York Lackawanna	Tom Smith Diana Irey Vaughan John Maher David Freed	Armstrong Washington Allegheny Cumberland

However, the northeast does serve an interesting role as Pennsylvania's political bellwether. Its' voting patterns are not only representative of the state, but in many respects, also the nation. As Table 1.6 points out, while Democrats have had an edge in registration, it is not one that they can always count on. This part of the state is home to many of the blue-collar, unionized, socially conservative voters who often decide elections. Known as Reagan Democrats in the 1980s, they came home to their party in the 1990s to support Bill Clinton, only to be fairly split in the presidential elections of 2000 and 2004 while reverting back to their party's allegiance in the last two contests. If you had to rely on only a few key precincts to predict the overall state vote, this would be a good place to examine.

Table 1.6 Democratic Share of Two-Party Registration Totals, Northeastern Pennsylvania

	1950	1952	1954	1956	1958	1960	1962	1964
Carbon	45%	44%	44%	48%	50%	53%	55%	52%
Lackawanna	57%	57%	56%	60%	63%	66%	66%	63%
Lehigh	49%	48%	48%	48%	50%	50%	50%	52%
Luzerne	27%	24%	24%	31%	33%	42%	48%	43%
Monroe	60%	57%	57%	58%	59%	59%	60%	59%
Northampton	62%	60%	60%	61%	62%	63%	60%	65%
Northeast Totals	**45%**	**44%**	**44%**	**48%**	**50%**	**54%**	**56%**	**54%**
State Totals	**41%**	**41%**	**41%**	**46%**	**48%**	**50%**	**52%**	**51%**

	1966	1968	1970	1972	1974	1976	1978	1980
Carbon	52%	51%	50%	53%	53%	56%	57%	56%
Lackawanna	64%	64%	64%	65%	66%	67%	68%	68%
Lehigh	52%	51%	52%	53%	53%	56%	56%	46%
Luzerne	43%	44%	48%	54%	56%	61%	63%	62%
Monroe	58%	53%	51%	53%	53%	55%	56%	53%
Northampton	65%	64%	64%	65%	66%	67%	68%	66%
Northeast Totals	**54%**	**54%**	**55%**	**58%**	**59%**	**62%**	**63%**	**60%**
State Totals	**51%**	**49%**	**50%**	**53%**	**54%**	**57%**	**58%**	**56%**

	1982	1984	1986	1988	1990	1992	1994	1996
Carbon	56%	56%	55%	55%	55%	56%	56%	55%
Lackawanna	68%	69%	69%	70%	70%	70%	70%	69%
Lehigh	54%	54%	53%	52%	51%	52%	51%	51%
Luzerne	62%	62%	60%	60%	61%	62%	62%	61%
Monroe	52%	51%	51%	48%	47%	48%	48%	48%
Northampton	65%	64%	63%	61%	61%	61%	60%	58%
Northeast Totals	**62%**	**61%**	**60%**	**60%**	**60%**	**60%**	**60%**	**58%**
State Totals	**56%**	**58%**	**56%**	**55%**	**54%**	**54%**	**54%**	**53%**

	1998	2000	2002	2004	2006	2008	2010	2012
Carbon	55%	55%	55%	55%	55%	58%	58%	56%
Lackawanna	68%	67%	68%	67%	68%	70%	71%	71%
Lehigh	51%	51%	51%	53%	53%	59%	59%	60%
Luzerne	62%	62%	61%	61%	61%	65%	64%	63%
Monroe	48%	49%	49%	51%	52%	58%	59%	59%
Northampton	57%	56%	55%	55%	56%	60%	60%	62%
Northeast Totals	**58%**	**58%**	**58%**	**58%**	**58%**	**62%**	**63%**	**62%**
State Totals	**53%**	**53%**	**54%**	**54%**	**54%**	**58%**	**58%**	**54%**

If you were to tell anyone under the age of 50 that Philadelphia was a Republican town a half-century ago, your comment would probably invoke more than a raised eyebrow. If you told someone—even a person who follows politics—that in Luzerne County (Wilkes-Barre), Republicans outnumbered Democrats in 1954 by more than three to one, you might expect a response of shock and bewilderment. In fact, only 10 other counties in the state provided a larger registration edge for the GOP in the elections of that year. The county's powerful Republican machine, under the leadership of future governor John Fine, dominated not just political life but also social and economic affairs there long after the New Deal. Fear of reprisals kept many from changing their party allegiances. Now, as any student of Pennsylvania politics undoubtedly knows, few counties in the state are as solidly Democratic. That's as clear an indication as any as to how politics in the Commonwealth can change.

Luzerne's "sister" county, Lackawanna (Scranton), has followed the path one would expect from such a blue-collar, unionized area. Its realignment began soon after Roosevelt was elected in 1932, and it was solidly Democratic by 1950. The Democratic share of registered voters today stands at 71 percent, third highest in the state. Lackawanna County is perhaps most famous for providing two of the state's most powerful political families of the past half-century, the Casey's and Scranton's.

The two counties in the middle of the northeast region share some similarities with their counties to the north and south, but they also have some important differences. Carbon County had coal and slate. Although it was once solidly Republican (though not to the same degree as Luzerne), it drifted into the Democratic column by the late 1950s. Unlike the counties to the north, its shift has been more muted. Monroe County, home of the Pocono resorts, is almost an anomaly today in Pennsylvania. It has had to deal with a population explosion, fueled by residents migrating from New York. Largely because of this, its political dynamics have been unpredictable lately. What had been one of the few Democratic counties in the state before the New Deal steadily moved into the other direction until 2004, when the parties became almost evenly matched. Two years later, however, the Democrats rebounded and increased their total by over 11,000 registered voters while the GOP remained the same. By 2012, the Democrats had gained an advantage of over 17,000, which translates to 59 percent of the two party registered vote, nearly a double-digit increase in just a six year period.

The two "sister" counties to the south, Lehigh (Allentown) and Northampton (Bethlehem and Easton) have many similarities. Lehigh, which is somewhat larger, has historically been more competitive politically. Republicans claimed 51 percent of registered voters in 1950, while decades later the Democrats moved into the lead with 53 percent by 2006. However, a Democratic surge, not unlike Monroe County experienced has vaulted them to 60 percent today. Northampton County has been more loyal to the Democrats historically, although some fraying has occurred here in recent years. As late as 1992, Democrats outnumbered Republicans, with 62 percent of all registered voters. However, the decade which followed saw that level of support drop to a low of 55 percent, though again, this most recent surge has moved the total back up to 59 percent by 2012.

Democrats have carried the northeast 70 of 106 times in statewide elections since 1950, one less than the southeast region and 19 more than they've won statewide. Nevertheless, these six counties in the northeast are an excellent indicator of what is going on throughout the rest of the state. In 17 presidential elections held since 1952, the Democratic share of the two-party vote in the northeast has been 51.8 percent, compared with 50.8 percent statewide, a difference of only one percent. Only once, in President Johnson's 1964 landslide, has the gap been more than three percentage points. For United States Senate elections, the Democratic share of the vote has been 48.0 percent, compared with 46.4 percent statewide, a difference of just 1.6 percent.

For gubernatorial elections, the difference between the region and the state has also been minimal as well, with Democrats garnering 53.4 percent in the former and 50.8 percent in the latter, a difference of less than three percent. Finally, in the 51 lower-tiered races held since 1950, only 14 times has the differential between the vote in the northeast and the vote statewide been more than three percentage points. Interestingly, seven of those 15 races featured someone from this region, skewing the results, since candidates' local roots tend to boost their numbers. In sum, while its relatively small population generally prevents it from being the determinant in statewide elections, the northeast perhaps remains the best predictor of who will be ultimately victorious.

CENTRAL PENNSYLVANIA

Known as the Pennsylvania "T," the 47 counties that range across the vast center of the Commonwealth make up the fifth and final region. This area begins in Lancaster County in the southeast and heads north and west until you hit the suburbs of Pittsburgh to the west and New York State to the north, all the while stretching back east to form a "T" shape. Describing this area as central Pennsylvania may not be purely accurate in a geographic sense, but it does describe the region's cultural state of mind. This is rural Pennsylvania, the state's Bible Belt. It is also, and not coincidentally, the bedrock of the Republican Party today.

Although it may be home to many culturally conservative voters like those who live in the southern United States, central Pennsylvania has had one major historical difference. Although southerners were largely Democrats until recently, central Pennsylvanians switched allegiances long ago, in the aftermath of the Civil War. It should be remembered that the only President of the United States from Pennsylvania was Democrat James Buchanan, who hailed from Lancaster County. Buchanan served as the Union was falling apart, and his inaction helped set the stage for the abolitionist Republican Party and Abraham Lincoln to take control. It should also be remembered that Pennsylvania was the only place in the north that the Confederate Army invaded. It was here—in Gettysburg, Adams County—that the decisive battle of the Civil War took place and the Union was ultimately preserved. Since then, central Pennsylvania hasn't changed much politically. Most of these 47 counties remain ever loyal both to conservatism and to Republicanism.

The Republican Party is supreme in much of the area, but the vast "T" has some pockets of Democratic strength (Table 1.7). In all, nine counties have a majority of registered voters for the Democrats: Berks, Cambria, Centre, Clinton, Dauphin, Elk, Erie, Indiana, and Mercer. In two others—Clearfield and Columbia,—they are essentially tied with the GOP. In 1950, six counties in this region were Democratic, although many are not part of this group today.

**Table 1.7 Democratic Share of Two-Party Registration Totals,
Central Pennsylvania**

	1950	1952	1954	1956	1958	1960	1962	1964
Adams	43%	42%	43%	46%	47%	48%	49%	46%
Bedford	38%	38%	40%	44%	44%	47%	48%	46%
Berks	64%	61%	61%	63%	64%	64%	64%	64%
Blair	30%	29%	30%	37%	38%	39%	39%	38%
Bradford	24%	23%	24%	28%	30%	31%	34%	33%

Cambria	55%	54%	55%	59%	58%	60%	62%	58%
Cameron	24%	24%	25%	29%	30%	32%	36%	35%
Centre	40%	38%	38%	40%	40%	40%	41%	41%
Clarion	46%	45%	45%	48%	48%	48%	49%	47%
Clearfield	47%	45%	46%	51%	52%	53%	54%	52%
Clinton	36%	35%	36%	41%	43%	45%	46%	44%
Columbia	56%	54%	54%	56%	57%	57%	58%	55%
Crawford	35%	33%	33%	35%	36%	38%	39%	39%
Cumberland	35%	32%	31%	36%	38%	40%	42%	39%
Dauphin	19%	17%	17%	27%	29%	32%	34%	28%
Elk	55%	53%	54%	57%	59%	59%	59%	58%
Erie	44%	43%	44%	48%	49%	50%	52%	52%
Forest	32%	30%	31%	39%	40%	43%	45%	40%
Franklin	39%	37%	38%	46%	48%	48%	48%	45%
Fulton	53%	52%	53%	55%	56%	56%	56%	53%
Huntingdon	28%	26%	26%	32%	33%	33%	37%	35%
Indiana	38%	36%	37%	44%	45%	45%	47%	44%
Jefferson	33%	33%	33%	42%	43%	44%	45%	41%
Juniata	45%	47%	47%	49%	49%	49%	49%	46%
Lancaster	26%	25%	25%	27%	28%	28%	29%	30%
Lebanon	27%	28%	28%	33%	34%	34%	35%	32%
Lycoming	39%	37%	37%	40%	42%	43%	44%	42%
McKean	25%	23%	22%	25%	27%	30%	32%	32%
Mercer	45%	44%	44%	48%	49%	49%	49%	50%
Mifflin	44%	43%	43%	47%	47%	47%	48%	47%
Montour	42%	40%	40%	45%	45%	46%	48%	46%
Northumberland	35%	32%	33%	38%	40%	42%	45%	42%
Perry	31%	29%	30%	37%	38%	40%	43%	38%
Pike	34%	30%	29%	34%	36%	37%	37%	35%
Potter	32%	31%	32%	36%	38%	40%	41%	36%
Schuylkill	28%	27%	25%	30%	31%	36%	41%	36%
Snyder	21%	19%	20%	26%	27%	28%	29%	28%
Somerset	41%	40%	41%	46%	46%	48%	49%	46%
Sullivan	40%	39%	40%	44%	45%	45%	46%	43%
Susquehanna	27%	26%	26%	34%	35%	36%	38%	35%
Tioga	18%	17%	17%	23%	24%	26%	30%	28%
Union	23%	21%	22%	26%	26%	26%	28%	27%
Venango	25%	24%	24%	30%	32%	34%	36%	34%
Warren	27%	26%	25%	31%	33%	36%	37%	35%
Wayne	20%	19%	19%	31%	33%	35%	37%	30%
Wyoming	24%	23%	22%	31%	33%	37%	37%	32%

	1966	1968	1970	1972	1974	1976	1978	1980
York	56%	55%	55%	56%	58%	58%	58%	57%
Central Totals	**38%**	**37%**	**37%**	**42%**	**43%**	**44%**	**46%**	**44%**
State Totals	**41%**	**41%**	**41%**	**46%**	**48%**	**50%**	**52%**	**51%**
	1966	**1968**	**1970**	**1972**	**1974**	**1976**	**1978**	**1980**
Adams	45%	43%	43%	44%	45%	48%	47%	44%
Bedford	44%	41%	39%	41%	41%	44%	45%	41%
Berks	54%	54%	55%	58%	59%	62%	63%	60%
Blair	37%	36%	35%	37%	38%	41%	41%	39%
Bradford	32%	31%	30%	34%	34%	35%	35%	33%
Cambria	58%	57%	57%	60%	61%	63%	64%	63%
Cameron	37%	37%	37%	44%	46%	50%	52%	49%
Centre	41%	39%	39%	46%	49%	52%	52%	46%
Clarion	47%	46%	46%	50%	50%	51%	51%	49%
Clearfield	50%	48%	48%	51%	52%	55%	55%	53%
Clinton	43%	41%	41%	46%	48%	51%	50%	47%
Columbia	55%	54%	54%	56%	56%	58%	59%	57%
Crawford	39%	38%	39%	42%	43%	46%	46%	44%
Cumberland	37%	33%	33%	38%	39%	43%	43%	39%
Dauphin	27%	24%	24%	36%	39%	44%	45%	39%
Elk	58%	57%	58%	59%	60%	62%	64%	63%
Erie	53%	53%	53%	57%	58%	61%	62%	61%
Forest	37%	35%	35%	41%	43%	45%	45%	43%
Franklin	45%	44%	43%	45%	45%	47%	47%	44%
Fulton	54%	51%	51%	54%	54%	56%	56%	53%
Huntingdon	34%	33%	33%	37%	38%	40%	41%	39%
Indiana	41%	39%	39%	44%	46%	48%	49%	47%
Jefferson	40%	39%	42%	44%	45%	46%	47%	46%
Juniata	45%	43%	43%	46%	48%	48%	47%	45%
Lancaster	30%	29%	29%	31%	31%	32%	32%	30%
Lebanon	32%	30%	29%	31%	31%	35%	36%	33%
Lycoming	42%	41%	41%	43%	44%	48%	48%	46%
McKean	31%	30%	30%	34%	35%	40%	39%	35%
Mercer	50%	49%	50%	52%	53%	55%	56%	56%
Mifflin	46%	45%	45%	46%	47%	50%	50%	47%
Montour	45%	43%	44%	51%	53%	53%	53%	48%
Northumberland	40%	38%	39%	45%	48%	50%	49%	46%
Perry	37%	34%	34%	39%	39%	42%	42%	36%
Pike	35%	34%	33%	36%	37%	48%	44%	42%
Potter	35%	33%	33%	39%	43%	47%	44%	41%
Schuylkill	35%	33%	34%	38%	41%	43%	43%	41%

Snyder	27%	26%	25%	27%	28%	30%	29%	26%
Somerset	46%	44%	44%	44%	44%	46%	46%	45%
Sullivan	41%	40%	39%	43%	45%	47%	47%	45%
Susquehanna	34%	33%	32%	36%	37%	39%	39%	37%
Tioga	27%	26%	25%	31%	31%	34%	35%	32%
Union	27%	25%	25%	30%	30%	32%	32%	30%
Venango	33%	32%	32%	35%	36%	39%	39%	37%
Warren	35%	34%	33%	38%	38%	42%	46%	44%
Wayne	29%	27%	26%	29%	30%	35%	35%	33%
Wyoming	30%	28%	28%	31%	33%	36%	36%	33%
York	56%	53%	52%	52%	53%	54%	54%	51%
Central Totals	**43%**	**41%**	**42%**	**45%**	**46%**	**48%**	**49%**	**46%**
State Totals	**51%**	**49%**	**50%**	**53%**	**54%**	**57%**	**58%**	**56%**
	1982	**1984**	**1986**	**1988**	**1990**	**1992**	**1994**	**1996**
Adams	44%	44%	43%	41%	41%	41%	39%	38%
Bedford	41%	41%	41%	42%	44%	41%	41%	39%
Berks	62%	59%	58%	56%	55%	55%	54%	52%
Blair	40%	39%	39%	39%	38%	39%	38%	38%
Bradford	33%	31%	30%	30%	30%	31%	31%	31%
Cambria	64%	66%	66%	68%	68%	68%	68%	67%
Cameron	48%	46%	44%	45%	49%	49%	47%	47%
Centre	45%	44%	44%	44%	43%	46%	46%	45%
Clarion	49%	49%	49%	49%	48%	49%	47%	46%
Clearfield	53%	52%	52%	52%	52%	53%	53%	50%
Clinton	48%	50%	49%	51%	51%	51%	50%	49%
Columbia	57%	57%	56%	55%	54%	54%	53%	52%
Crawford	45%	47%	45%	45%	44%	45%	43%	42%
Cumberland	38%	37%	36%	36%	35%	35%	35%	34%
Dauphin	38%	38%	38%	39%	39%	40%	40%	40%
Elk	64%	64%	63%	63%	63%	61%	61%	59%
Erie	62%	62%	62%	61%	61%	61%	58%	58%
Forest	43%	44%	43%	43%	44%	44%	43%	42%
Franklin	43%	42%	41%	39%	38%	38%	38%	36%
Fulton	53%	51%	49%	52%	49%	49%	49%	46%
Huntingdon	39%	40%	39%	39%	40%	40%	39%	38%
Indiana	48%	50%	50%	50%	51%	52%	52%	51%
Jefferson	45%	45%	45%	44%	45%	47%	48%	45%
Juniata	45%	44%	43%	44%	44%	43%	43%	42%
Lancaster	29%	29%	28%	27%	27%	28%	28%	28%
Lebanon	32%	33%	32%	31%	31%	32%	32%	32%

Lycoming	45%	44%	43%	43%	43%	43%	42%	41%
McKean	35%	36%	34%	33%	33%	35%	35%	34%
Mifflin	46%	45%	45%	45%	44%	45%	44%	43%
Mercer	54%	56%	56%	56%	56%	56%	55%	55%
Montour	48%	49%	49%	47%	49%	48%	48%	45%
Northumberland	48%	49%	50%	51%	51%	51%	51%	51%
Perry	34%	33%	32%	33%	32%	31%	31%	30%
Pike	41%	39%	38%	37%	37%	38%	38%	37%
Potter	41%	37%	36%	37%	38%	40%	37%	35%
Schuylkill	41%	41%	41%	42%	42%	43%	44%	43%
Snyder	26%	26%	26%	26%	26%	26%	26%	26%
Somerset	46%	49%	49%	49%	50%	50%	50%	49%
Sullivan	44%	44%	45%	44%	44%	43%	43%	41%
Susquehanna	37%	36%	36%	37%	35%	37%	36%	35%
Tioga	30%	29%	29%	30%	31%	30%	30%	30%
Union	30%	31%	31%	31%	31%	32%	32%	31%
Venango	39%	43%	43%	41%	41%	42%	42%	41%
Warren	42%	43%	42%	41%	42%	43%	43%	42%
Wayne	32%	32%	31%	30%	30%	31%	30%	31%
Wyoming	33%	32%	31%	31%	31%	33%	34%	33%
York	50%	48%	47%	44%	43%	44%	43%	42%
Central Totals	**46%**	**46%**	**45%**	**44%**	**44%**	**44%**	**44%**	**43%**
State Totals	**56%**	**58%**	**56%**	**55%**	**54%**	**54%**	**54%**	**53%**

	1998	2000	2002	2004	2006	2008	2010	2012
Adams	38%	37%	37%	36%	36%	39%	39%	38%
Bedford	39%	38%	37%	36%	36%	37%	36%	34%
Berks	52%	51%	51%	51%	52%	56%	57%	56%
Blair	38%	38%	38%	36%	36%	39%	39%	38%
Bradford	31%	32%	31%	32%	32%	35%	35%	34%
Cambria	67%	66%	67%	66%	66%	67%	66%	65%
Cameron	50%	47%	46%	46%	45%	46%	46%	46%
Centre	45%	45%	44%	46%	46%	53%	53%	52%
Clarion	46%	45%	44%	44%	44%	46%	45%	43%
Clearfield	51%	50%	50%	49%	49%	50%	50%	49%
Clinton	48%	48%	48%	49%	49%	53%	53%	51%
Columbia	52%	51%	51%	50%	49%	52%	51%	50%
Crawford	43%	43%	43%	44%	44%	47%	46%	45%
Cumberland	34%	34%	34%	34%	35%	40%	40%	39%
Dauphin	41%	42%	42%	45%	45%	51%	52%	52%
Elk	59%	59%	59%	58%	59%	60%	60%	58%
Erie	57%	57%	57%	56%	58%	62%	62%	61%

Forest	42%	41%	41%	42%	45%	48%	49%	46%
Franklin	36%	35%	34%	34%	33%	36%	35%	34%
Fulton	45%	43%	42%	39%	38%	37%	48%	36%
Huntingdon	38%	37%	37%	37%	37%	39%	39%	37%
Indiana	51%	51%	51%	50%	50%	52%	52%	51%
Jefferson	45%	44%	43%	43%	42%	43%	42%	40%
Juniata	41%	40%	39%	38%	37%	38%	38%	36%
Lancaster	29%	29%	29%	31%	31%	37%	37%	37%
Lebanon	33%	33%	32%	33%	33%	38%	39%	38%
Lycoming	41%	40%	40%	40%	40%	42%	42%	40%
McKean	35%	34%	34%	35%	35%	37%	37%	36%
Mercer	55%	55%	54%	54%	54%	55%	55%	54%
Mifflin	42%	40%	40%	38%	38%	37%	37%	37%
Montour	45%	44%	43%	43%	43%	46%	46%	45%
Northumberland	51%	50%	50%	48%	48%	49%	49%	48%
Perry	31%	30%	30%	29%	29%	32%	31%	30%
Pike	39%	40%	40%	41%	42%	46%	46%	46%
Potter	35%	34%	33%	34%	33%	35%	34%	32%
Schuylkill	50%	43%	43%	43%	44%	47%	48%	47%
Snyder	26%	26%	26%	27%	27%	30%	30%	30%
Somerset	50%	48%	47%	46%	46%	47%	46%	45%
Sullivan	41%	40%	40%	40%	40%	42%	42%	42%
Susquehanna	35%	35%	35%	36%	37%	39%	39%	38%
Tioga	30%	31%	30%	31%	31%	34%	34%	33%
Union	31%	31%	31%	33%	33%	39%	38%	38%
Venango	42%	42%	42%	41%	41%	43%	43%	42%
Warren	42%	42%	42%	42%	42%	46%	46%	44%
Wayne	31%	32%	32%	33%	34%	38%	39%	38%
Wyoming	33%	34%	35%	36%	36%	40%	40%	39%
York	41%	40%	40%	40%	40%	44%	44%	43%
Central Totals	**44%**	**43%**	**42%**	**42%**	**45%**	**46%**	**46%**	**45%**
State Totals	**53%**	**53%**	**54%**	**54%**	**54%**	**58%**	**58%**	**58%**

While Fulton County, located along the Maryland border, has shifted Republican, its political impact has been minor due to it being the third smallest county in the state (only trailing Cameron and Forest). Columbia County was solidly Democratic in 1950 (56 percent), but the GOP now has a slight edge. York, the other county that has switched allegiances, has been a political disaster in recent decades for the Democrats. For instance, in 1950, they could claim 56 percent of the registered two-party voters in the county. By 2006, their share of registered voters had dropped to just 40 percent, though it has inched back up to where it stands at 43 percent today. What has made the change even more important is that York has been a high-growth county. It now ranks seventh statewide in total population and second in the "T" behind only Lancaster County.

The other counties that were Democratic in 1950, Cambria and Elk, have maintained their party allegiances. The final county is Berks (Reading), and that provides an interesting case. In 1950, 64 percent of its registered voters were Democrats. However, by 2004, that number had slipped to just 50 percent. In recent years, however, Berks has experienced the same Democratic surge similar to the counties they border in southeast and northeastern Pennsylvania. Today, Democrats are back up to 56 percent, and though it appeared that it was heading in the direction of York County and becoming Republican just a short time ago, for now at least, that appears unlikely as the Democrats have pushed back.

Six other counties have switched to the Democrats in the past sixty years, one of which has the third highest population in the "T." Erie County has shifted from 56–44 percent Republican to 61–39 percent Democratic today. Indiana County has also changed, from 62 percent Republican in 1950 to now possessing a slight Democratic advantage. The third county in the region to switch has been Mercer, which has moved from 45 to 54 percent Democratic. In recent years, three others have flipped, with the youth vote being particularly influential. In sparsely populated Clinton County, home to just slightly more than 20,000 registered voters, the 5,000 students who attend Lock Haven University have contributed to a change in the areas politics. And of course in Centre County, home to Penn State University and the 45,000 students who attend its University Park campus has helped improved the Democratic share six percentage points since 2006, up to 52 percent overall.

The last county in the central Pennsylvania overtaken in registration by the Democrats is Dauphin. Unlike the student populations mentioned above, the driving force behind the shift here has been the importance of government workers. The political change that has transpired in Dauphin County is also symbolically important. This traditional bastion of Republican strength, in which the Democrats could claim just 19 percent of registered voters in 1950, is, of course, also home to the state capital in Harrisburg.

There are other, even more unlikely pockets within central Pennsylvania that have not been immune to the Democratic surge in recent years. In nine of the regions counties, Democrats have improved their share of registered voters by over five percentage points since 2004. These include such GOP strongholds such as Lancaster and Lebanon counties. Overall, between 1950 and 2012, Democrats—surprisingly—increased their registration advantage in 35 of the 47 counties. The GOP has had an increase in just ten, while one county, Potter, has remained unchanged. Most interesting, however, is that of the ten counties in this region that have become more Republican, all but one (Columbia) is located in the south-central portion. In all, the Democrats now can claim 45 percent of registered voters in the Central "T," far more respectable than the 38 percent recorded in 1950.

Nevertheless, Central Pennsylvania still remains largely the domain of the GOP, and thus it's no surprise that only a few Democrats have successfully broken through the carry the region. Democratic candidates have taken central Pennsylvania only ten times in statewide elections since 1950. Four of those belong to a candidate whose last name was Casey. Lyndon B. Johnson, who won handily in 1964, remains the only Democratic to carry the region at the presidential level. Though Robert Casey came very close in 2006, in United States Senate elections, no Democrat candidate has ever outpolled a Republican in the "T." Prior to that, the highest that Democrats have ever achieved in this region had been 45 percent on three different occasions (1958, 1964, and 1992). The loyalty that the Republicans have been able to count on from their supporters in central Pennsylvania is what Democrats in the southwest could only dream of. Indeed, if Democrats had ever achieved this consistency of support in their traditional southwestern base, the outcomes of many statewide elections would surely have been different.

CHAPTER TWO

UNITED STATES SENATE ELECTIONS IN PENNSYLVANIA

Until recently, the futility with which Democrats have contested United States Senate campaigns in Pennsylvania was largely unrivaled in American politics. However, with Robert Casey winning 2 of the last 3 senate elections held in the state, the numbers now appear much more respectable than they did at the time the first edition of this book was published. During the period of this study, Democrats have now won 5 of the 23 (22 percent) Senate elections held, subpar but a noticeable improvement from the 15 percent they recorded ten years ago. That the Democratic Party possessed a statewide registration advantage in 18 of these contests (78 percent) only exacerbates the years of disappointments that their partisan surely endured.

While the reasons for this phenomenon are many, one explanation rises above the rest. A sufficient number of Democrats residing in the party's political base—the southwest—have time and again crossed party lines, denying Democratic candidates an opportunity to take a seat in the Senate. The line-crossing has been especially true in several landmark elections, those closely contested races whose outcome ultimately determined who controlled the seat for the next generation.

That the prospects were rather poor in the middle of the 20th century is not surprising. At that time, Pennsylvania was one of the most Republican states in the nation. The GOP held a registration advantage of 59–41 percent statewide and an advantage in all but 11 of the state's 67 counties. The first Senate election of the second half of the 20th century set the stage for most of those that followed.

1950: DUFF/MYERS

With newspaper headlines blaring about the prospect that Communist Chinese intervention in Korea was about to lead to World War III, voters across the nation rejected President Truman's "Fair Deal," allowing the Republicans to pick up 5 seats in the Senate and 31 in the House of Representatives. In Pennsylvania, the GOP also had reason to rejoice, as their statewide candidate ejected a two-term Democratic senator while their gubernatorial candidate kept the Republicans ensconced in the governor's mansion. Further down the ballot, Republicans also held onto the offices of lieutenant governor and director of internal affairs (two positions no longer independently elected), while maintaining solid control of both state houses.

In the Senate contest of 1950, Democratic Majority Whip Francis J. Myers saw his political career come to an end at the hands of then-Governor James H. Duff. The progressive Duff had dispatched conservative Congressman John C. Kunkel of Harrisburg in the primary by more than 500,000 votes. It what was a big victory not just for Duff but also for the moderate wing of the Republican Party, who rallied around a call that "Grundyism must go." This was a reference to a former United States Senator and the founder of the Pennsylvania Manufacturers Association, Joseph R. Grundy. The archconservative Grundy backed Kunkel, along with a slate of statewide candidates, all of whom went down to defeat.

In the general election, the Senate contest was largely shadowed by the gubernatorial race—as is often the case when the two coincide in Pennsylvania. The Senate race received little attention, which is perhaps why Myers, the first Roman Catholic ever elected to the Senate from Pennsylvania, was completely surprised by his defeat, stating afterwards, "I can't understand it, we had no warning. It was a nation-wide trend. I don't know if the Korean War was the cause, or whether it was just a case of throwing the 'ins' out."

Table 2.1 Democratic Share of Two-Party Vote for Senate, Southeastern Pennsylvania

	1950	1952	1956	1958	1962	1964	1968	1970
Philadelphia	54%	59%	60%	59%	61%	58%	62%	55%
Bucks	41%	39%	48%	44%	46%	44%	40%	42%
Chester	35%	36%	37%	36%	38%	38%	34%	35%
Delaware	38%	39%	41%	37%	42%	41%	39%	37%
Montgomery	35%	34%	37%	34%	39%	37%	33%	38%
Suburban Totals	37%	37%	41%	37%	41%	40%	36%	38%
Southeast Totals	49%	51%	52%	50%	53%	50%	50%	47%

State Totals	48%	48%	51%	49%	51%	49%	47%	47%
Winning Party	R	R	D	R	D	R	R	R

	1974	1976	1980	1982	1986	1988	1991	1992
Philadelphia	50%	71%	49%	60%	56%	61%	74%	60%
Bucks	38%	49%	37%	34%	35%	29%	51%	47%
Chester	36%	38%	30%	25%	31%	21%	44%	45%
Delaware	37%	47%	37%	31%	44%	29%	50%	45%
Montgomery	30%	45%	32%	28%	31%	27%	52%	43%
Suburban Totals	35%	46%	34%	30%	36%	27%	50%	45%
Southeast Totals	42%	58%	41%	39%	45%	41%	60%	51%
State Totals	46%	47%	49%	40%	43%	33%	55%	49%
Winning Party	R	R	R	R	R	R	D	R

	1994	1998	2000	2004	2006	2010	2012
Philadelphia	76%	60%	77%	71%	84%	84%	87%
Bucks	44%	32%	42%	42%	59%	47%	52%
Chester	38%	26%	35%	38%	55%	47%	51%
Delaware	45%	31%	45%	46%	62%	56%	62%
Montgomery	47%	30%	45%	46%	62%	54%	59%
Suburban Totals	44%	30%	42%	44%	60%	51%	56%
Southeast Totals	56%	40%	54%	53%	67%	62%	67%
State Totals	49%	37%	46%	44%	59%	49%	55%
Winning Party	R	R	R	R	D	R	D

He shouldn't have been so surprised, considering that his opponent was not only one of the state's most popular governors but also one of its most productive. In addition, Republicans were still safely in the majority statewide. In defeating the Old Guard machine run by Grundy, Duff also set himself up as a major player in the presidential sweepstakes of 1952, and his relentless support of Eisenhower that year was particularly helpful for the former general that year.

On the campaign trail, Duff focused on the Republican-Progressivism of his gubernatorial term. Addressing the Pennsylvania Council of Republican Women convention a few days before the election, he proclaimed that "One is what the Republican Party has accomplished in Pennsylvania in providing go-forward, progressive, do-something government and the other is what the Democratic Party has failed to do in Washington." In addition, Duff railed against the power of Big Labor, charging "These labor bosses would ruin us here the same as they ruined England."

The Republican prevailed by 126,000 votes, winning 52 percent of the total and 50 of the state's 67 counties. Myers's Philadelphia, which was in its last year of GOP control, was not prepared to provide a Democrat with the huge pluralities that would come later. Duff's suburban numbers outdid Myers's 64,000-vote edge in the city, and the Republican emerged from the southeast with a 51-49 percent advantage (Table 2.1). Of the four suburban counties, the Democratic incumbent topped 40 percent only in Bucks.

The first Senate election of this study, however, established the trend that came to dominate those elections: that Democratic Party candidate's sorely underperformed in their southwestern political base. As Table 2.2 illustrates, Duff held the Democratic incumbent's margin to just 35,000 votes, a 4-percentage point lead in the nine southwest counties. Myers's 52 percent advantage in the region was 5 percentage points shy of his party's registration edge. Had Myers attained 57 percent of the vote in the southwest, he would have won a third term. The key was Allegheny County, where Myers received just 16,000 votes more than Duff in the Republican's home territory.

Table 2.2 Democratic Share of Two-Party Vote for Senate, Southwestern Pennsylvania

	1950	1952	1956	1958	1962	1964	1968	1970
Allegheny	52%	52%	53%	47%	58%	49%	49%	50%
Armstrong	45%	43%	48%	44%	49%	48%	42%	45%
Beaver	51%	55%	59%	52%	61%	53%	52%	55%
Butler	36%	38%	44%	40%	46%	45%	41%	47%
Fayette	58%	62%	63%	59%	62%	58%	59%	61%
Greene	62%	59%	65%	56%	61%	59%	57%	60%
Lawrence	46%	48%	54%	50%	53%	51%	48%	47%
Washington	59%	61%	62%	56%	62%	54%	52%	56%
Westmoreland	54%	57%	61%	55%	65%	53%	50%	56%
Southwest Totals	**52%**	**53%**	**55%**	**50%**	**58%**	**50%**	**49%**	**52%**
State Totals	**48%**	**48%**	**51%**	**49%**	**51%**	**49%**	**47%**	**47%**
Winning Party	**R**	**R**	**D**	**R**	**D**	**R**	**R**	**R**

	1974	1976	1980	1982	1986	1988	1991	1992
Allegheny	60%	33%	63%	39%	49%	33%	61%	49%
Armstrong	56%	36%	63%	41%	44%	24%	58%	47%
Beaver	68%	44%	73%	47%	58%	37%	69%	57%
Butler	65%	34%	61%	36%	38%	21%	47%	45%
Fayette	64%	51%	72%	52%	55%	45%	72%	56%
Greene	60%	52%	70%	52%	49%	37%	69%	58%
Lawrence	63%	50%	66%	50%	53%	36%	63%	57%
Washington	64%	43%	72%	47%	50%	33%	65%	54%
Westmoreland	65%	41%	69%	42%	50%	33%	59%	49%
Southwest Totals	**62%**	**37%**	**66%**	**42%**	**50%**	**33%**	**61%**	**50%**
State Totals	**46%**	**47%**	**49%**	**40%**	**43%**	**33%**	**55%**	**49%**
Winning Party	**R**	**R**	**R**	**R**	**R**	**R**	**D**	**R**

	1994	1998	2000	2004	2006	2010	2012
Allegheny	53%	39%	55%	52%	65%	55%	61%
Armstrong	46%	31%	43%	36%	50%	35%	33%
Beaver	55%	42%	55%	50%	62%	48%	51%
Butler	36%	30%	36%	35%	45%	32%	35%
Fayette	61%	50%	59%	52%	64%	50%	51%
Greene	61%	46%	56%	47%	64%	50%	48%
Lawrence	52%	44%	54%	46%	58%	44%	49%
Washington	55%	41%	54%	47%	59%	46%	48%
Westmoreland	47%	39%	47%	44%	54%	39%	42%
Southwest Totals	**52%**	**39%**	**52%**	**48%**	**61%**	**48%**	**53%**
State Totals	**49%**	**37%**	**46%**	**44%**	**59%**	**49%**	**55%**
Winning Party	**R**	**R**	**R**	**R**	**D**	**R**	**D**

The six counties of northeastern Pennsylvania demonstrated the competitiveness that would mark their voting behavior through the years, with each candidate receiving 50 percent, though Myers ultimately prevailed by a scant 2,700 votes (Table 2.3). Both candidates took an equal number of counties in the area, with Myers capturing Carbon, Lackawanna, and Northampton and Duff taking Lehigh, Luzerne, and Monroe.

Chapter Two

Table 2.3 Democratic Share of Two-Party Vote for Senate, Northeastern Pennsylvania

	1950	1952	1956	1958	1962	1964	1968	1970
Carbon	53%	47%	50%	52%	51%	54%	48%	46%
Lackawanna	54%	53%	52%	57%	33%	56%	55%	48%
Lehigh	46%	44%	46%	48%	48%	51%	46%	47%
Luzerne	48%	45%	49%	52%	54%	58%	54%	52%
Monroe	49%	41%	44%	50%	46%	49%	43%	46%
Northampton	54%	50%	53%	55%	55%	58%	56%	54%
Northeast Totals	**50%**	**48%**	**50%**	**53%**	**53%**	**56%**	**52%**	**50%**
State Totals	**48%**	**48%**	**51%**	**49%**	**51%**	**49%**	**47%**	**47%**
Winning Party	**R**	**R**	**D**	**R**	**D**	**R**	**R**	**R**

	1974	1976	1980	1982	1986	1988	1991	1992
Carbon	43%	52%	49%	47%	47%	33%	58%	53%
Lackawanna	46%	56%	55%	45%	46%	31%	64%	51%
Lehigh	39%	48%	44%	34%	40%	30%	52%	50%
Luzerne	41%	55%	52%	49%	50%	33%	62%	49%
Monroe	42%	48%	41%	37%	38%	27%	50%	49%
Northampton	**44%**	**54%**	**50%**	**43%**	**46%**	**37%**	**54%**	**54%**
Totals	**42%**	**53%**	**50%**	**43%**	**45%**	**31%**	**58%**	**51%**
Northeast Totals	**46%**	**47%**	**49%**	**40%**	**43%**	**33%**	**55%**	**49%**
Winning Party	**R**	**R**	**R**	**R**	**R**	**R**	**D**	**R**

	1994	1998	2000	2004	2006	2010	2012
Carbon	50%	42%	46%	41%	57%	45%	48%
Lackawanna	60%	40%	54%	43%	69%	60%	68%
Lehigh	46%	32%	42%	44%	58%	47%	56%
Luzerne	54%	35%	48%	42%	61%	51%	56%
Monroe	41%	34%	40%	43%	56%	48%	57%
Northampton	49%	35%	44%	44%	58%	48%	55%
Northeast Totals	**51%**	**36%**	**46%**	**43%**	**61%**	**50%**	**57%**
State Totals	**49%**	**37%**	**46%**	**44%**	**59%**	**49%**	**55%**
Winning Party	**R**	**R**	**R**	**R**	**D**	**R**	**D**

Central Pennsylvania provided the healthy majority that GOP candidates would come to expect. Overall, Duff received 56 percent of the vote there, earning a 135,000-vote plurality across the 47 counties (Table 2.4). His largest margins were in Tioga and Wayne counties, where he reached 72 percent of the vote, while his poorest showing was in Democratic Cambria County, which the

Republican lost by 10 percentage points. Although Myers's 44 percent may appear unimpressive, central Pennsylvania wasn't his problem. In fact, in only 4 of the other 23 Senate contests covered during the period of this study (1958, 1964, 1991, and 2006) would a Democratic candidate even match Myers's performance in the central "T."

Table 2.4 Democratic Share of the Two-Party Vote for Senate, Central Pennsylvania

	1950	1952	1956	1958	1962	1964	1968	1970
Adams	43%	36%	42%	45%	43%	45%	37%	40%
Bedford	44%	37%	42%	43%	39%	41%	29%	38%
Berks	52%	50%	51%	53%	51%	54%	48%	52%
Blair	38%	36%	44%	41%	35%	41%	31%	44%
Bradford	32%	24%	32%	34%	36%	38%	34%	29%
Cambria	55%	57%	58%	56%	54%	51%	45%	54%
Cameron	37%	30%	38%	37%	42%	46%	32%	46%
Centre	36%	36%	45%	42%	37%	38%	38%	36%
Clarion	48%	38%	45%	41%	45%	46%	36%	42%
Clearfield	51%	46%	53%	50%	44%	49%	38%	49%
Clinton	47%	42%	49%	48%	46%	50%	45%	46%
Columbia	51%	44%	49%	50%	46%	50%	45%	41%
Crawford	41%	35%	40%	42%	43%	46%	41%	47%
Cumberland	46%	35%	41%	43%	38%	39%	33%	36%
Dauphin	38%	38%	40%	42%	37%	40%	33%	35%
Elk	53%	47%	48%	49%	53%	54%	42%	52%
Erie	47%	44%	46%	46%	54%	50%	49%	53%
Forest	38%	30%	38%	39%	44%	42%	33%	24%
Franklin	40%	37%	45%	47%	43%	44%	40%	43%
Fulton	54%	46%	50%	51%	46%	46%	39%	46%
Huntingdon	37%	32%	41%	41%	39%	38%	35%	34%
Indiana	45%	41%	46%	45%	46%	42%	40%	43%
Jefferson	41%	36%	43%	41%	41%	40%	34%	40%
Juniata	47%	43%	48%	47%	44%	44%	39%	39%
Lancaster	33%	39%	34%	35%	33%	38%	31%	31%

Lebanon	42%	39%	44%	41%	34%	39%	31%	36%
Lycoming	51%	40%	46%	43%	43%	47%	40%	40%
McKean	32%	27%	30%	36%	39%	18%	36%	40%
Mercer	44%	45%	47%	48%	50%	51%	48%	49%
Mifflin	47%	42%	45%	43%	42%	47%	41%	36%
Montour	49%	39%	45%	43%	45%	50%	43%	41%
Northumberland	45%	40%	50%	45%	45%	50%	42%	40%
Perry	41%	32%	42%	42%	38%	39%	32%	35%
Pike	38%	27%	32%	36%	37%	38%	32%	30%
Potter	37%	29%	37%	40%	38%	41%	29%	45%
Schuylkill	44%	41%	44%	47%	47%	53%	44%	45%
Snyder	30%	21%	31%	30%	29%	32%	25%	25%
Somerset	45%	42%	46%	46%	44%	44%	37%	43%
Sullivan	45%	39%	45%	44%	46%	46%	41%	38%
Susquehanna	34%	26%	35%	36%	39%	39%	33%	32%
Tioga	28%	21%	28%	33%	35%	37%	30%	34%
Union	30%	21%	31%	28%	27%	31%	26%	27%
Venango	31%	28%	32%	33%	41%	41%	35%	39%
Warren	33%	29%	32%	37%	40%	46%	40%	42%
Wayne	28%	21%	31%	32%	33%	34%	29%	25%
Wyoming	33%	24%	33%	35%	34%	34%	30%	27%
York	50%	50%	50%	57%	48%	51%	42%	42%
Central Totals	**44%**	**40%**	**44%**	**45%**	**43%**	**45%**	**39%**	**42%**
State Totals	**48%**	**48%**	**51%**	**49%**	**51%**	**49%**	**47%**	**47%**
Winning Party	**R**	**R**	**D**	**R**	**D**	**R**	**R**	**R**

	1974	**1976**	**1980**	**1982**	**1986**	**1988**	**1991**	**1992**
Adams	38%	42%	38%	30%	38%	23%	44%	45%
Bedford	39%	40%	41%	32%	35%	22%	39%	40%
Berks	46%	48%	43%	35%	39%	27%	43%	47%
Blair	38%	39%	48%	28%	31%	19%	44%	41%
Bradford	25%	38%	35%	25%	28%	17%	40%	43%
Cambria	53%	43%	65%	45%	53%	35%	60%	50%

Cameron	40%	41%	46%	39%	33%	26%	39%	47%
Centre	33%	47%	48%	28%	38%	25%	45%	50%
Clarion	60%	39%	57%	34%	37%	20%	47%	45%
Clearfield	46%	48%	53%	41%	44%	30%	51%	51%
Clinton	35%	52%	45%	38%	44%	32%	57%	54%
Columbia	43%	53%	46%	39%	39%	24%	46%	48%
Crawford	41%	43%	48%	38%	35%	22%	53%	46%
Cumberland	33%	35%	33%	27%	32%	19%	37%	38%
Dauphin	33%	39%	36%	33%	34%	25%	45%	41%
Elk	57%	47%	61%	41%	47%	29%	50%	52%
Erie	43%	47%	60%	43%	42%	25%	55%	51%
Forest	46%	41%	50%	34%	36%	24%	47%	46%
Franklin	43%	45%	39%	34%	33%	21%	38%	40%
Fulton	42%	47%	46%	40%	39%	27%	40%	40%
Huntingdon	31%	40%	41%	27%	34%	20%	41%	42%
Indiana	48%	38%	55%	36%	41%	26%	55%	48%
Jefferson	49%	39%	54%	33%	38%	22%	45%	44%
Juniata	35%	43%	36%	36%	38%	24%	41%	40%
Lancaster	35%	32%	28%	20%	25%	19%	31%	36%
Lebanon	36%	36%	29%	26%	32%	20%	37%	37%
Lycoming	34%	45%	43%	33%	35%	22%	43%	44%
McKean	38%	39%	39%	30%	31%	25%	41%	45%
Mercer	48%	45%	55%	45%	45%	36%	60%	55%
Mifflin	30%	41%	43%	30%	37%	23%	44%	45%
Montour	38%	46%	43%	35%	37%	22%	46%	47%
Northumberland	41%	48%	46%	46%	42%	29%	52%	48%
Perry	29%	37%	34%	27%	29%	15%	34%	34%
Pike	36%	41%	36%	33%	31%	25%	44%	44%
Potter	40%	46%	37%	33%	30%	26%	35%	39%
Schuylkill	38%	50%	43%	41%	39%	27%	55%	46%
Snyder	23%	31%	29%	21%	23%	12%	32%	36%
Somerset	54%	38%	58%	37%	41%	25%	49%	44%
Sullivan	38%	47%	41%	38%	39%	27%	44%	46%

Susquehanna	31%	41%	35%	30%	29%	20%	46%	45%
Tioga	29%	37%	34%	28%	29%	23%	36%	40%
Union	26%	34%	33%	24%	27%	15%	38%	41%
Venango	49%	35%	50%	34%	37%	23%	50%	46%
Warren	37%	42%	41%	33%	36%	26%	48%	49%
Wayne	31%	37%	33%	26%	27%	17%	40%	42%
Wyoming	27%	38%	33%	28%	25%	15%	33%	42%
York	39%	40%	38%	30%	34%	21%	43%	44%
Central Totals	**40%**	**42%**	**44%**	**34%**	**36%**	**24%**	**45%**	**44%**
State Totals	**46%**	**47%**	**49%**	**40%**	**43%**	**33%**	**55%**	**49%**
Winning Party	**R**	**R**	**R**	**R**	**R**	**R**	**D**	**R**

	1994	**1998**	**2000**	**2004**	**2006**	**2010**	**2012**
Adams	37%	28%	32%	28%	45%	31%	38%
Bedford	34%	28%	26%	27%	42%	25%	26%
Berks	39%	30%	38%	40%	55%	44%	52%
Blair	38%	25%	30%	30%	44%	32%	35%
Bradford	32%	25%	27%	26%	43%	30%	36%
Cambria	59%	49%	50%	45%	64%	49%	49%
Cameron	36%	34%	29%	33%	48%	36%	38%
Centre	43%	30%	36%	42%	57%	48%	52%
Clarion	37%	28%	36%	32%	47%	33%	33%
Clearfield	43%	38%	36%	38%	55%	40%	36%
Clinton	51%	36%	39%	37%	54%	41%	45%
Columbia	46%	34%	35%	33%	51%	38%	46%
Crawford	36%	30%	35%	33%	49%	37%	38%
Cumberland	36%	26%	33%	29%	46%	34%	43%
Dauphin	43%	29%	42%	37%	53%	44%	55%
Elk	44%	41%	41%	39%	63%	45%	44%
Erie	47%	37%	44%	38%	66%	55%	57%
Forest	40%	30%	36%	33%	52%	40%	39%
Franklin	32%	27%	29%	25%	39%	26%	32%
Fulton	35%	30%	26%	23%	39%	23%	27%

Huntingdon	39%	25%	26%	29%	46%	32%	34%
Indiana	48%	35%	42%	39%	53%	40%	42%
Jefferson	36%	32%	32%	31%	45%	29%	28%
Juniata	38%	30%	29%	25%	42%	25%	32%
Lancaster	28%	23%	28%	30%	42%	32%	41%
Lebanon	34%	24%	34%	27%	45%	30%	38%
Lycoming	35%	27%	28%	29%	39%	30%	36%
McKean	30%	28%	31%	28%	46%	31%	37%
Mercer	47%	43%	49%	45%	57%	44%	50%
Mifflin	41%	27%	29%	26%	43%	24%	31%
Montour	42%	30%	31%	30%	47%	36%	41%
Northumberland	47%	36%	37%	33%	50%	38%	40%
Perry	34%	24%	27%	24%	40%	25%	33%
Pike	33%	32%	38%	35%	48%	37%	45%
Potter	26%	26%	25%	23%	36%	26%	28%
Schuylkill	47%	32%	38%	35%	54%	41%	44%
Snyder	31%	17%	24%	23%	37%	28%	32%
Somerset	44%	67%	41%	35%	51%	33%	33%
Sullivan	42%	50%	30%	31%	47%	33%	37%
Susquehanna	38%	27%	32%	30%	48%	35%	40%
Tioga	30%	26%	27%	24%	39%	28%	32%
Union	36%	24%	28%	32%	42%	35%	39%
Venango	41%	29%	40%	32%	48%	36%	36%
Warren	40%	30%	36%	32%	51%	37%	39%
Wayne	34%	27%	32%	30%	46%	34%	42%
Wyoming	36%	20%	30%	28%	45%	37%	44%
York	38%	28%	34%	36%	45%	32%	41%
Central Totals	**40%**	**31%**	**36%**	**33%**	**49%**	**37%**	**43%**
State Totals	**49%**	**37%**	**46%**	**44%**	**59%**	**49%**	**55%**
Winning Party	**R**	**R**	**R**	**R**	**D**	**R**	**D**

Nationally, it was indeed a victory for the GOP, or as they described it, for "two-party government." Of course, in Republican-dominated Pennsylvania, the

Democrats were the party desperately trying to achieve parity. But amid the negative national surroundings, it was surely something that the voters of this state were not quite ready to grant them. While it was a bad week for the Democrats, it could have been much worse. Several days before the election, President Truman narrowly escaped an assassination attempt.

1952: MARTIN/BARD

In 1952, Pennsylvania's other Senate seat was up. The contest was between Republican incumbent Edward Martin of Greene County and Democratic challenger Guy K. Bard, a former federal judge from Lancaster. This was an even more low-key affair, overshadowed by the presidential campaign. Martin, a one-time governor who had become a fixture in Pennsylvania politics, also had the benefit of Eisenhower's coattails, running up a 162,000-vote victory statewide, although he got 100,000 votes less than the top of ticket. As with Eisenhower, a major key to Martin's victory was how well he did in Allegheny County, losing by just 22,000 votes in that Democratic stronghold. In Philadelphia, he also ran slightly behind Eisenhower, losing the city by 173,000 votes. Although Martin's similarly ran behind Eisenhower throughout much of the state, his numbers were sufficient to send him back to Washington for a second term.

1956: CLARK/DUFF

Although previous Senate campaigns in Pennsylvania were largely obscured by presidential or gubernatorial contests, the 1956 race was different, largely because of the personalities involved. Former Philadelphia Mayor Joseph S. Clark on the Democratic side opposed Jim Duff, who harbored higher political ambitions but first needed to win reelection to a second term. Clark had already cemented his place in the Pennsylvania's political history in 1951, when he helped engineer a realignment of Philadelphia's political scene, upsetting the GOP machine that had dominated the city for well over half a century.

Philadelphia's shift would enable the Democrats to finally narrow the huge registration gap that they had faced in the state since the Civil War. Just six years earlier, when Duff was first elected, Republicans possessed 70 percent of the two-party registration numbers in Philadelphia and 59 percent in the state. Now, the Democrats had narrowed the gap to just 2 points in the city and just 8 in the state. In addition, a Democrat, George Leader, now resided in the Governor's mansion, only the third to do so since Abraham Lincoln's presidency.

While the opportunity for the Democrats to advance their political fortunes in the state may have ripened, they also faced with the daunting task of running against not just the popular Duff, but also President Dwight D. Eisenhower, who headed the Republican ticket. Not surprisingly, Duff sought to attach himself to the Eisenhower, who by then considered himself a fellow Pennsylvanian. The incumbent Senator also tried to center much of his campaign on what he called Eisenhower's "program for peace"—in reference to the president's opposition to sending in troops to support Great Britain and France in the Suez Crisis in the Middle East. Otherwise, Duff focused his attacks on Clark's record as mayor of Philadelphia, arguing that Clark was a wild spender who had repeatedly raised taxes.

Despite Eisenhower's popularity, Clark didn't shy from attacking the president directly, on both international and domestic matters. He chided the President and Secretary of State John Foster Dulles on their Middle East policy, saying that it had caused the most humiliating diplomatic defeat in U.S. history. On domestic policy, the Democrat charged that the hard-money policy of the Eisenhower Administration had caused unnecessary hardship without helping to hold down the cost of living.

Campaigning as an unabashed liberal, Clark focused on issues such as minimum wage, social security, and immigration reform and on overturning what was the scourge of labor unions, the Taft-Hartley Act. He also suggested eliminating the filibuster rule in the Senate, a procedure used by opponents of civil rights legislation to thwart reforms in that area. That position later became the thesis behind Clark's much-heralded book *The Sapless Branch*. The Democrat also repeatedly attacked the incumbent's attendance record, one of the worst in the Senate. The 73-year old Duff was vulnerable to this charge by his more youthful opponent. That and the fact that Duff had made a lot of enemies over the years both inside and outside his party probably were enough to make the difference.

The result was one of the closest elections in Pennsylvania history, with Clark prevailing by a little less than 18,000 votes statewide (of 4.5 million cast). It was so close that Clark wasn't determined the victor until 50,000 military ballots had been counted. The election also produced a phenomenon that would become one the hallmarks of Pennsylvania Senate elections—ticket splitting. Although it would later be Democratic Senate candidates "cut" from the ticket more often than not, this time the tables were turned. Except for Duff, Republicans had a clean sweep, winning not just the presidential contest (by more than 600,000 votes), but also every statewide office. The Republicans also increased their numbers in both the national congressional delegation and in both chambers of the state legislature

Clark reaped the political benefits of being the former mayor of the state's largest city. He captured a 170,000-vote plurality in Philadelphia, which was particularly impressive considering that the GOP still maintained a registration edge of 33,000. In the suburbs, Duff failed to balance the city vote, carrying the four counties by only 109,000 votes, although his party held a 386,000-vote advantage in registered voters. Bucks County, where Duff managed only a 5,000-vote victory, proved particularly disappointing to the incumbent.

Across the rest of the Commonwealth, traditional voting patterns largely held. The Republican carried all but four counties in the central "T": Berks,

Cambria, Clearfield and York (which he lost by only 149 votes), on the way to a 165,000-vote advantage. Clark's Philadelphia ties dragged him down somewhat in southwestern Pennsylvania, although he did carry the region by 10 percentage points. The Democrat managed only a 41,000-vote edge in Duff's Allegheny County. Clark's overall victory came despite Democratic defections in the state's second most populous county, where his party held a 161,000 edge in voter registration. Future Democrats would not be so fortunate. In the bellwether northeast, the race was about as close as it was statewide, although Duff grabbed 3,800 more votes. Overall, Clark carried only 15 of the state's 67 counties, but in it is the actual votes that count, and there the Democrat had just a few more.

1958: SCOTT/LEADER

With Clark's victory coming on the heels of fellow Democrat George Leader's upset gubernatorial win two years earlier, Democrats certainly couldn't be faulted for feeling that a new era had developed in Keystone State politics. Indeed, with the retirement of incumbent Senator Edward Martin and the decision by Leader to run (state laws precluded a second gubernatorial term), they were now clearly favored to capture Pennsylvania's other senate seat as well.

In what would be a harbinger of things to come, however, George Leader's attempt to move from the governor's mansion to the United States Senate in 1958 managed to just come up a little short. Unquestionably, Leader's two-point loss to Republican Hugh Scott that year was due primarily to his poor showing in the southwest. In that traditional Democrat bastion, voters resoundingly rejected their candidate in favor of a Republican who hailed from Philadelphia, of all places. The difference between the percentage of Democrats in the region (61 percent) and Leader's final numbers (47 percent) was a staggering 14 percentage points. Had Leader merely approximated Pittsburgh Mayor David Lawrence's 55 percent total in the southwest in that year's gubernatorial contest (which was nevertheless a poor showing also considering Lawrence's background in the region), he would have been off to Washington, perhaps the first of many trips.

Instead, Leader's career was derailed in the very heart of southwestern Pennsylvania, Allegheny County. Despite a Democratic Party registration advantage of almost 182,000 votes, the Republican Scott outpaced his opponent by 33,000 votes. Although Leader's proposal as governor to enact the state's first income tax certainly didn't help, more than anything the defeat of the reform-minded Leader was attributed to a number of Democratic Party officials who resented his attempts to scale back the state's patronage apparatus.

Specifically, the case that stoked their ire involved J. Franklyn McSorley, whom Leader had selected to head the Pennsylvania Turnpike Commission. Sometime later, however, the governor accused him of providing an automobile and a driver to a former chairman in return for his counsel. McSorley was initially suspended from his position and later indicted and convicted for his wrongdoing. He served four months in a Dauphin County prison. Described as "a man of many friends in Pittsburgh," McSorley gained revenge when the "friends" ganged up on the governor and extracted their own retribution in Allegheny County.

Elsewhere in the Commonwealth, the results were somewhat mixed. While Leader carried Philadelphia by 133,000 votes, he couldn't match Clark's numbers of the 1956 election. But that Philadelphia was Scott's hometown and that he had served in Congress for several terms needs to be figured into the equation. Leader also did a reasonable job holding down Scott's numbers in the Philadelphia suburbs, although he trailed by 128,000 votes in the region. In central Pennsylvania, the York native ran fared far better than Clark, holding Scott's advantage to 132,000 votes in this traditional GOP stronghold. Leader also carried all but Lehigh County in the tightly competitive northeast, on his way to a 24,000-vote plurality in this area.

In the end, however, infighting within the Democratic Party, particularly in southwestern Pennsylvania, was the determining factor. Democrats clearly had no one to blame but themselves. The party had squandered a golden opportunity to take total control of the Senate delegation. Instead, this would mark the sudden end of what had appeared to be a promising political future for the young former governor from York County (he was only 40 years old at the time of the defeat). Leader would never seek elective office again. On the other hand, Hugh Scott went on to national prominence, serving two more terms until his retirement 18 years later, in 1976, concluding his career as the Senate Minority Whip.

The significance of this defeat for the Democrats is impossible to measure, but state historian Paul B. Beers perhaps summed it up perfectly in his 1980 book, *Pennsylvania Politics*: "The supposition is not farfetched that had Governor George M. Leader won a U.S. Senate seat in 1958, he would have gone to be the Democrats' presidential or vice-presidential candidate in 1968, 1972, or 1976. The plain-spoken, liberal, and highly principled George Leader seemed destined for national prominence. His positions had appeal, and he could have been the right Pennsylvanian at the right time."

1962: CLARK/VAN ZANDT

Joe Clark managed to win a tight reelection in 1962, this time by 2 percentage points over Congressman James Van Zandt of Blair County. With the Scranton-Dilworth gubernatorial race taking center stage, few seemed to notice the Senate race. It probably didn't help that the campaign focused more on Clark's personality than on anything else. Van Zandt, a Republican from Altoona, criticized the incumbent repeatedly not just for being a liberal, but also for being a visionary and a dreamer.

On policy, Van Zandt mainly trotted out the Cold War rhetoric commonplace for the day, questioning his opponent's anti-Communist credentials. Van Zandt assailed Clark for his association with the Americans for

Democratic Action organization and his support of the Kennedy Administration's policy toward Cuba and China. Responding, Clark charged that his opponent was using disreputable campaign tactics. "He has attacked Americans for Democratic Action, a strong anti-Communist organization founded by Eleanor Roosevelt, as being soft on communism.... Representative Van Zandt has had the gall to attempt to smear his opponent with Red paint.... This outworn trick of low-level politics is, in this case, as ridiculous as it is reprehensible."

Clark used his own hyperbole, charging that Van Zandt was "trigger-happy" and "we would have declared war unilaterally" had it been up to him. Even in his victory speech, the victorious Clark couldn't resist one final jab. Commenting on what he called the "Red smear" tactics of his opponent, he remarked, "It seems clear that McCarthyism is not yet dead."

Voters in southwestern Pennsylvania were the difference again, although this was one of the rare times that went in favor of the Democrats. Clark recorded a 198,000-vote advantage (58 percent) in this nine-county area, almost double his previous result. Perhaps making amends for the Leader debacle, Allegheny County alone produced a 108,000-vote advantage (58 percent) for the senator from Philadelphia. In Westmoreland County, Clark almost doubled Van Zandt's numbers, carrying it by more than 38,000 votes (65 percent). The only county in the region that the Republican carried was Armstrong, and that by a mere 572 votes.

Clark needed every bit of this southwestern support, because elsewhere in the state he did little to expand his margins from his 1956 cliffhanger. He carried his hometown of Philadelphia by slightly more than 180,000 votes, an increase of just 10,000. In the suburbs, he ran 109,000 votes behind his opponent. Six years of incumbency didn't seem to help much in central Pennsylvania, where Clark lost by 184,000 votes (57–43 percent). Van Zandt carried all but Berks, Cambria, Elk, Erie, and Mercer Counties in the "T." The only other area outside the southwest that Clark showed any noticeable improvement was in the competitive northeast. A region he had lost six years earlier provided him with a 29,000-vote margin in 1962.

Statewide, Clark picked up 103,000 more votes than his challenger, and although it looked like a landslide compared with his first election, it was close nonetheless and certainly indicates that he had done little to enhance his support over the course of his first term. Against a candidate such as Van Zandt, who was not the best the GOP had to offer, it was enough for victory. Against a stronger challenger in his next election, however, the vulnerability would be exposed. In fact, if western Pennsylvania had provided Clark with the margin it did in the 1956 battle, his winning margin would have been less than 8,000 votes. This was one time—a rarity, as we will soon witness—that the Democratic base of southwestern Pennsylvania actually delivered for the party. No one could predict that 1962 would be the last time in the 20th century that a Democrat from Pennsylvania would win a full term in the United States Senate.

1964: SCOTT/BLATT

In his first attempt to win reelection to the United States Senate, Hugh Scott couldn't have faced a more daunting political climate—1964. With Lyndon B. Johnson rolling to a record-breaking victory against Senator Barry Goldwater nationally, negative coattails must surely have caused many in his camp to worry about their fate. Pennsylvania was no exception, with the President coasting to a 1.46 million-vote plurality (65 percent). That Scott survived in that environment against a strong challenger is a testament to both his political skills and his political luck.

For just as Democratic infighting had torpedoed Scott's previous challenger, it would once again in 1964, this time in the form of Allegheny County native Genevieve Blatt. The challenger, noted for her trademarked flowery hats, was currently serving her third term as Pennsylvania Secretary of Internal Affairs. She had made state political history when she became the first woman ever to hold statewide office with that victory in 1954. As in the previous Senatorial race, when George Leader had run, enough Democrats in the southwest abandoned their party's nominee to send the Philadelphia Republican back to Washington.

This time the seeds were sowed in a bitter spring primary battle that pitted Blatt against Supreme Court Judge Michael A. Musmanno. The judge was a colorful personality in his own right, known as the court's prime orator. Musmanno, who, like Blatt, was from Allegheny County, had the support of much of the state's Democratic Party organization. The one exception was Senator Clark, whose vociferous support of Blatt went so far as to accuse Musmanno of changing his name years earlier to appear more Jewish when he was practicing law in Philadelphia. Some in the party, particularly Musmanno's friends back home in the Pittsburgh area, would not forget four years later, when Clark himself was back on the ballot.

At first, Blatt appeared to be the winner by a slim 491 votes, but a dispute arose over approximately 5,000 questionable ballots in Philadelphia. These "wrong-line ballots" materialized when the state Election Bureau mistakenly left spaces below and beside the candidates' names for voters to use. Musmanno had enough of an edge among those ballots that counting them would have thrown the election his way. The case went before Musmanno's own Supreme Court, where to the astonishment of most observers, the justices ruled against their colleague. The outcome of the race wasn't decided until August 21—115 days after the primary—when the Election Bureau finally certified Blatt's 491-vote victory. That didn't prevent Musmanno from continuing the appeals process, all the way up to the United States Supreme Court. The Court finally put an end to the battle by refusing to hear the case on October 10th, less than one month before the general election.

The impacts of the primary on Blatt's general election campaign were devastating, not just in terms of the time and money spent, but also in regard to enemies accumulated. In the fall campaign, Blatt not surprisingly attempted to tie the Republican Scott to the widely unpopular Goldwater campaign. The sharpest exchange between the two candidates occurred two days before election day, when both addressed the Philadelphia chapter of the NAACP. Speaking first, the Democrat said, "the American people have been confronted with a candidate for the Presidency on the Republican ticket who says most emphatically that we are not our brother's keeper; that state's rights come before human rights; that we should use our national power to get our own way in the world."

While noting that other prominent Republicans had personally distanced themselves from the Arizona Senator, Blatt said that "here in Pennsylvania, my opponent has not done so. He has never said whether he agrees or disagrees with Barry Goldwater on any specific point." Perhaps the strongest charge leveled by the Democrat, however, was that Scott was appealing to voters "not as Americans concerned about the future welfare of the families and country, but on the basis of their race, or their national origin, or religion."

All of this brought a stinging rebuke when moments later Scott addressed the convention. With the Democrat no longer in the hall, the Senator stated that his opponent was in no position to criticize him, proclaiming, "When she can show my record, when she can wear my robe, when she can do what I have done, then she can." He continued, "I get a little tired of these holier-than-thou righteous appeals. She appeals to you by using hogwash and trying to make all of you hate me. Aren't you through with hate? How insidious this was."

As the votes were counted, Allegheny County again emerged as the deciding factor. In the Leader fiasco six years earlier, Allegheny County Democrats had at least damaged a candidate who was from outside their region, but with Blatt they turned on one of their own. Despite Johnson 233,000-vote plurality in the county, Scott carried it once again, and although his 17,000-vote advantage was smaller than six years earlier, it proved to be the difference.

Blatt fared better in the rest of the region, but she still ran markedly below the presidential ticket. She also lost the two GOP-leaning counties of Armstrong and Butler. The only two counties in the west that provided her with large majorities were the Democratic strongholds of Fayette and Greene counties. With Democrats claiming 60 percent of the registered voters in the southwest, and LBJ on his way to a 446,000-vote cushion across the region, Blatt managed only a 9,000-vote plurality in what was her political backyard. Democrats in the rest of the state understood that it was once again their base of Allegheny County that had robbed their candidate of the brass ring.

Elsewhere in the Commonwealth, Scott's numbers largely paralleled his 1958 effort. He trailed his opponent in Philadelphia, his hometown, by 142,000 votes, 9,000 votes larger than the gap in 1958. In the suburbs, Scott increased his plurality to 144,000 votes, which negated Blatt's city edge. Interestingly, central Pennsylvania failed to provide the incumbent Republican with the numbers one might expect. Scott carried the region by only 10 percentage points, a 138,000-vote advantage but only a slight increase from his 1958 effort against the central Pennsylvanian George Leader.

Even more surprising, however, was the strength that Blatt demonstrated in the northeast. In this six-county area, she scored a 62,000-vote plurality against the incumbent. Scott carried only Monroe County (which had the lowest population in the region), and his margin was only 263 votes. Blatt also carried the coal county of Luzerne by 25,000 votes, despite a 27,000-voter registration edge that the GOP still possessed. While some of this can no doubt be attributable to LBJ's coattails, it was a very impressive effort nonetheless.

The statewide results revealed one of the closest Senate campaigns in the state's history. On election night, unofficial tallies fixed Scott's lead at just 19,456 votes. Blatt, who two years earlier had survived an Internal Affairs race by just 1,313 votes, held out hope that a recount of approximately 129,000 absentee ballots might change the outcome in her favor. But by the end of the second canvass, it became apparent that the incumbent was indeed the winner, this time by 71,000 votes. While Blatt's quest to become Pennsylvania's first female senator came up short, she would make history once again years later, when Governor Milton Shapp appointed her as the first woman to serve on the Commonwealth Court.

1968: SCHWEIKER/CLARK

However disappointing for Democrats the Scott victory was, they paled in comparison to what awaited them in 1968. Even though Hubert H. Humphrey was carrying the top of the Democrat ticket to victory statewide, Congressman Richard S. Schweiker of Montgomery County pulled off one of the biggest upsets in the nation by knocking off the powerful Senator Joseph S. Clark. What was particularly surprising was the sheer size of Schweiker's victory, the challenger winning by 6 percentage points statewide. Interestingly, Schweiker hadn't even been the first choice of the party faithful. Clark thought he had caught a break when William Scranton, the popular former governor, wouldn't allow himself to be talked out of retirement.

Although it has become part of Pennsylvania political folklore that Clark's strong advocacy of gun control doomed him, other issues hurt the incumbent as well. Vietnam dominated much of the conversation during the campaign, and the challenger proved more nimble in presenting his position than the more experienced incumbent, who was a member of the powerful Senate Foreign Relations Committee. Both candidates sought de-escalation of the war, but while Clark called for the immediate unconditional suspension of U.S. bombing, Schweiker put forth a plan for step-by-step de-escalation demanding a North Vietnamese response at each step. This was ultimately the option chosen by President Johnson.

The Clark campaign also made the costly mistake of agreeing to a series of four half-hour television debates. Before the debates, the 42-year-old third-term congressman was unknown in much of the state. Speaking to reporters in the campaign's aftermath, Schweiker's campaign manager, David Newhall, stated that the debates solved the biggest problem they faced: "Our problem from the beginning," Newhall said, "was a lack of statewide name recognition. If I had been in Clark's corner, I would have agreed to one debate and that would have been it. Then, I couldn't have been charged with not debating him and he wouldn't get the exposure he needed." Perhaps emblematic of what went wrong with the Clark campaign was that the senator showed up at the wrong polling place to vote on election day. (Clark, who had recently moved after remarrying, was promptly directed to the proper location.)

Clark's poor showing in the southwest sealed his fate. Again, memories of the 1964 primary battle lingered among many Democrats in the region, and they proved costly to the Clark campaign. Ultimately, the incumbent ran 4,000 votes behind the challenger in the southwest event though 62 percent of voters in the region were registered Democrats. An incumbent who ran as much as 13 points behind his party's number of registered voters had many problems.

Again crucial was Allegheny County, which Schweiker carried by slightly less than 9,000 votes. The 1968 election marked the third time in the past four elections that this seat of Democratic Party power had thrown its political weight to the Republican. Clark fared poorly in the rest of the area, too, dropping Armstrong, Butler, and Lawrence counties while managing only a 615-vote plurality in populous Westmoreland. The overall gap between registered Democratic voters in these nine counties and Clark's final numbers was a devastating 310,000 votes.

Ironically, Philadelphia voters provided their former mayor with an impressive 194,000-vote advantage, slightly eclipsing their level of support in his two previous, successful attempts. The figure is less impressive in the context of the overall campaign, as Humphrey carried the city by 272,000 votes, considerably more than Clark managed in his own hometown. Furthermore, the GOP suburbs provided huge numbers for their candidate. Schweiker, a Montgomery County native running as a favorite son, rolled up a 196,000-vote advantage in the suburbs. This was double Richard Nixon's total and almost double what Clark's previous foes had recorded. With Philadelphia's vote essentially balanced out in the suburbs (Schweiker narrowly won the southeast as a whole), and southwestern Pennsylvania deserting him, there was little opportunity for the incumbent elsewhere.

Certainly not in central Pennsylvania, as the liberal Clark was held to an astonishingly low 39 percent across the region's 47 counties, home to many of the state's most conservative voters. The Democrat failed to carry even one county in the region, reaching a level of ineffectiveness rarely seen by an incumbent in sparsely populated Snyder County (Middleburg), where Clark received just 25 percent of the vote. Schweiker's numbers in the central "T" were so large—a 297,000 vote advantage—that even if Clark had run well in the southwest it probably wouldn't have mattered.

Similar to Genevieve Blatt four years earlier, the Democrat performed relatively well in the northeast despite the trends statewide. Although Clark's numbers slipped somewhat from his 1962 contest, he still attained a 21,000-vote edge (52 percent) overall. This was built on his strong tallies in the three counties that he won in the region: Lackawanna, Luzerne, and Northampton.

For the second straight time, the Democratic senatorial candidate ran far behind the party's presidential candidates, both of whom carried the state. Rather than merely costing them a chance to control both Senate seats as was the case in 1964, however, this time Democrats were left completely empty-handed. It would take a tragedy almost a quarter-century later to finally turn that around.

1970: SCOTT/SESLER

After a string of intense and even ferocious campaigns, the 1970 Senate contest was a much more subdued affair. As usual, it was overshadowed by that same season's gubernatorial contest, itself rather low key by Pennsylvania standards. Seeking to make history as the first person elected to three straight terms in the U.S. Senate was incumbent Hugh Scott. By now, the Republican with the trademark pipe had become a powerful force in Washington, having risen to the office of Senate Minority Leader. This left Democrats in a difficult position of trying to find someone willing to take on the Chestnut Hill native. Their inability to recruit a top-tiered challenger forced them to settle on 42-year-old State Senator William Sesler of Erie. Although the youthful Democrat was already into his tenth year in the State Senate, he was still virtually unknown outside his home county.

Not surprisingly, Sesler's main problem was name recognition, and he ultimately traveled 100,000 miles trying to increase his presence in the minds of voters across the state. Those efforts were largely hamstrung, however, by a lack of money, which limited him to only a few commercial spots. By his own estimate, the challenger had only about $100,000 for all media advertising, which was just under half of his total campaign budget.

On the issues, Scott stressed his experience in Washington and pointed out that as Senate Minority Leader he was much better able to advance the state's interests. Sesler attempted to counter this theme by arguing that the incumbent had repeatedly placed his political allegiances to the Nixon Administration ahead of those of his fellow Pennsylvanians. The incumbent Republican, who stressed his moderate credentials, successfully positioned himself in the middle on most issues, thereby pushing his challenger further left than where he needed to be politically. The Vietnam War never became a major issue in the campaign. The Republican Senator largely supported the Administration's policy, and although his opponent tried to distinguish himself from the incumbent on the decision to intervene in Cambodia, he had been generally hawkish on the war himself.

Scott may have felt somewhat vulnerable on the issue of gun control by virtue of his strong support of the 1968 gun registration act. He clearly sought to avoid the wrath of hunters, who had claimed credit for Clark's defeat, by later publicly admitting that he made a mistake in supporting all sections of the gun control act. He also admitted regret in supporting failed Supreme Court nominee

G. Harrold Carswell, which Sesler posited was further evidence of Scott's equivocation on major issues.

The incumbent prevailed by a comfortable 220,000 votes, a 6-point victory, yet Sesler ran better in southwestern Pennsylvania than either of Scott's two previous, much better known rivals. In Allegheny County, Scott for the first time failed to carry the county, as Sesler eked out a 2,100-vote advantage. That this would stand as the best the Democrats could muster in three tries in their political base against Scott is clear evidence of the Philadelphian's political abilities. In the southwest as a whole, Sesler compiled a 35,000-vote plurality, again stronger than his predecessors, but still far from what a Democrat would ordinarily need to win statewide.

Although Sesler was a candidate from the opposite end of the state and virtually unknown to the average voter, his 61,000-vote margin in Philadelphia was disappointing. He ran 9 points behind Shapp's gubernatorial numbers. In the suburbs, Scott enjoyed his usual success, achieving a 140,000-vote advantage. Throughout the southeast region as a whole, the incumbent prevailed by 79,000, easily his best showing ever.

Predictably, central Pennsylvania delivered its usual margin for the Republican candidate, this time in the form of 176,000 votes. Sesler carried only four counties in the vast "T": Berks, Cambria, Elk, and his home county of Erie located in the far northwest quadrant. Scott carried the northeast by a narrow 699 votes, taking all but Luzerne and Northampton counties. Interestingly, normally reliably Democratic Lackawanna threw its support to Scott, by 3,300 votes.

This was the last campaign for the three-term senator, whose career would end under a dark cloud after it was disclosed that he had accepted illegal payments from Gulf Oil Corporation. In defeating a variety of opponents in both good political times and bad, there's no question that Scott enjoyed some breaks along the way. That shouldn't minimize what he was able to achieve politically. He battled Democrats and won, and battled the more conservative elements of his party and won. While others had been unable to withstand the turbulent times, Senator Hugh Scott had always prevailed. He also kept alive another tradition, one that had been a hallmark of Pennsylvania politics for generations: that there was no more potent or enduring political appeal in the state than that of a solid, moderate Republican.

1974: SCHWEIKER/FLAHERTY

Regionalism has always been a factor in Pennsylvania politics, as it is in almost every state. In California, the battle lines form north and south, colliding somewhere around Santa Barbara. In the Buckeye State, Columbus serves as the gateway to southern Ohio, and there are huge economic, cultural, and political differences between the industrial areas in the north, such Cleveland, Akron and Toledo, and the more conservative farming areas spreading out to Cincinnati in the south. In New York State, New York City serves as the divide between those who reside there or those who live "upstate."

So it's not surprising that in a state as large and diverse as Pennsylvania, regionalism and geography also shape the state's political environment. There are unique differences in the political attitudes of those from various parts of the Commonwealth, but one distinctive rivalry stands above all others: that of the state's two largest cities, Philadelphia and Pittsburgh. This is often most clear when a prospective statewide officeholder comes from one of these two cities. Candidates must take special care in minimizing their own provincial interests so that they are viewed as acceptable to the rest of the state. Hugh Scott, a Philadelphia native, did an exceptional job walking this tightrope throughout his career, and he was rewarded with three terms. Others, however, have been less adept and have watched as their careers collapsed under the weight of their narrow, regional appeal.

The 1974 Senate campaign in Pennsylvania produced one such individual. He was a man who would become ubiquitous in statewide politics over the next decade, Pittsburgh Mayor Pete Flaherty. The 1974 contest pitted Flaherty against incumbent Republican Richard S. Schweiker. To advance to the general election, Flaherty first had to fight off a tough primary challenge by State Insurance Commissioner Herb Denenberg of Philadelphia, whom he ended up defeating by 38,000 votes. Throughout his two terms as mayor, Flaherty had built a reputation as a political maverick. Instituting cost-cutting measures, he contended that cutting taxes would improve services for the city's residents. He tried to portray Schweiker, who had built a moderate-to-liberal voting record in the Senate, as a big spending deficit advocate.

Although Schweiker emphasized his votes for budget-slicing measures, he was most adept at distancing himself from President Nixon, who had resigned in disgrace several months before the election. Running in 1974 posed a special burden on just about any Republican officeholder, but Schweiker's well-known run-ins with the Administration had the effect of inoculating himself against a post-Watergate backlash. He also counted on the strong labor support that he had built up over the years to cut into this traditionally Democratic voting bloc. Flaherty's own collisions with unions while mayor only made this clearer.

Interestingly, for the first time since the 1962 Clark–Van Zandt tilt, a Democrat demonstrated real success in the southwest. Flaherty carried the region by a whopping 201,000 votes, although the 62 percent recorded was still 4 percentage points less than the number of registered Democrats in the region. Not only did Flaherty carry every county in the region; he also reached at least 60 percent in all but Armstrong. In Allegheny alone, he topped the incumbent by 93,000 votes. If those numbers had been approximated by any of the previous Democratic candidates, any of them would have been successful. That Flaherty could enjoy this lead in the southwest and still lose by 248,000 votes statewide highlights what a regional candidate he was. It is difficult to think of any other candidate in Pennsylvania whose support was so concentrated.

Philadelphia, where Democrats had a 334,000-vote registration advantage, provided Flaherty with a slight 4,500-vote plurality. This was partly because Schweiker received as much as 40 percent of the black vote, according to estimates. Flaherty received more votes in his hometown of Pittsburgh than he did in the much larger City of Brotherly Love. In the suburbs, not surprisingly, Schweiker had a margin of 185,000 votes, holding Flaherty below 40 percent in each of Philadelphia's four suburban counties. In his native Montgomery County, Schweiker got 70 percent of the vote and defeated his challenger by 83,000 votes.

Perhaps most surprising, given Schweiker's generally liberal voting record compared with Flaherty's own sometimes more conservative approaches, the incumbent trounced the Democrat in central Pennsylvania by 217,000 votes (60 percent). Snyder County again gave the Republican his biggest plurality of any county, an astonishing 77 percent. Even the Democratic counties in northeastern Pennsylvania turned their backs on their party's candidate. Flaherty failed to carry even one of the six counties there, losing by 51,000 votes, a difference of 14 percentage points. In traditionally competitive Lehigh County, Schweiker amassed a 14,000-vote victory, a 61 percent share. Outside of Philadelphia, the easternmost county that Flaherty carried was Elk, which is a long way from the New Jersey border.

Discussing the campaign with reporters, the Republican also attempted to thrust himself into the national spotlight. "Unless we mend our ways and change our approaches and attitudes," Schweiker said, "our party could become extinct." He added that while other progressive Republicans like him—Jacob Javits of New York and Charles Mathias of Maryland—had survived the Watergate trauma, many on the more conservative side of the spectrum had lost. This attempt to make the GOP more progressive would seem more than a little ironic just two years later. Then, the mercurial Schweiker confounded just about everyone by accepting conservative Ronald Reagan's offer to serve as his running mate. Reagan was making an 11th-hour attempt to wrest control of the Republican Party nomination from President Gerald Ford. After Reagan's challenge fell short, the two-term senator found that he had alienated many of his former political allies. He would never run for elected office again. He would remain in government for several years, however, after newly elected President Reagan repaid him by asking him to serve as Secretary of Health and Human Services.

1976: HEINZ/GREEN

With the retirement of Senator Scott in 1976, Pennsylvania found itself with an open Senate contest for the first time in twenty years. Both parties fielded exceptional candidates—both of them young, aggressive, and on the political move. This battle pitted two incumbent 38-year old Congressmen, Democrat William Green III from Philadelphia and Republican H. John Heinz III from Pittsburgh. Green had easily defeated State Senator Jeanette Reibman of

Northampton County in the primary, while Heinz had been forced to survive a bruising battle against Philadelphian Arlen Specter, whom he outlasted by just over 26,000 votes.

The stakes were made higher because both men had to relinquish their safe House seats to run. The risks were great but the rewards were greater as each stretched to reach his lofty ambitions. There was a sense that this wasn't just a contest to hold the seat for the next six years, but to control it for generations. The winner would also be strategically positioned to become a major player in national, even presidential, politics.

This contest between Green, son of the former Democratic Party boss in Philadelphia, and Heinz, multimillionaire heir to the famous pickle and ketchup fortune, was more a regional battle than a partisan or ideological one. Both men had built up liberal voting records in Congress. Both could also count on the support of labor, divided along the state's east-west lines. Because of the Democrats' registration advantage of 750,000, Heinz essentially campaigned as an independent, rarely mentioning his Republican affiliation. Conversely, of course, Green took great pains to stress that he was the Democratic nominee.

Given that the candidates agreed on many of the basic issues, it's no surprise that the campaign rhetoric focused primarily on personalities and ethical questions. The tone of the campaign turned increasingly nasty. Heinz attempted to tie Green to what he claimed were the corrupt administrations of Governor Milton Shapp of Pennsylvania and Mayor Frank L. Rizzo of Philadelphia. He even went as far as accusing Green of "gutless leadership" by not repudiating his Democratic colleagues. Heinz also charged Green, the son of the former Philadelphia power broker, with being a product of machine politics. Heinz also exploited the regionalism issue on the campaign trail out west by repeatedly claiming that Green would be responsive only to a handful of Philadelphia ward leaders.

The Democrat didn't shy away from leveling his own attacks. Green tried to attach Heinz to the Nixon Administration, claiming that the Republican had caved in on several key legislative issues over the years in response to pressure from the White House. Green also criticized Heinz for accepting $6,000 in illegal campaign contributions from Gulf Oil Company in his 1972 congressional campaign. In response, Heinz maintained that he was unaware of the items and blamed campaign aides for failing to notify him. To avoid being connected to Hugh Scott and Scott's ethics troubles, Heinz allegedly made clear that he didn't want an endorsement from the outgoing senator.

During the final few weeks of the campaign, with polls showing Green trailing by about 9 points, the Democrat shifted his message to one solitary issue—his opponent's personal spending on the race. Heinz spent more than $2 million in all, and more than half of that was on a television advertising, the likes of which the state had never seen. On the stump, Green accused Heinz of trying to buy the election. The Philadelphian finally seemed to have a theme that resonated: "Green versus Heinz: It's the man against the money." As election day approached, even Heinz's aides conceded that the spending issue had made an impact. When the polls finally opened, most observers viewed the race as a tossup.

As the votes were being tallied, Green jumped out to an early lead, based on his strong showing in his hometown of Philadelphia. He ultimately carried the city by startling 306,000 votes, a huge 71 percent. This was almost 50,000 votes more than presidential candidate Jimmy Carter would get from the city in his winning effort. Ordinarily, it would have been more than enough for a comfortable Democratic victory, but 1976 was no ordinary year and John Heinz was no ordinary opponent.

The Pittsburgh congressman had parlayed his vast resources to minimize Green's regional advantage in the southeast suburbs. Heinz carried the four counties by 73,000 votes, running especially strong in Chester County, where he recorded 62 percent. Delaware and Montgomery were reasonably close, however, and Green achieved a virtual draw in Bucks County, where the Democrats enjoyed a brief interlude as the majority party. In the southeast region as a whole, Green emerged with a 233,000-vote advantage (58 percent).

Green also ran reasonably well in northeastern Pennsylvania, taking the six counties there by a combined 27,000 vote. He was most successful in the far northeast counties of Lackawanna and Luzerne, which he carried by 56 and 55 percent, respectively. Heinz more than held his own in Lehigh, however, defeating Green by 3,400 votes in that battleground, and he narrowly took Monroe County.

Heinz also pulled in traditional Republican leads in central Pennsylvania, where he won by 231,000 votes, dropping only 3 of the region's 47 counties. Interestingly, those three—Clinton, Columbia, and Schuylkill—were places that Democratic candidates generally don't win. On the other hand, Heinz carried the few counties in the region that do contain Democratic strength, such as Cambria and Erie. No doubt the issue of regionalism affected voters in both those areas.

The most impressive aspect of Heinz's victory was his ability to parlay his favorite-son status in the southwest. He walked away with a 280,000-vote advantage (63 percent) across these nine counties. Green's Senate aspirations were destroyed in the very heart of Democratic power, Heinz's home of Allegheny County, which the Republican carried by 212,000 votes, a 67-33 percent advantage. Green carried only three counties in the southwest—Fayette, Greene, and Lawrence—and each of those by only a narrow margin. That all of this had occurred while Jimmy Carter was tallying an 88,000-vote plurality in the same nine counties is also striking.

In the end, regionalism won out over partisanship, as Democrats in the southwest ignored their candidate's message. Had Bill Green been able to shore up his partisan base in the southwest to some extent (as Heinz had accomplished in the Philadelphia suburbs), he would have won the race. But the 31-point gap between the number of voters registered as Democrats in the southwest and their actual voting preference would go down as one of the greatest examples of crossover appeal that any candidate has ever achieved.

For Heinz, the United States Senate and a very bright future awaited, until tragedy struck 15 years later. Bill Green, despite his election three years later as Mayor of Philadelphia, would move on to relative obscurity. Taking the risk and coming up short, he found solace on election night in a Rudyard Kipling poem titled "If," which his father had asked him to memorize when he was a boy:

"If you can make one heap of all your winnings / And risk it on one turn of pitch-and-toss / And lose, and start again at your beginnings / And never breathe a word about your loss..."

1980: SPECTER/FLAHERTY

With Senator Richard Schweiker's announcement that he would not seek reelection in 1980, Pennsylvania had its second consecutive open-seat contest. The race featured a pair of candidates who had one thing in common that both would surely have preferred to forget (but that only one ultimately could): Both had previously lost two other bids for major statewide office. Perhaps only in the Keystone State, with its bizarre political machinations, could such a circumstance be possible.

The Republican, Arlen Specter, had an extensive history—even on the national scale—when he served as counsel for the Warren Commission, investigating the assassination of President Kennedy. A short time later, he was elected district attorney of the Philadelphia. Originally a Democrat, he switched parties, lost a mayoral election in 1967 by only 11,000 votes to incumbent James Tate (despite the huge registration disadvantage), and then saw his career temporarily sidetracked six years later, when his bid for a third term as district attorney went down to defeat.

Specter had attempted a comeback in the 1976 senate race but was overpowered by John Heinz in the GOP primary. He ran for governor two years later, but once again a Republican from the west, Richard Thornburgh, dashed his hopes. Now, at 50 years of age, Specter appeared to be looking at his political career though the rear-view mirror when he decided to set up a law office in Atlantic City, New Jersey. At that point, Schweiker unexpectedly announced his decision not to seek another term. Specter still believed that if he could grab the nomination, his moderate credentials would place him in a strong position in the general election. Getting the nomination would not be easy, however, because standing in his way was the candidate whom Governor Thornburgh had handpicked to run, Delaware County Councilman Bud Haabestad. Haabestad also had the endorsements of Senators Schweiker and Heinz as well as of Philadelphia GOP boss William A. Meehan. Additionally, State Senator Edward Howard of Bucks County joined the primary race, along with five lesser-known candidates. While Specter and Haabestad each recorded huge numbers in his home county, Specter ran strong enough in northeastern Pennsylvania, while holding his own in the rest of the state, to prevail by about 37,000 votes.

Waiting for him in the general election, was the former mayor of Pittsburgh, Pete Flaherty, who was also making his third attempt at statewide office in recent years. Flaherty had lost general-election match-ups to Thornburgh in 1972 and Schweiker in 1974, and the 1980 election would be the final opportunity for the 56-year-old erstwhile Pittsburgh golden boy. In the primary, Flaherty had needed to survive a crowded field of eight Democratic contenders, his biggest threats coming from State Representative Joseph Rhodes of Pittsburgh, who had the support of labor and most newspaper endorsements, and from C. DeLores Tucker of Philadelphia, formerly secretary of the commonwealth. The Democratic field had also included several other names that would later dot the Pennsylvania political landscape: former Iowa Congressman Ed Mezvinsky, (later attorney general nominee in 1988), State Senator Craig Lewis (later auditor general nominee in 1992), and Temple University Law School Dean (and its future President), Peter Liacouras. Flaherty's name recognition overwhelmed his opponents, and he ended carried every county on his way to an easy primary victory.

The general election would ultimately decide which man could shed the perennial-loser label and adopt a new reputation for resilience and being a political survivor. For the vanquished, it would be the final political chapter in a career that would fail to meet the ambitions he had once envisioned.

Flaherty's strategy was to win big in the southwest while narrowly carrying Philadelphia, as he had in his two previous statewide bids. He also hoped that the support of several labor groups could help spell the difference in the swing towns of northeastern Pennsylvania. He had lost both Lackawanna and Luzerne counties in the past. Specter, meanwhile, had long promised that he could prevail in his home of Philadelphia if given the chance in a general election, despite the Democrats' 7-2 registration advantage. To help win in Philadelphia, Specter accumulated a number of endorsements among the city's Democratic leadership, including prominent black leaders such as City Councilman (and future Mayor) John Street.

Along with winning Philadelphia, Specter also counted on rolling up big margins in its suburbs and, of course, in the strongly Republican central Pennsylvania. As in previous Senate contests involving his predecessor Schweiker, big labor was split, an advantage for any Republican. Specter also successfully distanced himself from Governor Thornburgh, who had become very unpopular in the black community, primarily because of his proposals to sharply reduce the state's welfare rolls. Finally, the political environment of 1980, in which Ronald Reagan would score a sweeping victory over incumbent President Jimmy Carter, provided an added bonus.

Together, it was enough to allow Arlen Specter to grasp what had eluded him for so long—a statewide office. He beat Flaherty by 108,000 votes. Specter delivered on his promise to carry Philadelphia (by 12,000); achieving what Republicans hadn't been able to do in years. In the Philadelphia suburbs, Specter ran strong as expected, building up a 251,000-vote advantage. He held Flaherty to less than 40 percent of the vote in all four counties (reaching a high of 70 percent in Chester), including a huge 96,000-vote advantage in populous Montgomery County. Overall, Specter outpolled his Democratic opponent by 263,000 votes in the southeast region. The odds of any Democrat's overcoming numbers like that in a region centered by Philadelphia are long indeed.

Interestingly, Flaherty ran relatively well for a Democrat in central Pennsylvania, losing by 176,000 votes in the region. He ran especially strong in the counties peripheral to his western base, such as Cambria (65 percent), Clarion (57 percent), Erie (60 percent), and Mercer (55 percent). Specter's moderate credentials probably cost him votes in the state's Bible belt; indeed on some social issues, the Democrat had the more conservative posture. In fact, it's difficult to believe that a Democrat who managed to carry ten counties in the state's "T," including 55 percent in Indiana County, would have lost.

Flaherty, however, ran poorly in the Democratic-leaning northeast. Specter won the region by 1,600 votes, reaching a high of 59 percent in Monroe County. He even carried competitive Lehigh County by 12,000 votes (56 percent) and came within 102 votes of carrying Northampton County. Only the counties of Lackawanna and Luzerne turned out impressive numbers for Flaherty.

Unlike the previous Democratic candidates, Flaherty was able to deliver his southwestern political base, even surpassing his showing six years earlier against Schweiker. This time, he carried all nine counties in the region en route to a 333,000-vote advantage (66 percent). Flaherty achieved his highest percentage in Beaver County, where he captured 73 percent, a 37,000-vote edge. In his Allegheny County home, the Democrat defeated Specter by 151,000 votes (63 percent). This was one time that Democrats couldn't lay the blame on the southwest.

The 1980 contest also marked the end of three straight Senate elections that shaped up as classic east-versus-west battles. In each case, geography would be a major determinant of the outcome. Twice the Democrats fielded the candidate from the southwest and once from the east. It didn't seem to matter, though—no matter which regional side they lined up on, the result would be the same. A political party that had a registration advantage of approximately 700,000 voters had allowed another set of competitive seats, this time open seats in the Senate, to slip through its fingers again.

1982: HEINZ/WECHT

In 1982, for the first time in memory, Pennsylvania didn't have a competitive Senate election. Democrats were unable to come up with a strong challenge to the popular, well-financed Heinz. They settled on Cyril Wecht, an Allegheny County commissioner and a forensic pathologist, who had gained some renown over the years for his outspoken criticism of the Warren Commission. Wecht had previously been the county coroner, and it was rumored that he had served as the model for the fictional television character Quincy.

Senator Heinz pledged not to spend his own money this time, and he didn't need to, outspending the Democrat by nearly 7 to 1 anyway. With the challenger unable to get his message out to the public, the campaign received scant attention from the press and the voters. Not that it would have mattered, as Heinz was arguably the safest GOP incumbent in the nation in what was a difficult midterm election cycle for the his party.

Wecht focused his campaign attacks on the economy, charging, in particular, that Heinz had been unsuccessful in fighting the Reagan Administration's free-trade policy on steel imports. But despite a statewide unemployment rate of more than 11 percent, Heinz successfully distanced himself from the president by emphasizing his opposition to constitutional efforts to prohibit abortion and to allow prayer in public schools. Heinz was again the beneficiary of support from the labor community, including the United Mine Workers, the Pennsylvania State Education Association, the Teamsters and the Pennsylvania AFL-CIO. Only the United Steelworkers spurned him in favor of Wecht.

Thus, it came as a surprise to no one that Heinz won going away, defeating Wecht by more than 724,000 votes statewide. The only region in which Wecht had any success was in Philadelphia, where the overwhelming registration edge gave the Democrat a 105,000-vote plurality (60 percent). The incumbent Republican reaped a 247,000-vote advantage in the suburbs, holding Wecht to just 25 percent in Chester County and 28 percent in Montgomery County. Among the four counties, the best Wecht could do was 34 percent in Bucks County, which he still lost by more than 46,000 votes.

Wecht captured no counties in the 47 that spread out across the central "T," trailing the incumbent by a whopping 381,000 votes in the region. His campaign reached its nadir in Lancaster County, arguably the "capital" of central Pennsylvania, where Wecht attracted just 20 percent of the vote. Heinz also rolled up big margins in northeastern Pennsylvania, again claiming victory across the board, for a 46,000-vote advantage. Most impressive were the results in the usually competitive Lehigh County, where Heinz walked away with a 23,000-vote plurality (66 percent) over the Democrat.

In southwestern Pennsylvania, the home of both candidates and an area where Wecht needed to score impressively to entertain any notions of an upset, Wecht was overwhelmed. Heinz took 61 percent of the vote—an 113,000-vote edge in Allegheny County alone—on his way to compiling a 154,000-vote victory margin in the region. Heinz carried Westmoreland by 18,000 votes or 58 percent. Wecht staved off total defeat by narrowly winning Fayette and Greene counties. If Heinz had picked up a few more votes in those two counties, he would have been able to pull off a most unusual feat—winning every county in the state except Philadelphia. As it was, however, 64 of 67 was an impressive showing.

1986: SPECTER/EDGAR

Unlike the 1982 campaign, which was uncompetitive from the outset, the 1986 race gave the Democrats much more confidence in their effort to unseat the incumbent, this time Senator Arlen Specter. First, the year was shaping up as a good one for the party (in fact, the Democrats would ultimately regain control of the U.S. Senate). Also, they had an attractive candidate in Congressman Bob Edgar, 43, of Delaware County, who had demonstrated an uncanny ability to win close elections. But while Specter may have appeared to lack the popularity that Senator Heinz, his GOP colleague, enjoyed, he made clear in this campaign that he wasn't going to let slip away what he had worked so hard to achieved back in 1980. It was testament to his grit and determination that the Edgar campaign, which once held so much promise, would somehow never quite get off the ground.

Edgar had been first elected to the House of Representatives in the post-Watergate year of 1974. Unlike other Democrats, who were swept in during the anti-Nixon fervor that season, his success owed largely to local issues; internal disputes, and corruption charges that had rocked the powerful Republican Board of Delaware County Supervisors—the so-called War Board. Edgar, only 31 years of age at the time, was a minister in the American Methodist Church and had been serving as Protestant chaplain at Drexel University. His stunning 16,000-vote victory that year marked the first time a Democrat had held that congressional seat since before the Civil War. In the years afterward, he had won a series of hard-fought, hotly competitive battles, often by razor-thin margins in a district that Republicans dominated by a 2-1 ratio.

The Democratic nominee had continued to defy the odds in the 1986 primary, when he battled State Auditor General Don Bailey of Westmoreland County for the right to oppose Specter. In a race that divided Democrats largely along geographic lines, the Democrat from the east prevailed by just slightly less than 25,000 votes. Surely, his supporters had every reason to believe, despite the challenges of knocking off an incumbent; "Miracle Bob" would somehow find a way to pull it out again in the fall.

Edgar ran a personal campaign, his message primarily focused on the idea that there were "two Arlen Specters." Back home, he argued, Specter had tried to burnish an image as a moderate-to-liberal voice of political independence, while in Washington he would come down on the side of the Reagan Administration whenever it was crucial. Edgar also depended on a cadre of volunteers, many of them young people who had worked in various grassroots causes, to overtake the incumbent, who outspent him by about $5 million to $2 million.

The Specter campaign responded that their peace activist opponent was weak on defense issues and, in general, far too liberal for most Pennsylvanians. They also complained that their opponent was running a negative, sometimes even nasty, campaign. "I had thought, given his background and my background, that we could approach a campaign based upon the issues," Specter said afterward. "Instead, he personalized it from the start."

Nevertheless, it came as a bit of a surprise that Specter dispatched the challenger with such apparent ease, prevailing by more than 458,000 votes statewide (57 percent). In a battle of southeastern candidates, Edgar carried Philadelphia by only 61,000 votes and was drubbed in the suburbs. Specter took a 174,000-vote plurality in those four counties, including a 24,000-vote victory (56 percent) in the Edgar's Delaware County base.

Specter also carried all but one county, Cambria, in central Pennsylvania on his way to a 309,000-vote advantage. His 64 percent in the region nearly matched Heinz's numbers of 1982. Specter's tally was far more impressive, however, considering the strength of his opponent. Specter also bested Edgar in every county in the northeast, leaving the challenger 31,000 votes behind. Only Luzerne County, which Specter won by only 825 votes, was close.

Edgar was also disappointed in southwestern Pennsylvania, where he needed to record big victories to remain competitive. Yet Specter won— narrowly—by less than 5,000 votes. Only Butler and Fayette counties performed up to expectations for the Democrat, while Specter easily carried Armstrong and Butler counties. In the rest of the southwest, in places such as Allegheny and Westmoreland counties, the competitors were locked in a virtual tie, which is tantamount to a Republican victory. Unlike Edgar's other campaigns, the 1986 Senate race had little suspense for the Congressman and his troops. "Edgar's Eighth Miracle," as it was called, had clearly failed to materialize.

1988: HEINZ/VIGNOLA

Whereas Bob Edgar's candidacy had once brought promise, few Democrats harbored any illusions that their candidate in 1988, Joe Vignola, had any chance of winning against John Heinz. As in the 1982 contest, Heinz faced a candidate, this time in the 39-year-old former Philadelphia city controller, who was largely unknown outside his hometown. Once again, he vastly outspent his opponent, raising more than $5 million, 10 times the amount that Vignola's campaign spent.

Traveling around the state in a station wagon, Vignola spoke in favor of increased spending on education, health care, and other domestic programs, and paying for them with large cuts in the defense spending. He accused Heinz of showing "no leadership, no stature" and "no clout" and for being more concerned about Wall Street than Main Street. Mostly, Vignola ran a positive campaign; it certainly lacked the nastiness that was present in Wecht's campaign against Heinz. Knowing that he was running well ahead, the incumbent had no need to run anything except a low-profile campaign. One Democratic consultant, observing that ward leaders and committee people had already given up, predicted on the eve of the election that their candidate was "about to become Heinz's 58th variety."

Although it came as no surprise that Heinz won comfortably, the sheer magnitude of his victory eclipsed even his triumph over Cyril Wecht. The Republican carried every county in the state except Philadelphia, on his way to an overwhelming 1.49-million vote victory margin, earning 67 percent of the total vote. While Philadelphia delivered a 135,000-vote margin for Vignola, Heinz did so well in the suburbs—winning by almost 400,000 votes—that he still walked away from the southeast with a 257,000-vote advantage (59 percent).

Heinz also trounced his opponent in the southwest, by 333,000 votes (67 percent), which included an 183,000-vote spread in Allegheny County. Vignola fared poorly in the northeast, too, losing by 142,000 votes, a 36-point difference. The magnitude of Heinz's triumph in central Pennsylvania is what was most striking. As expected; he carried every county, and he held Vignola to a paltry 24 percent, a margin of 753,000 votes. The challenger's best showing was the 36 percent he received in Mercer County. His poorest showing was an anemic 12 percent in Snyder County. That all this happened to a political party that enjoyed a 551,000-registration advantage was a huge embarrassment for the Democrats. At least they had reason to suspect that they had hit rock bottom in a statewide Pennsylvania election.

1991: WOFFORD/THORNBURGH

Thus as the last decade of the 20th century arrived, Pennsylvania continued to have two entrenched Republican senators, individuals from opposite ends of the state who appeared ready to occupy their seats well into the future. Then, on April 4, 1991, tragedy struck. On his way to a meeting on Medicaid reform in Philadelphia, the 53-year-old John Heinz and six other people were killed (including two children on the ground) when a helicopter collided with his plane over a schoolyard in Lower Merion Township, Montgomery County. The death of the popular senator dealt a devastating blow not only to his family and friends but also to citizens across Pennsylvania. Additionally, the loss of the state's most popular politician remade Pennsylvania's political landscape.

With Governor Robert Casey naming Heinz's successor, the Democrats laid claim to a Senate seat for the first time since Joe Clark's defeat in 1968. After flirting with several prominent celebrities, such as Chrysler former CEO Lee Iacocca, an Allentown native, Casey went into his own cabinet and tapped Secretary of Labor Harris Wofford. Because Wofford was not widely known outside the state's political establishment, his selection excited few. Many thought that the governor had squandered a golden opportunity. It didn't help that to fill the remaining three years of Heinz's term the new senator would be forced to defend the seat later in the year.

After Heinz's widow, Teresa, declined an invitation from the state's GOP leadership to run, attention immediately shifted to former Governor Richard Thornburgh, who would require little persuasion. It was no secret that Thornburgh, then serving as attorney general in the Bush Administration, was interested. When the opportunity arose, he jumped in. From the outset, Thornburgh was viewed as a heavy favorite. In fact, one poll taken during the summer gave him a 40-point lead. Even within the Democratic Party, Wofford was viewed as a caretaker, an interim senator holding the seat until Thornburgh could legally assume it.

Few paid attention to the race during the summer. By early September, Thornburgh was already on the air with television ads. Wofford, meanwhile, struggled to raise both money and awareness for his campaign. Then something unexpected happened: The Wofford campaign—specifically his message of universal health care—began to resonate. The defining moment, according to Senator Wofford himself, was the first television debate between the two competitors, on September 6, when Wofford more than held his own. National officials took notice, and the Democratic Senatorial Campaign Committee, which had been dragging its financial feet, promptly handed over $500,000.

Weeks later, on October 18, in their only other debate, Thornburgh turned in another lackluster performance. And, again, the surprisingly aggressive Wofford kept Thornburgh on the defensive, with charges that his opponent was out of touch with the middle class. After that debate came a flurry of favorable press, which, the Democrat later stated, "opened the floodgates."

Although he had never run for public office, the 65-year-old Democrat had been around American politics his whole life, boasting an impressive resume. In the 1960s, he served with President John F. Kennedy, helping to found the Peace Corps, and later with the Reverend Dr. Martin Luther King Jr., in civil rights struggles. Possessing an antiestablishment streak, Wofford was one of the first whites ever to graduate from Howard University Law School. He was arrested while protesting outside the 1968 Democratic National Convention (the charges were later dropped). In more recent years, he had twice been a college president—of Bryn Mawr in suburban Philadelphia and at Old Westbury in Long Island, New York. Wofford was inexperienced in the art of the sound bite, and his speaking style in the early months of the campaign reflected his professorial background.

Somehow, though, his unconventional style seemed to fit the mood of the times. Beginning with that first debate, he began to hammer his opponent on education, tax cuts for the middle class, and, most of all, affordable health care. He crafted the classic line "If criminals are entitled to a lawyer, working people should be entitled to a doctor." In the aftermath of the Persian Gulf War, with the economy mired in recession, his campaign had developed a cogent theme: that the government needed to "take care of our own." For a man who had such an elite background to serve as a vehicle for such a populist message seemed unlikely, but it worked. He was the right candidate at the right time. Conversely, the Thornburgh campaign message, that the candidate was an insider who had contacts within the corridors of power in Washington, was decidedly the wrong one.

Although Thornburgh's campaign strategists may have sensed that they were in serious trouble by the time the second debate had concluded, it was too late to change the central message of their candidate. According to Greg Stevens, Thornburgh's media consultant, "The major thing I would do differently is to have defined Wofford earlier and not let him get up a head of steam. But I defend the thinking. Here you're sitting on what appears to be a strong lead—that doesn't argue for attacking your opponent." A late counterattack on the health care issue, specifically that 90 percent of Pennsylvanians already had insurance and that the type of plan Wofford offered would jeopardize their health security, was too little too late. When the votes were counted, Wofford had delivered a knockout blow to Thornburgh, winning by 338,000 votes statewide for a 10-point victory.

Finally, after years of underachieving, a Democratic candidate for the United States Senate had united the party and maximized its vote-getting potential. Not only did Wofford carry Philadelphia by a three-to-one margin and a 218,000-vote plurality; he also ran ahead of Thornburgh in three of the four Republican-dominated Philadelphia suburbs (Chester County being the sole exception). Although Wofford carried his home county, Montgomery, by only 6,000 votes, that was a huge accomplishment for a Democratic in a statewide campaign. The only hope Thornburgh might have had would have been to sweep his home of southwestern Pennsylvania, the way John Heinz did in 1976.

This time, however, southwestern Democrats did not let their party down. Wofford rolled up a 182,000-vote margin (61 percent) in the region, winning every county except Butler. He scored as high as 72 percent in loyal-Democratic Fayette, and reached 69 percent in Beaver and Greene counties. Most important, he racked up a 108,000-vote margin, or 61 percent, in Allegheny. With Philadelphia and Pittsburgh, the twin pillars of Democratic strength, fully onboard along with the southeast suburbs, there were hardly enough votes elsewhere for the Thornburgh campaign to succeed.

Although Wofford hailed from the leafy Main Line, his populist message played exceptionally well in the economically distressed towns of the southwest. Other than Pittsburgh-native Pete Flaherty's two unsuccessful attempts, Wofford ran better than any other Democratic candidate in memory. Unlike Flaherty, however, Wofford had experiences and credentials that also appealed to the more socially liberal voters in the eastern part of the state.

Wofford had brought back Democratic voters with his populist economic message in the southwest, and the message also resonated in the blue-collar towns of the northeast. The Democrat carried all six counties in the region, exceeding Thornburgh by 53,000 votes. Wofford reached 60 percent in both Lackawanna and Luzerne counties. Even in the Republican dominated "T," Wofford surpassed normal projections for a Democrat, carrying 10 of its 47 counties and holding Thornburgh to a 115,000-vote plurality.

Again, however, it was Wofford's ability to unlock those Democratic votes in southwestern Pennsylvania that held the key to his victory. Given that it was the only election of any significance held in the off year of 1991, the outcome made national headlines and provided the Democratic Party with momentum going into the next year's presidential contest. The victorious Wofford proclaimed in its aftermath that his election signaled the first day of the end of the Bush Administration. In retrospect, it would be hard now to argue otherwise.

1992: SPECTER/YEAKEL

By the spring of 1992, the newly energized Democrats seemed primed for taking Pennsylvania's other Senate seat as well. They had a fresh political face in Lynn Yeakel, an activist who was director of Women's Way, a charitable organization dedicated to assisting low-income women. Yeakel, who came from Delaware County in southeastern Pennsylvania, had shocked the establishment by easily defeating the party's endorsed candidate, Lieutenant Governor Mark Singel, in the primary. In late spring and early summer, it appeared that Arlen Specter, the Republican incumbent, was also likely to fall.

By then, Specter faced problems on several fronts. He had received a great deal of criticism for his handling of Anita Hill during her testimony before the Senate Judiciary Committee on Clarence Thomas' nomination to the United States Supreme Court. In addition, as the year unfolded it became evident that President Bush was in deep political trouble both nationally and across Pennsylvania. An unemployment rate of 7.6 percent along with a recession that rocked the nation placed both Bush and Specter in a precarious position. Specter's biggest problem was that he faced a political environment, later dubbed the "the year of the woman," that was tailor-made for Yeakel. The Thomas hearings had struck a political and cultural nerve nationwide, and no one was more closely identified with the hearings than Specter. As the general-election campaign opened, everything was in place for the Democrats to lay claim to both United States Senate seats.

Although President Bush's troubles would continue unabated, Specter showed amazingly resilience heading into the fall campaign. He outworked and outflanked his inexperienced opponent at every turn. He spent the summer months not simply solidifying his GOP base but going right for the heart of his opponent's traditional Democratic one. First, he carved away at the Democrats' support in the African-American community, particularly in Philadelphia, where many leaders appeared openly ambivalent about the candidacy of a wealthy amateur from the suburbs. Specter gained key endorsements from several influential black Democrats in the city. It didn't help that Yeakel's family belonged to a country club that had no black members, a fact that further alienated many rank-and-file voters. Next, Specter, who is Jewish, went after voters in that community when it was reported that Yeakel's Bryn Mawr Presbyterian Church had sponsored seminars on the Arab-Israeli conflict that were criticized as being anti-Semitic.

Specter also went after leaders in the Democratic Party establishment, particularly in his hometown of Philadelphia, whom he had worked with on local issues for his entire career. Yeakel, who ran against and beat the party hierarchy in the primary, never reached out to recruit ward leaders to her campaign. One anonymous party official commented afterward that some in the organization wanted to see her lose because otherwise they'd lose power with a U.S. senator who didn't owe them anything. The Specter camp evenhanded out thousands of dollars in "street money," getting Philadelphians—including Democrats—to work for him on election day.

The Yeakel campaign suffered from a series of political gaffes, such as mispronouncing names and places ("Juanita County"). Specter outspent Yeakel two to one, $8 million to $4 million. This prevented the Democrat from airing her first television ad until September 23, long after Specter's attacks had already taken hold. But through it all, she remained competitive, and on the eve of the election the race was viewed as a virtual tossup.

Although Yeakel led through the early part of the evening (which is typical for Democrats in Pennsylvania), her hopes faded as the rural counties reported later in the night. By midnight, it became clear that Specter had successfully withstood his most difficult challenge as an incumbent senator, ultimately prevailing by 133,000 votes, a 3 percent win.

Lynn Yeakel did carry Philadelphia by 122,000 votes, far surpassing what any of Specter's previous opponents had accomplished in the city. Nevertheless, the total was 73,000 votes shy of what Democratic presidential candidate Bill Clinton was pulling at the top of the ticket. In the suburbs, Yeakel ran respectably for a Democrat, particularly a challenger, dropping the four counties by a combined 92,000 votes. But her performance in Montgomery County was disappointing. This county, which had simultaneously elected its first Democrat in a century to its congressional seat and given Bill Clinton his largest plurality in the suburbs, had become the least reliable of the four suburban counties for the GOP. Specter, however, enjoyed his strongest showing there, winning by 39,000 votes, a 14 percent advantage, which even topped his showing in Chester County.

Yeakel's problem wasn't central Pennsylvania either. Although Specter carried it handily, his 174,000-vote margin was far from overwhelming and well within what a Democratic could afford to lose the region by and still be successful statewide. Yeakel carried six counties in all, including Centre and Clearfield counties, which are rarities for a Democrat. She also came close to winning several other counties, such as Indiana, Northumberland, and even Warren.

Specter, however, ran well in northeastern Pennsylvania, holding his opponent to a 6,600-vote edge. Ordinarily, a Democrat must do several percentage points better than the 2-point win Yeakel recorded in the region. Lackawanna, which she barely won and Luzerne, which she narrowly lost, were particularly damaging to her candidacy. They combined to produce a net advantage for the Democrat of only 177 votes. Only Northampton County, which Yeakel took by 7,000 votes (54 percent), came close to meeting Democratic expectations.

More than anything else, however, Democratic voters in the southwest were again the determining factor. As had occurred so many times before, their party's candidate would succumb to ticket-splitters in their political base. In a stroke of luck for the Specter camp, Yeakel's ability to introduce herself to voters in the region was greatly hampered by an ongoing newspaper strike in Pittsburgh. She ran strong in some of the region's smaller counties but ended up narrowly losing the two largest, Allegheny and Westmoreland. The differences between her vote and the Democratic registration figures in the two counties were 12 and 11 percentage points, respectively. It's remarkable how close she came to victory considering how poorly she ran in those Democratic-vote-rich counties. If she had run reasonably well there, she would have toppled the incumbent.

Today, Lynn Yeakel's Senate campaign can be looked on in a different light. Given her inexperience, and the fact that she was unknown to the public before she started, coming as close as she did to defeating one of Pennsylvania's most accomplished politicians of the 20th century indicates that she did a lot of things right. In the final days of the campaign, she rediscovered the issue that had taken her so far in the spring—voters' anger over the economy and her opponent's incumbency. After losing the Democratic primary for governor two years later (against the man she defeated in this 1992 Senate race, Mark Singel), Yeakel narrowly lost a state senate race to an incumbent in 2000 and bowed out of politics for good. With grit and determination, Specter demonstrated once again that he would not relinquish what he had worked so hard to achieve in 1980. To withstand the political winds of 1992, he must have calculated that he needed to run a perfect campaign—and that's precisely what he did.

1994: SANTORUM/WOFFORD

Because the 1991 special election gave Harris Wofford only the right to serve out the remainder of the late Senator John Heinz's term, he was forced to stand before the voters just three years after his surprising victory. This was poor timing for any Democrat, because the 1994 midterms were a political minefield. Despite relative peace and prosperity, the nation had become disenchanted with the Clinton Administration during its first two years. Democrats had become demoralized in response to Clinton's missteps, while most Republicans couldn't wait to get to the polls and take out their anger. The feeling was only exacerbated as election day drew nearer, when the President's plan to reform the nation's health care system was finally shelved.

Because of this, Wofford, who had made the issue of health-care reform the centerpiece of his 1991 campaign, now appeared incapable of delivering what he had promised. And in 36-year-old two-term Congressman Rick Santorum he faced an opponent who was much more aggressive than the overconfident Thornburgh had been three years earlier. Santorum was first elected in 1990, when he pulled off one of the biggest upsets in the nation by surprising incumbent Congressman Doug Walgren. After arriving in Washington, Santorum gained recognition as one of the "gang of seven," a group of first-term Republican watchdogs who ultimately blew the lid off the House banking scandal, in which a number of members were charged with bouncing checks from the government payroll office. Behind a theme of more individual freedom and less government, Santorum ran a much more ideologically driven campaign than is typical for Republicans in the state.

Historically, Pennsylvania Republicans had been successful positioning themselves as moderate consensus builders who strove to occupy the political middle ground. In the primary, Santorum brushed aside a challenge from Joe Watkins, a 40-year-old ordained Baptist minister and businessman who tried to make the case that his opponent was outside the mainstream of the state party. Endorsed by former Congressman Jack Kemp, Watkins claimed that he was the candidate who could rightly proclaim to follow in the tradition of Hugh Scott and John Heinz. But although he had been a staff person to former President Bush and to Dan Quayle when Quayle was a U.S. senator, Watkins was unable to raise money or garner support from prominent Pennsylvania Republicans or the state organization. He was also highly critical of the National Republican Senatorial Campaign Committee for not supporting his efforts "as a qualified, serious, black candidate."

After the primary, Santorum had no desire to moderate his approach or to blur the differences between him and Wofford; he was on a mission to carry out his conservative principles. Santorum's ambitions, however, came close to being derailed, when on October 18, in a speech at La Salle University, he told the crowd that the retirement age of 65 was ridiculous and should be raised to at least 70. The Wofford campaign videotaped the event and saturated the airwaves with television commercials showing a clip of the challenger making the comments. Denouncing Santorum for "pitting generation against generation," the Democratic incumbent charged that Social Security was a "sacred trust" that should not be violated. The Santorum camp admitted that within a few days their internal polls showed their candidate experiencing a double-digit decline. According to their estimation, however, they were saved by an extensive grassroots organization that immediately began working to minimize the damages.

Conversely, Wofford's campaign was sluggish from the outset. It was slow to define the challenger in the early stages, when he was still relatively unknown in much of the state. The campaign built a message that was almost entirely based on negative ads, putting forth little effort to highlight their own candidate's strengths. It was as if the Democrats had seemingly forgotten to reintroduce the man that voters had so warmly embraced just a few short years before. Perhaps the turning point was a brilliant set of positive "kitchen table" ads that Santorum began running one month before the election. In it, the challenger sat calmly discussing his views, projecting a positive image that separated him from the onslaught of negativity that was dominating this and every other campaign.

Although Wofford carried Philadelphia by 202,000 votes, the impact was somewhat lessened by an exceedingly low turnout in the city. A strong indicator of how discouraged many Democrats were, is that in the 1991 special election (a typically light turnout), Wofford received 331,638 votes in the city, which translated to 74 percent. In the 1994 election, Wofford increased his share to 76 percent, but he generated only 293,007 total votes, 39,000 votes less.

Wofford's inability to run strong again in the Philadelphia suburbs also hurt him. In the 1991 election, he had carried three of the four counties and ran even with his Republican opponent there. Now, even though he lived in Montgomery County, the Democrat lost all four rather handily, lagging 72,000 votes behind Santorum. In central Pennsylvania, Wofford's numbers also declined significantly, and he lost the region by 250,000 votes, taking only Cambria and Clinton counties. Santorum even snatched normally Democratic Erie County, where he benefited from having the region's favorite son, Tom Ridge, lead the way in the gubernatorial race. Santorum also ran well in the northeast, losing only Lackawanna and Luzerne, while holding Wofford's overall edge to slightly more than 7,000 votes.

Despite those problems, Wofford could have won if he had recorded half the margin in the southwest that he had against Thornburgh when he built up an 182,000-vote advantage. But the populist economic message that played so well for Wofford in 1991 had been negated by a stronger economy and largely drowned out by a focus on social issues such as abortion and gun control. For the conservative Santorum, who came from Allegheny County, it was enough to hold the Democrat to just 52 percent in the southwest. This marked a 9 percent drop from Wofford's numbers just three years earlier and 17 points below his party's registration.

The final tally showed an 87,000-vote plurality for the young Republican, a tremendous victory for his party both statewide and nationally. Not long before, the Democratic Party had finally won a Senate seat in Pennsylvania and then reclaimed the Presidency, which appeared to be the beginning of a bright new era for the party. On this night in 1994, however, that all appeared to be a distant memory. The party's governing coalition, which had dominated American politics for half a century, had largely collapsed, leaving the party faithful shattered. For Democrats in Pennsylvania, the feeling had to be even worse. Once again, they found themselves on the short end of a U.S. Senate election. The sting of another defeat was a painful reminder of how the party almost always seems to find a way to lose Senate elections in Pennsylvania.

1998: SPECTER/LLOYD

After surviving a difficult election in 1992, Senator Arlen Specter had an easy one in 1998. Democrats had a difficult time finding an opponent. Their pool of credible candidates was thinner than it had been at any other time in the past half century. Philadelphia Mayor Ed Rendell was the exception, but he had little interest in taking on his old friend and boss in the Philadelphia District Attorney's office. Rendell clearly had his sights set on the governor's mansion.

The eventual nominee was State Representative William Lloyd, 50, of Somerset County. Lloyd was widely respected in the legislature for his intellect, but he entered the campaign virtually anonymous to voters outside his home county. Unfortunately for him, he exited the race in about the same fashion. With Governor Tom Ridge's reelection campaign, it would be hard to think of a time when Pennsylvania had two more lopsided elections at the top of the ticket. Neither campaign attracted the attention of the media or the voters.

Driving around the state in his 1996 Dodge Stratus, Lloyd hoped that the impeachment process of President Clinton could backfire on Specter and turn out Democrats eager to take revenge. He tried to nationalize the campaign, arguing that a vote for Specter wasn't just a vote for a moderate Republican but also a vote for Trent Lott as majority leader. Lloyd's campaign was so low on cash, however, that he could not produce an advertising campaign of any magnitude. As a result, few took notice. Lloyd was further handicapped because he hailed from a remote area that provided him with neither a large base of support nor a major media market.

The only question on election day was whether Specter could surpass John Heinz's victory margin in 1988 (he didn't). He did, however, carry every county in the state except Philadelphia and Somerset, Lloyd's home county. That this Republican-leaning county thought highly enough of Lloyd to give him an 8,000-vote plurality (67 percent) might have been some solace to the candidate as the returns came in.

It was a sweeping victory for the incumbent. Specter carried 64 percent of the vote in the northeast, including a remarkable 68 percent in usually competitive Lehigh County. In the central "T," the Republican rolled up a 390,000-vote margin (69 percent), reaching a high of 83 percent in Snyder County. The only county in southwestern Pennsylvania where the Democrat was even competitive was Fayette, which he ended up losing by 42 votes. Statewide, Specter rolled to a 785,000-vote victory margin earning 64 percent of the vote, just 3 percentage points short of John Heinz's mark.

2000: SANTORUM/KLINK

Senator Santorum's first reelection campaign, however, shaped up to be much more competitive. The staunch conservative was a more polarizing figure than previous Republicans were, and Democrats were eager to turn him out. Believing that Santorum's initial victory was a fluke owing to the political environment of 1992, they wanted to prove that someone from the right wing of the GOP couldn't survive long in statewide politics. After a bruising primary battle of six Democrats, including State Senator Allyson Schwartz of Philadelphia and Tom Foley, the former Secretary of Labor in the Casey Administration, Democrats believed that in Congressman Ron Klink they had just the nominee to topple Santorum. In fact, Klink's basic message in the primary was that he would give the party its best chance at victory.

Klink, 49, a four-term Congressman representing five counties in the Pittsburgh area, presented an interesting match-up for Santorum. A traditional liberal on economic policy, he had strong support in the labor community, but he took a conservative posture on the state's hot-button issues of abortion and gun control. Democrats hoped that his positions might negate some of Santorum's appeal among more socially conservative Democrats, especially in the northeast and in the central "T." They also hoped to attract Democrats back to their party in Pittsburgh and its environs, where Klink was already well known to the voters. In the southeast, particularly Philadelphia, the hope was that he could ride a huge turnout and presidential candidate Al Gore's coattails straight to the Senate.

Unfortunately for Klink, his conservative positions alienated him from many in the Democratic Party, particularly southeast liberals. He had a difficult time raising money from some of the traditional sources; many simply would not contribute to a pro-life Democrat whom they didn't know and who lived at the other end of the state. Campaign financial reports showed Klink falling further behind the incumbent. Eventually, he was even forced to mortgage his home for $300,000. By the time the campaign drew to a close, the challenger had raised just half of the $9 million his opponent had accumulated, and he had spent much of that to win the primary. The money factor was crucial, because it prevented Klink from establishing a strong presence in much of the state. This was painfully evident in the expensive Philadelphia media market, where the Democrat failed to run even one television commercial. Worse yet, Klink seemed to spend little time campaigning in the area. In a major blow to his campaign, the Reverend Vernal Simms, president of the Black Clergy of Philadelphia and Vicinity, endorsed Santorum shortly before the election. Simms said that although he would have liked to do otherwise, Klink never gave him the opportunity, ignoring repeated requests to meet with the organization's representatives.

Despite polls showing him trailing by double digits, the large number of undecided voters still gave Klink a glimmer of hope that he could pull off an upset. Many undecided voters were in Philadelphia, offering hope that they would pull the straight party lever. On the strength of an exceptionally large turnout in the city, the strategy partly worked. Klink registered an impressive 277,000-vote plurality in Philadelphia, although he ran 50,000 votes behind Gore. It seemed that the candidate was a victim of the "cutting" that had plagued other Democratic candidates in the past. For instance, one report said that in a South Philadelphia division, the local Democratic committee had highlighted every party name except Klink's on the sample ballots handed out to voters.

The lack of ads hurt Klink in the southeast GOP suburbs. Gore ran strong there, winning three of the four counties. If Klink had managed to do as well there, he could have made the race tight. But suburban Republicans were mostly unwilling to cross party lines for someone they knew little about. Additionally, Klink's conservative posture on social issues probably alienated him from Republicans who had been defecting for candidates such as Clinton and Gore.

Klink's strategy also was derailed in the more rural areas of the state. He lagged 469,000 votes behind Santorum in the "T," failing to win even one county. Santorum reached 59 and 56 percent, respectively in the Democratic-leaning counties of Elk and Erie. Santorum also crushed Klink in the

Democratic northeast. While the Democratic candidate's political portfolio closely resembled that of former Governor Casey, a tremendously popular figure during his time, it didn't seem to translate into votes. Interestingly, the only county Klink carried of the six in the region was Casey's Lackawanna. Santorum dominated everywhere else, including the swing Lehigh Valley (Lehigh and Northampton counties), where he enjoyed a 29,000-vote edge.

Klink topped Santorum by 52,000 votes in the battleground of the southwest, home to both candidates, but he needed much more. Klink had a 59,000-vote advantage in Allegheny County, although even that margin fell short of what Democratic expectations had been at the start of the campaign. Santorum whittled away at Klink's numbers in some of the surrounding counties, winning handily in Armstrong, Butler, and, most importantly, in the battleground of Westmoreland, where he prevailed 10,000 votes, a 6-point advantage.

In contrast to other campaigns, however, this defeat couldn't be placed squarely on the shoulders of Democrats in the southwest. Blame could be spread evenly across the Commonwealth. The Klink campaign posted large numbers among African-American voters in Philadelphia, but it never mounted a strong enough challenge to take advantage of the high turnout engendered by the presidential contest.

For Santorum, being able to carry all but eight counties en route to a 327,000-vote, 7-point win was a great accomplishment. It demonstrated that his initial triumph was not a political accident as his critics had charged. Instead, he won validation for both his policies and his style. He could now assume a role as a dominant figure not only in state politics, but in national politics as well.

2004: SPECTER/HOEFFEL

In 2004, 74-year-old Arlen Specter was attempting to win a historic fifth term to the United States Senate, yet he almost failed to reach the fall campaign. That's because he was forced into a tough primary fight with three-term Congressman Pat Toomey of Lehigh County. Toomey tapped into the anger that many Pennsylvania conservatives had harbored over the years concerning Specter and some of his liberal positions. Although Specter outspent him, Toomey benefited enormously from the support of several Washington-based conservative groups, particularly the Club for Growth, which launched a massive advertising campaign against the incumbent. This allowed Toomey to increase his name recognition outside the Lehigh Valley dramatically and enhance the credibility of his candidacy.

Toomey closed remarkably strong as election day approached, and as the votes were being counted, it became obvious that Specter would be fortunate to survive. In fact, the challenger held the lead for a time fairly late in the evening before falling to a 2-point defeat.

Shaken by the primary and forced to start all over again financially, Specter appeared somewhat vulnerable. The Democratic challenger was another three-term Congressman, 53-year-old Joe Hoeffel of Montgomery County, who initially appeared to benefit from running unopposed for his party's nomination. The Republican also faced the added prospect that the Constitution Party candidate, James Clymer, would drain votes from him on the right.

Aside from Specter's primary woes, it appeared at the outset that Hoeffel had several strategic advantages in bracing for the fall campaign. In fact, the Hoeffel challenge appeared remarkably similar to the one Specter had faced 18 years earlier, when Congressman Bob Edgar opposed him. Both were young and hardworking, and both cultivated an image of honesty and sincerity. Both also represented districts in the Philadelphia suburbs, which provided them with a base of support in a traditionally GOP stronghold. Indeed, Hoeffel increased his visibility within the city after part of his congressional district was moved there after redistricting in 2000. Unfortunately for the Democrats, however, the dynamics of this race also bore strong similarity to Edgar's disappointing bid.

As he had before, Specter trumpeted his ability to deliver federal money to Pennsylvania for a myriad of projects, a manifestation both of his seniority and of his seat on the powerful Senate Appropriations Committee. Like previous Democratic opponents, Hoeffel tried linking the incumbent to a Republican president, but he found an elusive target in the light-footed Specter. In fact, the pummeling that Specter endured in the spring—that he was too liberal—only served to inoculate him against charges in the fall that he was too conservative. Specter also lined up his usual share of endorsements among Democratic notables, including Ron Klink.

But perhaps the most devastating blow the Hoeffel camp received was when the Pennsylvania AFL-CIO endorsed the Republican incumbent. They had supported Hoeffel during his congressional campaigns, but by not at least staying neutral in the Hoeffel-Specter contest, they sent a clear signal of how they viewed the race. Specter's support from the labor community and several other traditionally liberal groups diminished Hoeffel's ability to keep up financially. By election day, Specter had raised approximately four times as much as his opponent. Finally, Governor Rendell's long relationship with Specter precluded him from providing more than just lukewarm assistance.

Hoeffel benefited from the coattails of presidential candidate John Kerry in Philadelphia, where straight ticket voting gave Hoeffel a 270,000-vote plurality. But Specter managed some inroads in his old hometown, holding the Democrat to 90,000 votes less than the presidential ticket. In the suburbs, Hoeffel, like Edgar, failed to take advantage. Specter carried the region by 147,000 votes, including a smashing 24-point victory in Chester County. Even in his Montgomery County home, Hoeffel ran 28,000 votes behind Specter.

Despite the problems he had faced in the primary, Specter ran as strong as ever in the "T," winning all 47 counties and scoring a 600,000-vote windfall. In fact, Hoeffel reached 40 percent of the two-party vote totals in only four counties: Berks (40 percent), Cambria (45 percent), Centre (42 percent), and Mercer (45 percent). The veteran Republican also walked off with a victory in the northeast. He even carried the twin Democratic counties of Lackawanna and

Luzerne by 14 and 16 points, respectively. In the southwest, the challenger managed to carry only Allegheny and Fayette counties, and both were by small margins.

When the race was over, Specter had breezed to a comfortable 591,000-vote margin. This marked the fifth term for a man who appeared to be heading toward retirement from politics until Dick Schweiker announced that he was stepping down in 1980. Whether the winds were at his back, such as when Specter was first elected in 1980, or in his face, as in 1992, Specter ultimately prevailed. He had also survived one heart-bypass surgery and two brain tumors (both of which were benign) and, prior to this contest, Hodgkin's Disease. After dropping three campaigns in a row back in the 1970s, he has demonstrated an unmatched level of persistence and resilience.

The year 2006 also marks the 50th anniversary of Joe Clark's victory over Jim Duff, the last time a Democrat defeated an incumbent Republican. What appeared to be the dawn of a new era politically for the Democrats would eventually turn into a political nightmare and a national embarrassment. For Democrats and the long, painful suffering they'd endured, derailing Rick Santorum's political career is perhaps the one thing that could wipe all those sorrowful memories away.

2006: CASEY/SANTORUM

March 5, 2005. That was the day the 2006 United States Senate race in Pennsylvania was decided. It was the day in which State Treasurer Robert Casey Jr., announced that he was going to challenge two-term incumbent Rick Santorum. Despite the millions of dollars which would later be spent, the debates, and the television and radio ads, the glare of the national spotlight, there really was little that Santorum, the powerful chair of the Republican Senate Conference, could do to stop the inevitable.

While 2006 proved to be a disaster for the GOP nationally, most pinned the blame on the growing unpopularity on the Bush Administration and especially the ongoing war in Iraq. And while Casey benefited from this political climate, many of the most serious wounds Santorum received during this campaign season were entirely self-inflicted. For the early part of his political career, Santorum had cultivated a reputation for himself as that of a reformer, of working-class roots, who championed basic conservative values. On some economic issues, such as trade protectionism, there was even a strain of populism that certainly appealed to many of the state's voters. However, throughout his second term, he had developed a larger national following, particularly among conservative evangelicals that would shatter his overall popularity statewide and perhaps better reflect the political profile of a senator from state much more conservative in nature than Pennsylvania.

The following is a synopsis of those political blunders. First, there was the tragedy of Terry Schiavo. Schiavo was a 41-year-old Florida woman who had been in what doctors labeled a persistent, vegetative state since 1990. For years, her husband, Michael, whom the courts had assigned the power of legal guardian, had fought to convince the state courts to remove her feeding tubes. Schiavo's parents, Robert and Mary Schindler, disagreed, and insisted that their daughter was conscious while offering to personally take care of her. Finally, in 2005, after years of battles in the Florida courts, it had reached a point were Terri Schiavo's feeding tubes were about to be removed.

With much of the nation engrossed as the drama unfolded, it was now time for Washington to get involved. In what became known as the "Palm Sunday Compromise," President George W. Bush signed into law legislation effectively transferring the case to the Federal Courts (in fact, it only applied to this particular case). Amidst protests and vigils, the battle waged on, until Pinellas County Judge George Greer basically decided to ignore the United States Congress and signed a judicial order forbidding Schiavo's removal from the hospice. Six days later, with her feeding tubes removed, Terri Schiavo succumbed.

In the aftermath, public opinion polls ran strongly in opposition to the congressional intervention in the case. And no other politician was as outspoken or became as identified with the ordeal than Senator Rick Santorum. He announced that, "We need to do something to stop this unconscionable act on the part of the Florida Court. Terri Schiavo is a daughter, a sister, and most importantly, a person. We cannot allow an innocent person to be put to death." For this, he was criticized for offering up language that not only smacked of hyperbole but was even exploitative in nature. However, with the nation transfixed and the television cameras rolling, Santorum's role may best be remembered for his decision to pay a personal visit to Schiavo's parents. That a lawmaker from a state a thousand miles away was compelled to interject himself in this manner for many smacked of grandstanding, at best, and brash political opportunism, at worst. That he also found time to rake in $250,000 at a fundraiser while in the Sunshine State also certainly didn't help matters.

Second. The Book. In "It Takes a Family," Santorum's seeming retort to Hillary Clinton's "It Takes a Village," the senator cemented his reputation as both a major voice among Christian conservatives nationally and major critic of contemporary American liberalism. However, while as a philosophical treatise or sociological tract on family-related issues it may have been thought-provoking, as a political document it was a disaster. While sincere, the overall theme of the book that emerged for much of the general public was that women who decided to pursue a career rather than being a stay-at-home mom were being selfish. One quote that stood out in particular was that radical feminists had succeeded in undermining the traditional family by convincing women that professional accomplishments were the key to happiness. This was so damaging that Santorum attempted to deflect the criticism he received by suggesting that his wife had helped him write it. Overall, that the book was portrayed as an attack upon working women severely undercut the support he once enjoyed in places like the Philadelphia suburbs. The bottom line is that political books are supposed to advance ones political objectives, not detract as this one most certainly did.

Lastly, the home in Virginia. While most of Santorum's troubles related to his outspokenness on issues, this was one that even his ideological allies were left scratching their heads over. Santorum had claimed his legal address was a house in Penn Hills, a suburb of Pittsburgh. However, local television crews eventually began staking out the home in order to determine whether or not he still truly lived in this Pennsylvania residence. What these news reports would reveal was a property with high weeds, peeling paint, and worse, piles of mail stacked up on the front doorstep. When the cameras looked inside the house, it was empty. Clearly, the Senator and his family did not live there anymore.

Compounding the problem was that rather than living in this modest home valued at $106,000 in western Pennsylvania, Santorum also possessed another property, this one assessed at $600,000. However, the real problem was that the more impressive home, and the one in which he was living wasn't located in the state at all, but rather in Great Falls, VA. Democrats and the press had a field day with this, and many from western Pennsylvania couldn't help but recall the irony since it was similar to a charge made by Santorum against incumbent Congressman Doug Walgren when he first won election to the United States House of Representatives.

However, if this wasn't enough to alienate even a few of his ideological supporters, one final aspect of this issue would soon come to light that would make it even harder to ignore. Though the Senator was obviously living in Virginia, it was reported that he was billing the Penn Hills School District around $40,000 annually to educate each of his five children in the Western Pennsylvania Cyber Charter School. This issue infuriated voters in western Pennsylvania, and one would guess, particularly those who lived in Penn Hills that were picking up the tab.

Revealingly, rather than attempt to soften his image during the campaign Santorum almost seemed to relish all of the controversy. He may have tried to soften his image by focusing on items such as his work on behalf of AIDS victims in Africa. Over the past 15 years in public office he had also developed a number legislative accomplishments as well as a position in the senate GOP leadership which could have served as a political asset. Instead, he decided to press forward on the social issues.

When he did go on the offensive, however, some of Santorum's attacks on the Democratic candidate backfired anyway. In what was dubbed his "Gathering Storm" speech, Santorum attempted to rally the crowds on the need to fight "Islamofascism." Positioning himself as a modern-day Winston Churchill, he contrasted his aggressive, battle-ready persona with that of the laidback Casey. All of this may have been effective, however, he went much too far and sounded desperate when he charged that as State Treasurer, Casey had made investments that sponsored international terrorism.

As for the Casey campaign itself, their strategy of running a low key campaign, while allowing the incumbent himself to be the story never really allowed the incumbent senator an opening he could exploit. Santorum charge that Casey had spent too much of his time campaigning rather than actually showing up for work may have been effective if the Democrat was an unknown quantity. But the Casey family name had been around far too long in Pennsylvania for this line to take root. It was another reason why Casey would prove to be the perfect candidate for this race; socially conservative himself on issues like gun control and abortion, Santorum didn't even have much success rallying his supporters along those lines.

By the time election day finally arrived, the final outcome was no surprise. However, the sheer enormity of Casey's victory was shocking. The Democrat won by over 700,000 votes, taking 59 percent overall. Generally, when they do lose, incumbent US Senators do so by narrow margins, but Santorum's defeat was the second biggest defeat in state history. Only Democratic Senator Joe Guffey's 1946 thrashing at the hands of Governor Edward Martin was worse.

It's instructive to note how Santorum had dominated the state in his previous election, carrying 58 of the state's 67 counties, and all but three counties that were located outside of the southwest region. This time, he managed to win just one, Butler County that was located outside of the central Pennsylvania. While his numbers dropped considerably across the entire Commonwealth, his biggest decline was in the Philadelphia suburbs where he dropped from 58 percent to just 40 percent. Even in the central "T," the only region he managed to carry with 51 percent, his numbers declined 13 points since his last election.

Defeats of this magnitude are usually the end of one's political career, but not so with Santorum. The support he engendered in this campaign among Christian Conservatives for continuing to press on and fight the fight, would serve as the foundation to a surprisingly strong presidential bid in 2012. He eventually would come in second to eventual GOP nominee Mitt Romney. One can only wonder if he had toned his rhetoric down, brushed aside his desire to author a book and stuck to his core economic principles that perhaps things could have been different. Had his approval ratings remained credible, Casey may not have jumped in at all to challenge him and he might have faced a much weaker Democrat. Had he withstood that 2006 tide, his presidential ambitions for 2008 would have been perfectly served up before him.

2010: TOOMEY/SESTAK

Heading into the elections of 2010, Democrats had been on a roll both nationally and in Pennsylvania. Nationally, they now controlled not only the White House and both chambers of congress but also held a 60-vote filibuster proof majority in the US Senate for the first time since December 1978. In Pennsylvania, they controlled both of the US Senate seats for the first time since January 1947 and 12 of the state's 19 congressional seats. They held the governor's mansion and outnumbered the GOP in the state house of representatives. Additionally, a recent surge had lifted their advantage in overall registration advantage to 1.2 million over the Republicans. They even controlled 27 of the state's 67 counties, the most since 1978, including flipping such GOP strongholds such as Bucks, Centre, Dauphin, and Montgomery counties. However, on November 2, 2010, much of this came crashing down.

While the White House was not at stake in this midterm election, the Republicans were able to pick up six senate seats (though they did not take control), and a whopping 63 house seats (where they did take control) and now held more seats in the latter than they did at any time since 1946. They also controlled 39 of the nation's 50 governorships and held more state legislative seats than they did since the 1928 elections. In Pennsylvania, they would win back the Governorship, the state house, maintain control of the state senate, and pick up five US House Seats flipping the balance of that delegation. But perhaps the biggest loss of all for the Democrats was seeing control of the US Senate delegation, one that they had waited over a half-century to enjoy, slip away with the narrow victory by Pat Toomey over Joe Sestak.

The story of this campaign really begins on April 28, 2009, when Senator Arlen Specter announced that he was leaving the Republican Party and becoming a Democrat, once again. He had originally flipped parties 44 years earlier when the Philadelphia Democratic Party rebuffed his interest in running as the city's District Attorney. Specter, who was Assistant DA then ran as a Republican and was able to defeat the individual who was both the incumbent, and his boss, James Crumlish, Jr. However, circumstances had now changed, and spurred on by two long-time friends, Vice President Joe Biden and Governor Ed Rendell, he announced that his future in the GOP was untenable, stating "I'm not prepared to have my 29-year record in the United States Senate decided by the Pennsylvania Republican primary electorate, not prepared to have that record decided by that jury."

Specter had only narrowly defeated Pat Toomey back in the 2004 GOP primary, and clearly that was going to be even tougher to navigate this time around. He explained that his former party's shift to the right, some of which was due to the migration of roughly 200,000 Republicans over to the Democratic Party, robbed him of many of the moderates that he could always count on. He had also engendered the wrath of many in the GOP by being one of two Republican Senators (Senator Olympia Snowe of Maine) was the other, to support President Obama's controversial $787 billion economic stimulus package, the cornerstone of the newly elected Democrat's first year agenda. Because of the Republican filibuster, these two votes were vital to get to the 60 vote threshold necessary to invoke cloture, thus subsequently allowing the bill to come to the floor for passage.

With his announcement, Specter also became the Democratic Party's 59th seat in the senate, and with Al Franken on the verge of winning a disputed contest in the state of Minnesota, thus allowing the Democrats to achieve the elusive 60 vote caucus, only further exacerbated the contempt that many of his former supporters now felt, starting at the top with the Chairman of the

Republican National Committee, Michael Steele, who labeled him "Benedict Arlen."

As a Democrat, however, the 80 year old Specter, would now be forced to stand before an electorate that could well remember all of the battles they had fought (and largely lost) to the five-term senator. Many would not be so quick to embrace him. Despite the full support from President Obama, the national party and the statewide Democratic apparatus headed up by Rendell, Congressman Joe Sestak of Delaware County, a retired Navy Admiral, who had been eyeing the race, could not be dissuaded from challenging Specter in the Democratic primary.

Almost immediately, the race drew national headlines and controversy when Sestak hinted that the Obama Administration had offered him a high-level White House job if he abandoned his campaign. Although the official report subsequently made clear that he had only been approached (by former President Bill Clinton) and there were no illegalities involved, the entire affair looked messy and reflected unfavorably upon both Democrats.

Although early polls indicated a sizeable lead for Specter, much of that could be attributable to Sestak's low degree of name recognition throughout the state. It was also clear that the challenger, who had $3 million left over from his previous congressional race, possessed the resources necessary to rectify that situation. In addition, while the incumbent certainly had the benefit of highlighting all that he had accomplished for Pennsylvania voters during his thirty years in the senate, this argument also came with a price. Sestak and his supporters countered that this was proof that the incumbent had been in office too long, that he was an opportunist, the "poster child" for everything that was wrong in Washington, D.C.

However, the tipping point in the contest may have been an ad unveiled by Sestak's camp as primary day drew near which reminded Democratic voters of the incumbent's past. In it, Specter was being endorsed by another president, George W. Bush, who, flanked by Senator Santorum proclaimed that the Pennsylvania senator was a firm ally whom he could count on. This spot, originally run six years earlier may have helped him prevail in that 2004 primary battle against Toomey, but those words would come back to haunt him dearly now among the Democratic party electorate.

Specter responded with a series of ads questioning his opponent's naval record, but that misfired badly and only made things worse. Challenging the veracity of someone with Sestak's military credentials, he once served on the National Security Council and headed an anti-terrorism unit after 9/11, only alienated more voters within the Democratic Party electorate. Specter attempted to combat this by arguing that over the years he had fought often with GOP leaders and had supported Democratic causes on a number of important issues throughout his career. In reality, during his short stint as a Democratic senator he voted consistently with the majority in his new party—much more than he ever did with his old one.

But ultimately Spector's past meant more to a majority of Democrats than the present in what would be his last campaign. Sestak continued to gain throughout the spring and pulled even in the polls one month before the primary. Many doubted that his campaign organization, or lack thereof (he possessed neither a campaign manager nor much in the way of a field operation) could defeat the entire organization of the Democratic Party, but he did and in a fashion few would have predicted, taking 54 percent of the vote, a roughly 80,000 vote margin statewide.

Nevertheless, the Democratic Party was itself now badly split and unprepared to take on the fight in the general election. Sestak, who had bucked the party establishment to win its nomination, would find it much more difficult to win in the general without its support. Waiting for him in the general election would be a Republican opponent who also had a history of facing off once against Arlen Specter in a primary, this one the 2004 GOP race when he was defeated. However, the comeback of Pat Toomey was about to unfold.

There is an old adage in American politics that if you challenge an incumbent within your own party you better win—because your career is probably finished. That Pat Toomey was able to defy this within the GOP is impressive, that he was able to do it without any serious opposition within his own party is remarkable. That no other prominent Republican office-holder across the state was willing to run for the nomination, and essentially step aside for Toomey, a former three-term congressman from Lehigh County, suggests that many felt they had erred by supporting Specter in their 2004 battle and they now bore no ill will towards him. Perhaps many felt that Toomey was right all along, that Specter ultimately couldn't be trusted and now admired Toomey for stepping forward in 2004. Whatever the reason, only Peg Luksik, several times a candidate for statewide office attempted to seek the GOP nomination and that proved to be no contest at all as the state party rallied around Toomey, and he brushed her aside with ease.

Toomey was fortunate in that he could avoid both the personal and financial scars of a primary battle. The Democrats, however, destroyed one another which would prove to be insurmountable to Sestak in the fall. While the Democrat had to begin fundraising from scratch after spending his resources in the primary, Toomey was able to campaign from the beginning with a full war chest, grabbing a lead that he would truly never relinquish.

While both candidates tried to portray their opponent as an extremist, the campaign itself was relatively mild considering the high stakes. Sestak spent much time criticizing his opponent's role as head of the conservative think tank, Club for Growth, where he served as president after his defeat in the 2004 primary. The Club for Growth wreaked havoc on GOP organizations in a number of states, purging the party of those whom they considered too moderate and not consistently supportive of conservative issues. They had fought hard with Specter while he was still in the GOP and had helped defeat other moderates in primary battles along the way.

Toomey, a former Wall Street trader, who spent his years in the House of Representatives taking a hard line on fiscal issues, responded with a vision that focused on "More Jobs, Less Government." He attacked Sestak for not only supporting the agenda of President Obama, but for pushing an agenda even further left, with a greater stimulus package and a "public option" in the President's Affordable Care Act. Toomey also pressed Sestak on his support for the cap-and-trade energy tax, arguing that it would be economically devastating for a manufacturing state like Pennsylvania. Like many Democrats across the nation, Sestak also had to fend off charges that he voted in lock step with the leadership, particularly Speaker of the House Nancy Pelosi, a charge that would resonate among not just conservatives but also moderates, particularly outside the southeastern part of the state.

Though Sestak began to draw closer after Labor Day, the unwelcome political climate of 2010 was just too much for the Democrat to overcome. Trying to tie the earnest appearing Toomey to the more extremist elements in the Tea Party movement was ultimately ineffective. While Toomey did enjoy an overall financial advantage (with $15 million) owing largely to his head start on the fall campaign, Sestak was able raise enough money, taking in $12 million.

However, Sestak's unwillingness to unite his campaign with the state party organization, in fact, he continued to battle them throughout the fall, may have been decisive. He avoided appearing with other Democrats on the ballot thereby running any sort of coordinated effort; he even removed the word "Democrat" from his campaign literature. This would alienate some within the leadership of the party and leave others to wonder why they should go out of their way to help him. The question remains, could the party have been able to push him first across the finish line if he had given them the the opportunity? Given the environment, it was no surprise that there was the sharp decline in turnout among voters in many of the core Democratic groups (African-Americans, Latinos, single women, and college students) who had voted in record numbers two years earlier. Their indifference would cost the party dearly in 2010.

Toomey's 80,000 vote victory was among the closest senate races in the nation. In the southeast, he was able to capture Bucks and Chester counties, thus stemming the overall advantage that Democrats had enjoyed there in recent years. Here, Sestak's overall margin was approximately 150,000 fewer than the 450,000 vote margin that Casey had garnered in the most recent senate election. Strategically, this was also important since Sestak was unable to accumulate in his political backyard the margins that he would need to offset the losses that he would face elsewhere across the state. Toomey also fought the Democrat to a draw in the northeast, though interestingly, he lost his own home county, Lehigh by six percentage points.

In the Central "T", Toomey captured all but one of the 47 counties in this region, Eric County, and his roughly 365,000 vote edge here more than offset his loses in the southeast. However, as has been the cases for many of the previous Democratic Party failures in races for the US Senate, once again, the southwest would be their ultimate undoing. That both candidates hailed from the eastern part of the state, made the southwest the clear battleground. Whoever broke through here would go on to the US Senate.

Carrying Allegheny County by a tepid 40,000 votes (55 percent) was troubling; however, the final nail in the Sestak campaign was his inability to carry any other county in this traditionally Democratic region. Despite the fact that Democrats enjoyed a registration advantage in the southwest of almost a half million votes, Toomey took the overall region by 30,000. Of particular note, was Toomey's performance in GOP-trending Westmoreland County. That the GOP candidate was able to amass a 28,000 vote margin (61 percent) here, despite a Democratic registration advantage of 42,000 is a good indicator of not only Sestak's problems but also what the Democrats themselves now face in the southwest. For the two candidates from eastern Pennsylvania, this geographically neutral battleground of the southwest would serve as the microcosm for the GOP victory.

Toomey's victory was also significant from a geographical standpoint in that he became just the third individual from the Lehigh Valley to ever hold statewide office. Only George Wolf of Easton, who was elected Governor in 1828 and Richard Brodhead, also of Easton, who was selected to the United States Senate in 1850, preceded him. While there is no clear reason why the state's third largest metropolitan area has been so underrepresented historically, one theory is that because the Lehigh Valley lacks its own media market, its politicians get overshadowed in the huge Philadelphia market. Whatever the reason, we'll have to wait and see whether it takes another 150 years for the next candidate from the area to be as successful.

2012: CASEY/SMITH

Interestingly, Senator Casey's campaign for reelection proved more difficult in many respects than the one he faced when he captured the seat over Rick Santorum in 2006. The reasons for this were several. First, he now had a record in the senate he would be forced to defend, and votes on the Affordable Care Act, and the stimulus bill were a political target. Second, the environment in 2014 was much different than it was six years earlier, and though not the minefield that it was for Democrats two years earlier, still posed some difficulties. The national forces, with an especially close presidential contest, would not allow him to simply coast to victory. Secondly, his opponent this time was not going to be someone who was as politically damaged as Rick Santorum had been.

Though he didn't have the good fortune of running against a widely unpopular incumbent, he benefited from the GOP's inability to recruit a top-tier challenger, perhaps someone from the congressional delegation to take him on. Their nominee, farmer and former coal company executive Tom Smith defeated several others in the spring primary. Most notably, that list included former State Representative Sam Rohrer of Berks County, who had the support of a number of conservative Christian organizations. Rohrer had also run two years earlier for the GOP nomination for governor but was easily defeated by the eventual winner, Tom Corbett. Corbett and the state Republican Party endorsed Chester County venture capitalist Steve Welch, a former Democrat, but he finished a distant third.

Smith was also once a registered Democrat (though he also heavily contributed to a number of conservative causes in recent years), invested more than $5 million of his own money into the primary. His ability to saturate the state's airwaves with advertisements leading up to the primary was the crucial element allowing him to separate himself from the rest of the field. This was the first attempt at elected office for Smith, who still lived on the family farm that he grew up on in Armstrong County, which was a central element of the image he burnished as a political outsider. What separated Smith from previous Democratic candidates who had challenged incumbent Republicans for US Senate races and ultimately never became competitive, was money—he had lots of it and was prepared to spend however much was necessary.

While Casey started out with a lead of over 20 points at the start of the summer, his opponent's financial resources (Smith personally loaned himself over $12.5 million for the general) allowed the GOP candidate to get on the air long before the incumbent started running ads himself in mid-September. The centerpiece of the challenger's message was that he would fight to change Washington, specifically attacking Casey by labeling him "Senator Zero," while pushing for traditionally conservative causes such as a balanced budget amendment and a flattening of the tax code.

Casey meanwhile kept a very low profile campaign right through a large part of the fall, until polls began to indicate that his lead was beginning to slip. When the Democrat did respond with a message built around attacking "Tea Party Tom Smith," some contended that the attacks weren't sufficiently focused enough and had the unintended consequence of further enhancing the Republicans name identification across the state. Casey was noticeably upset by the "Senator Zero," remark as well as Smith's charge that he didn't author a single bill his first term in office. The Democrat fired back that his record of getting results for the people of Pennsylvania is what truly counted, citing his own legislative accomplishments in items such support for the payroll tax cut. He also highlighted his role in working to include special provisions for women and military personnel to be included within the Affordable Care Act itself.

Though polls indicated that Smith was within striking distance heading into the final weeks, his lack of experience on the campaign trail was evident in a speaking style that was hardly polished and even worse, being prone to gaffe. The most damaging occurred while relaying a personal anecdote about his daughter who had become pregnant outside of marriage. As he continued to recount the experience, Smith stated that from a father's position, out-of-wedlock pregnancy was similar to rape, a commented that drew the ire of many, including some Republicans.

Despite a moderate degree of national attention and some outside money coming in, Smith was unable to close the gap and the incumbent pulled away as the election drew near. Casey's overall victory margin of approximately 500,000 was about 200,000 votes shy of his first election back in 2006. It's important to note that, however, that it was also about the same amount more than President Obama received on election night in 2012, reflecting the different political climate.

In the southeast, Casey's and Obama's numbers were virtually identical, with the senator taking one percent more overall at 67 percent. Casey could also be credited with carrying each of the counties, while the President narrowly lost Chester. There was only a slight difference between the two Democrats in the northeast, with the senator doing slightly better in each of the six counties and registering two percent more overall at 57 percent. Their numbers were similar in Central Pennsylvania as well, with Senator Casey getting 43 percent in the region, while the President lagged two points behind him. Each carried Centre, Dauphin, and Erie counties, while Casey also added Berks to his ledger.

The largest variation in the statewide vote between the two Democratic winners occurred in the southwest. While Casey's support fell far short of his effort in this region in 2006 when he took 61 percent, he still managed to maintain a majority with 53 percent of the vote. This time, however, he carried only three of the counties, Allegheny, Beaver and Fayette, the latter two quite handily. It should be noted that this was a significant drop from his previous encounter with Santorum, a westerner himself, when he was able to carry every county in the region.

Despite some decline in the support he received, Bob Casey had accomplished what no other Democrat had done in a half-century, which was to win reelection. And after all of those decades of disappointments, that was surely good enough for both he and his political party.

CHAPTER THREE

PENNSYLVANIA GUBERNATORIAL ELECTIONS

1950: FINE/DILWORTH

Between the end of the Civil War and the time this study began in 1950, the Republican Party controlled Pennsylvania's chief executive office, just as it generally controlled politics in the state. During that roughly 100-year time span, only two Democrats—Robert E. Pattison in 1882 and 1890 and George H. Earle in 1934—enjoyed the pleasure of residing in the gubernatorial mansion. For the Democratic Party, this constituted an anemic success rate of just 12.5 percent (3 of 24 elections), a figure made even worse because incumbents were constitutionally prevented from succeeding themselves; hence, every contest was for an open seat. Nevertheless, Democrats felt a cautious sense of optimism as Governor Jim Duff's term neared its completion in the fall of 1950.

Their candidate was Richardson Dilworth, a wealthy patrician from Philadelphia who along with Joe Clark and other reformers would finally wrest control of Philadelphia's government from the Republicans. Dilworth, who was the city treasurer, faced Republican John Fine, a judge from Luzerne County. Fine had been forced to wage a brutal primary battle against Philadelphia millionaire Jay Cooke. Cooke was the candidate of Joseph Grundy—a former U.S. Senator and the founder of the Pennsylvania Manufacturers Association—and his political machine. Lycoming County Judge Charles S. Williams, a former newspaperman, also entered the race. Fine, however, had the support of the popular Duff, which boosted him to an almost 200,000-vote victory over Cooke, who finished second.

The general election dominated the state's political landscape (which included the Myers-Duff Senate contest), as is usually the case. In a ferocious and personal battle (even by Pennsylvania standards), each candidate traded barbs over such items as their labor records (Fine fending off charges that he was anti-labor), cronyism (Dilworth promised to overhaul the state bureaucracy and abolish the patronage system), and communism (Fine proclaimed that unless we stop our opponents, the city, county, state and nation were headed toward a totalitarian state). Both candidates were guilty of demagoguery: Dilworth, for instance, charged that the Republicans wanted to repeal the 20th century, which was fairly standard boilerplate compared with Fine's assessment that he no longer had an opponent but "rather a psychiatric problem heading for political extinction."

With President Truman's popularity at extraordinarily low levels, the midterm elections of 1950 provided a propitious political landscape for the GOP. In a state where the Republicans were already well entrenched, it all proved too much for Dilworth or any other Democrat to withstand. With United States Senator Francis J. Myers also being sent home in defeat (by Governor Duff), the first campaign of the second half of the 20th century would end as most in the first half had ended: triumphantly for the Republicans. Indeed, the election was a major setback not only for the Democrats but also for their allies in the organized-labor community. Unions had devoted unprecedented energy across the nation, as well as more than $1 million, to elect a more pro-labor Congress, but they fell far short of their expectations.

The results, however, were not entirely negative for the Democrats, given their historically disadvantaged position. The Fine-Dilworth contest was one of the closest races in the state's history, with the Republican winning by just 86,000 votes, far below the usual GOP margin. Dilworth amassed a 77,000-vote advantage in his hometown of Philadelphia, which was on the verge of a dramatic partisan shift. Fine's 71,000-vote margin in the Philadelphia suburbs offset most of Dilworth's city total, but Dilworth's 40 percent in the four suburban counties—where Democrats had only 17 percent of the registered voters— was far greater than his party generally achieved (Table 3.1).

**Table 3.1 Democratic Share of Two-Party Vote for Governor,
Southeastern Pennsylvania**

	1950	1954	1958	1962	1966	1970	1974	1978
Philadelphia	55%	58%	62%	57%	58%	64%	70%	52%
Bucks	44%	49%	47%	40%	43%	56%	55%	42%
Chester	38%	40%	38%	32%	33%	47%	45%	31%
Delaware	41%	41%	40%	37%	34%	46%	50%	39%
Montgomery	39%	38%	38%	34%	33%	51%	49%	34%
Suburban Totals	**40%**	**41%**	**40%**	**36%**	**35%**	**50%**	**50%**	**37%**
Southeast Totals	**50%**	**52%**	**53%**	**48%**	**48%**	**57%**	**60%**	**45%**

State Totals	49%	54%	51%	44%	47%	57%	54%	47%
Winning Party	**R**	**D**	**D**	**R**	**R**	**D**	**D**	**R**

	1982	**1986**	**1990**	**1994**	**1998**	**2002**	**2006**	**2010**
Philadelphia	64%	64%	71%	73%	63%	85%	89%	83%
Bucks	38%	40%	59%	39%	30%	65%	70%	45%
Chester	31%	33%	53%	36%	24%	58%	65%	44%
Delaware	35%	40%	55%	41%	30%	66%	74%	53%
Montgomery	32%	34%	50%	44%	33%	68%	72%	52%
Suburban Totals	**34%**	**37%**	**54%**	**40%**	**30%**	**65%**	**71%**	**49%**
Southeast Totals	**48%**	**49%**	**61%**	**53%**	**41%**	**72%**	**77%**	**60%**
State Totals	**49%**	**51%**	**68%**	**47%**	**35%**	**55%**	**60%**	**46%**
Winning Party	**R**	**D**	**D**	**R**	**R**	**D**	**D**	**R**

Dilworth carried the six counties of northeastern Pennsylvania by 137 votes, despite the GOP's registration advantage of 53,000 there, a ten-percentage point edge (Table 3.2). In Fine's home county of Luzerne, Dilworth held Fine's margin to under 11,000 votes. Even in central Pennsylvania, where the Democrats held a majority of registered voters in just 6 of its counties and only 38 percent of registered voters, Dilworth ran surprisingly well, particularly for a Philadelphia Democrat, taking 43 percent of the vote (Table 3.3).

**Table 3.2 Democratic Share of Two-Party Vote for Governor,
Southwestern Pennsylvania**

	1950	**1954**	**1958**	**1962**	**1966**	**1970**	**1974**	**1978**
Allegheny	52%	58%	54%	46%	53%	63%	57%	52%
Armstrong	45%	52%	44%	40%	46%	60%	50%	60%
Beaver	51%	62%	57%	49%	57%	68%	59%	67%
Butler	37%	47%	41%	36%	41%	59%	46%	58%
Fayette	58%	67%	60%	53%	58%	64%	56%	67%
Greene	63%	70%	56%	53%	56%	67%	51%	64%
Lawrence	45%	54%	53%	44%	47%	57%	50%	64%
Washington	59%	65%	57%	51%	58%	68%	57%	66%
Westmoreland	54%	65%	57%	49%	57%	69%	56%	66%
Southwest Totals	**52%**	**60%**	**55%**	**46%**	**53%**	**64%**	**56%**	**58%**

State Totals	49%	54%	51%	44%	47%	57%	54%	47%
Winning Party	**R**	**D**	**D**	**R**	**R**	**D**	**D**	**R**

	1982	1986	1990	1994	1998	2002	2006	2010
Allegheny	49%	57%	72%	52%	43%	55%	60%	50%
Armstrong	53%	55%	69%	47%	36%	40%	41%	29%
Beaver	61%	67%	76%	57%	44%	54%	55%	44%
Butler	46%	47%	67%	38%	32%	36%	39%	28%
Fayette	64%	69%	83%	64%	49%	58%	59%	44%
Greene	64%	67%	79%	59%	48%	54%	55%	46%
Lawrence	62%	61%	73%	50%	41%	53%	55%	41%
Washington	52%	62%	75%	54%	47%	52%	53%	40%
Westmoreland	57%	61%	75%	51%	42%	46%	46%	32%
Southwest Totals	**52%**	**59%**	**73%**	**52%**	**43%**	**52%**	**43%**	**48%**
State Totals	**49%**	**51%**	**68%**	**47%**	**35%**	**55%**	**60%**	**46%**
Winning Party	**R**	**D**	**D**	**R**	**R**	**D**	**D**	**R**

Table 3.3 Democratic Share of Two-Party Vote for Governor, Northeastern Pennsylvania

	1950	1954	1958	1962	1966	1970	1974	1978
Carbon	52%	53%	52%	45%	48%	57%	55%	45%
Lackawanna	54%	57%	58%	50%	50%	54%	57%	45%
Lehigh	47%	52%	49%	41%	44%	62%	56%	41%
Luzerne	46%	53%	53%	49%	51%	59%	56%	48%
Monroe	50%	55%	47%	40%	41%	53%	49%	41%
Northampton	54%	61%	54%	49%	53%	67%	60%	45%
Northeast Totals	**50%**	**55%**	**54%**	**48%**	**49%**	**60%**	**57%**	**45%**
State Totals	**49%**	**54%**	**51%**	**44%**	**47%**	**57%**	**54%**	**47%**
Winning Party	**R**	**D**	**D**	**R**	**R**	**D**	**D**	**R**

	1982	1986	1990	1994	1998	2002	2006	2010
Carbon	58%	57%	70%	47%	41%	57%	61%	41%
Lackawanna	57%	68%	82%	58%	42%	61%	73%	55%
Lehigh	43%	44%	63%	40%	31%	58%	63%	45%
Luzerne	57%	64%	81%	53%	35%	54%	68%	47%
Monroe	44%	46%	64%	41%	29%	49%	60%	46%
Northampton	48%	52%	68%	44%	33%	60%	64%	46%
Northeast Totals	**52%**	**58%**	**73%**	**48%**	**35%**	**57%**	**66%**	**47%**
State Totals	**49%**	**51%**	**68%**	**47%**	**35%**	**55%**	**60%**	**46%**
Winning Party	**R**	**D**	**D**	**R**	**R**	**D**	**D**	**R**

More than anything else, it was the Democratic Party base of southwestern Pennsylvania that cost Dilworth the governorship. Despite a registration advantage of more than 187,000 voters (57 percent), the Philadelphian carried the area by just 42,000 votes (Table 3.4). Allegheny County, where Democrats had a 142,000-voter registration advantage, was most disappointing to the Democrats: Dilworth outpolled Fine by only 24,000 votes. Fine's achievement there was quite remarkable. Although he hailed from the other side of the state, it was his performance in the heart of Democratic Party power that ultimately kept executive control of the state's government in his party's hands.

Table 3.4 Democratic Share of Two-Party Vote for Governor, Central Pennsylvania

	1950	1954	1958	1962	1966	1970	1974	1978
Adams	42%	50%	44%	39%	37%	46%	45%	37%
Bedford	44%	51%	44%	36%	37%	43%	39%	41%
Berks	54%	62%	52%	45%	48%	62%	58%	46%
Blair	38%	49%	41%	33%	39%	52%	41%	47%
Bradford	33%	39%	35%	32%	30%	36%	36%	25%
Cambria	54%	63%	60%	45%	48%	59%	56%	63%
Cameron	38%	44%	39%	35%	37%	50%	40%	42%
Centre	40%	49%	43%	33%	39%	51%	50%	38%
Clarion	47%	50%	38%	36%	40%	52%	44%	55%
Clearfield	50%	56%	48%	42%	45%	56%	50%	53%
Clinton	48%	54%	47%	41%	43%	60%	56%	40%

Columbia	52%	58%	49%	40%	41%	47%	51%	43%
Crawford	41%	46%	44%	37%	38%	54%	40%	44%
Cumberland	45%	48%	42%	33%	33%	45%	46%	30%
Dauphin	38%	43%	42%	34%	32%	43%	51%	33%
Elk	53%	56%	51%	42%	51%	64%	47%	59%
Erie	48%	55%	49%	47%	52%	59%	47%	46%
Forest	38%	45%	38%	38%	35%	45%	44%	50%
Franklin	41%	47%	20%	38%	39%	48%	50%	34%
Fulton	54%	59%	51%	43%	46%	51%	50%	44%
Huntingdon	37%	46%	40%	35%	36%	44%	41%	38%
Indiana	44%	49%	44%	39%	41%	54%	49%	50%
Jefferson	39%	44%	40%	37%	39%	49%	42%	51%
Juniata	48%	54%	46%	42%	39%	47%	51%	39%
Lancaster	34%	42%	35%	29%	27%	37%	36%	27%
Lebanon	40%	46%	39%	31%	34%	46%	46%	35%
Lycoming	50%	54%	43%	36%	41%	49%	41%	38%
McKean	32%	33%	37%	35%	36%	42%	38%	34%
Mercer	44%	52%	49%	42%	47%	58%	48%	50%
Mifflin	46%	51%	41%	36%	39%	47%	56%	41%
Montour	48%	54%	43%	41%	40%	47%	47%	38%
Northumberland	45%	51%	44%	41%	40%	51%	50%	41%
Perry	40%	46%	41%	35%	35%	44%	47%	31%
Pike	38%	38%	37%	32%	28%	34%	38%	34%
Potter	39%	45%	41%	35%	33%	43%	44%	36%
Schuylkill	44%	46%	47%	43%	43%	58%	53%	42%
Snyder	30%	36%	29%	26%	26%	33%	35%	24%
Somerset	45%	52%	47%	39%	40%	49%	45%	58%
Sullivan	45%	53%	45%	42%	39%	41%	41%	39%
Susquehanna	33%	40%	37%	35%	35%	39%	36%	32%
Tioga	28%	34%	33%	31%	30%	37%	35%	25%
Union	31%	36%	28%	24%	26%	35%	33%	24%
Venango	31%	38%	35%	33%	38%	50%	37%	50%
Warren	33%	39%	38%	35%	39%	50%	39%	38%

Wayne	28%	30%	33%	29%	28%	30%	33%	27%
Wyoming	34%	39%	35%	28%	27%	37%	34%	28%
York	51%	62%	54%	43%	43%	51%	50%	39%
Central Totals	**44%**	**50%**	**44%**	**38%**	**40%**	**50%**	**47%**	**41%**
State Totals	**49%**	**54%**	**51%**	**44%**	**47%**	**57%**	**54%**	**47%**
Winning Party	**R**	**D**	**D**	**R**	**R**	**D**	**D**	**R**

	1982	**1986**	**1990**	**1994**	**1998**	**2002**	**2006**	**2010**
Adams	39%	41%	71%	36%	20%	33%	43%	27%
Bedford	44%	46%	61%	35%	22%	31%	38%	22%
Berks	44%	45%	62%	39%	30%	56%	57%	41%
Blair	42%	46%	68%	36%	19%	31%	40%	27%
Bradford	35%	38%	56%	31%	20%	33%	44%	28%
Cambria	55%	70%	80%	69%	36%	44%	61%	42%
Cameron	48%	47%	65%	42%	28%	36%	45%	30%
Centre	40%	43%	59%	42%	27%	43%	54%	45%
Clarion	48%	48%	65%	37%	26%	35%	42%	29%
Clearfield	53%	57%	74%	42%	33%	43%	50%	36%
Clinton	57%	51%	71%	45%	33%	49%	56%	39%
Columbia	53%	54%	68%	42%	32%	43%	51%	34%
Crawford	44%	46%	67%	23%	26%	37%	42%	33%
Cumberland	40%	37%	66%	37%	19%	37%	41%	30%
Dauphin	53%	44%	72%	45%	25%	43%	46%	32%
Elk	52%	61%	77%	40%	36%	42%	61%	38%
Erie	47%	49%	72%	25%	26%	43%	58%	50%
Forest	44%	46%	65%	29%	19%	34%	47%	33%
Franklin	41%	39%	64%	33%	25%	30%	39%	23%
Fulton	49%	47%	62%	36%	36%	30%	38%	21%
Huntingdon	39%	44%	66%	36%	26%	32%	40%	27%
Indiana	47%	55%	70%	48%	37%	42%	49%	35%
Jefferson	45%	49%	67%	36%	28%	31%	38%	25%
Juniata	50%	44%	74%	38%	24%	30%	35%	21%
Lancaster	29%	28%	73%	29%	18%	33%	42%	29%

Lebanon	44%	43%	70%	36%	19%	36%	42%	26%
Lycoming	54%	47%	67%	32%	23%	32%	41%	27%
McKean	37%	40%	57%	32%	24%	34%	46%	28%
Mercer	58%	55%	70%	39%	39%	46%	52%	42%
Mifflin	44%	45%	70%	40%	23%	32%	38%	21%
Montour	50%	53%	69%	37%	27%	39%	47%	32%
Northumberland	63%	56%	74%	45%	34%	43%	51%	32%
Perry	46%	39%	66%	36%	17%	27%	31%	21%
Pike	42%	39%	55%	34%	28%	38%	53%	36%
Potter	39%	46%	58%	29%	24%	28%	37%	24%
Schuylkill	59%	52%	70%	44%	39%	53%	56%	37%
Snyder	38%	34%	64%	28%	20%	28%	36%	24%
Somerset	50%	55%	72%	49%	28%	33%	45%	28%
Sullivan	47%	49%	59%	35%	25%	37%	50%	29%
Susquehanna	38%	44%	68%	35%	23%	34%	55%	31%
Tioga	38%	43%	57%	30%	23%	30%	41%	24%
Union	43%	37%	66%	31%	24%	34%	43%	31%
Venango	42%	50%	67%	31%	27%	38%	45%	31%
Warren	40%	42%	69%	28%	25%	41%	55%	33%
Wayne	34%	46%	63%	34%	25%	35%	52%	32%
Wyoming	38%	47%	69%	33%	19%	36%	54%	34%
York	40%	40%	71%	39%	21%	34%	44%	29%
Central Totals	**45%**	**46%**	**69%**	**37%**	**25%**	**39%**	**47%**	**33%**
State Totals	**49%**	**51%**	**68%**	**47%**	**35%**	**55%**	**60%**	**46%**
Winning Party	**R**	**D**	**D**	**R**	**R**	**D**	**D**	**R**

Nevertheless, Democrats could find comfort in their narrowing of the traditional Republican advantage. Dilworth received over 400,000 more votes for governor statewide than John Rice had received as the Democratic candidate just four years earlier. Asserting in the days after the election that his party could no longer be considered a mere minority opposition, a spokesperson for the Democratic State Committee claimed that Pennsylvania was now a real two-party state. Perhaps that could be chalked up to political spin at the time, but it was indeed prophetic of the changes that were about the sweep across the Commonwealth.

One of the best known, although not truly surprising, aspects about Pennsylvania politics over the past half century is how the major parties have alternated control of the governorship every eight years. It isn't necessarily peculiar, because governors have been constitutionally limited to two terms since the state's 1968 constitutional convention. Generally, incumbents have been able to use the powers of their offices to win reelection handily. Also, because the seat is term limited, stronger candidates for the party out of power usually bide their time until the seat opens up in the next cycle. Thus, many challengers that incumbents faced could be categorized kindly as being less than formidable. When the seat is open after eight years, a combination of factors— including a public appetite for change and a motivated party seeking to escape its stretch in the wilderness—have also contributed to this phenomenon. Not only has power changed hands consistently every eight years; the aggregate vote for each party during the 54 years of this study has been an identical 50 percent.

While the flip-flop nature of these contests has developed into a trademark of Pennsylvania politics, geography has been a factor. One reason Democrats have fared better in gubernatorial contests than in contests for other offices is that they have done a better job of holding onto their voters in the southwest. The average southwest vote for Democrats in gubernatorial contests has been 55 percent, compared with 51 percent in senatorial elections. The 55-percent figure is less than the 65 percent of voters registered as Democrats in the southwest over the time of this study, but this improvement has had a big impact through the years. Although the number of southwest votes for Democrats in gubernatorial elections is still less than the Democrats' share of registered voters, achieving 55 percent has been enough to help the Democrats considerably in the governors' races.

1954: LEADER/WOOD

The election of George Leader in 1954 over Lieutenant Governor Lloyd Wood remains one of the key events in Pennsylvania's political history. Leader, a state senator from York County, became the first Democrat to be elected governor since George H. Earle in 1934—and only the second since 1895. The Earle election, coming on the heels of FDR's triumph two years earlier, eventually proved to be only a momentary setback for the GOP rather than the political realignment that was sweeping much of the rest of the nation. Numerous charges of corruption in the Earle administration hampered the Democrats (although they were relatively mild by Pennsylvania standards), and control of statewide politics remained well within the grasp of the GOP. Pennsylvania was a strong party state, and the hands that controlled the levers of power were unmistakably those of the Republicans. Leader's election, however, finally signaled an end to GOP domination, as some voters no longer worried that their services would be cut if they changed their voter registration. The impact was so acute that by the end of the decade, Democrats would even overtake Republicans in the number of registered voters statewide.

With his victory, the 36-year-old Leader became the second-youngest governor in Pennsylvania history. Only Robert E. Pattison, also a Democrat, and just 32 years old when elected in 1882, was younger. Leader was the proprietor of one of the largest chicken farms in the state, but he was anything but a political novice. He had succeeded his father in the state senate, and he had dropped a close race for state treasurer in 1952, which nevertheless brought him invaluable name recognition across the state in the 1954 gubernatorial primary, Leader had fended off a tough challenge from William "Doc" McClelland, the five-time coroner of Allegheny County. McClelland, a former quarterback at the University of Pittsburgh who had been a longtime foe of the Lawrence organization, came within 66,000 votes of taking the nomination.

In the general election, Leader's message was critical of Republican Party policies on state issues such as coal, steel, and farming, and he was outspoken about the direction of the national Republican Party. Leader also sprinkled in the traditional corruption charges that Democrats tossed at the long-dominant GOP machine. On the eve of the election, Wood, who was a turkey grower from Montgomery County and had been a state senator, tried to refresh voters' memories about when the Democrats were in control of state government: "Our Democratic opponents have no record of accomplishment to offer. In fact, having in mind the scandals, the unemployment, the destruction of industry that were the only accomplishments of the last Democratic administration in Pennsylvania, you may have noticed that in this campaign your Democratic candidates have carefully avoided any discussion of the Democratic record." That record, established while the Democrats controlled state government almost 20 years earlier, "was something they want you to forget, " according to Wood.

But in contrast to what had happened during the 1950 gubernatorial contest, the national surge in 1954 was Democratic, and it helped carry Leader to an easy 279,000-vote victory (he tallied 54 percent of the total vote). Republicans had hoped that they could hold the Democrat to a 50,000-vote margin in Philadelphia and Allegheny counties. That would be offset by votes in the GOP strongholds of Lancaster and Dauphin counties and the four Philadelphia suburban counties. When it was over, however, the Republicans had lost Allegheny County by 88,000 votes and Philadelphia by a startling 116,000. This came even though the GOP had a 230,000-voter registration edge in Philadelphia. Leader's combined advantage in the state's two largest metropolitan areas was 204,000 votes. The southwestern region produced an 187,000-vote plurality (60 percent). Voting in the two areas alone produced a daunting task for any GOP candidate to overcome elsewhere in the state.

In northeastern Pennsylvania, where the Republicans enjoyed a registration advantage of almost 70,000 voters, Leader ran slightly better than he did statewide. He carried the region and all six of its counties by 44,000 votes (55 percent). Democratic Northampton County provided the biggest margin: 61 percent. It was in some of the most traditional Republican spots, however, that

Wood's candidacy ultimately sank. He managed 59 percent in suburban Philadelphia but just 49 percent in Bucks County.

Perhaps Leader's most impressive political achievement was in the 47 counties of central Pennsylvania. The 1954 election was one of the few times a Democrat from that region has been nominated for statewide office, and the York County native demonstrated its utility as a political base for the party. Altogether, Leader carried 19 of the counties, but, more important, he defeated his opponent by 8,000 votes in the heart of GOP country, an area where they maintained an edge of 400,000 registered voters. Cambria County gave the Democrat the largest share of the region's vote (62 percent), while Berks and the candidate's home county of York contributed 61 percent. Leader even fared well in Lancaster County, where he held his opponent to just 58 percent of the vote, far below the usual Republican total.

With the Democrats bound not to repeat their failures of the most recent time that they had held the reins of power in the state, 20 years earlier, Leader's election clearly signaled the beginning of a new era in Pennsylvania politics.

1958: LAWRENCE/MCGONIGLE

Leader's successor was a longtime fixture in Democratic Party politics statewide, Pittsburgh Mayor David Lawrence. However, despite his victory, it is worth noting Lawrence's disappointing performance in his own southwestern base. In fact, his opponent, Arthur McGonigle, a Reading businessman who had built Bachman Bakeries into the world's largest pretzel factory, was from the opposite end of the state. McGonigle was a surprise choice to head the GOP ticket when he defeated two rivals better known to the public—Harold Stassen, a former candidate for president, and William Livengood Jr., the former state secretary of internal affairs—in the primary.

Lawrence, who had served as head of the Democratic Party in Allegheny County during the Earle Administration, was seeking to establish a second consecutive Democratic administration for the first time in the 20th century. His abilities as an organizer certainly were noticed on the GOP side, and barring a major breach, many predicted that a Lawrence victory could usher in a quarter century of Democratic rule. It was certainly no accident that he had been elected four times as mayor of Pittsburgh.

The 69-year old Lawrence was something of a surprise and a compromise choice as the Democratic candidate for governor. Although he had always wanted the job, he thought that his religious faith—he was a prominent Catholic layman in a state that had never elected a Catholic—would be a deterrent. Richardson Dilworth had shown some interest in running again, but that was squelched by State Senator Joseph M. Barr, chair of the party's State Committee, and by Lawrence himself after Dilworth made a statement favoring the recognition of Red China—a comment that would come back to haunt him repeatedly through the rest of his career. Lieutenant Governor Roy E. Furman decided to run, but he was never taken seriously after being described by his boss, Governor Leader, as unfit to succeed him. Lawrence, who was seen as satisfactory to all parties, trounced Furman in the primary by more than 500,000 votes.

After a lackluster start, the inexperienced McGonigle (making his first bid for public office) ran both an energetic and a forceful campaign. He hit Lawrence hard on several key issues, particularly law enforcement and taxes. McGonigle charged that while serving on the state Board of Pardons during the Earle administration, Lawrence had helped free more than 1,000 convicts. In addition, McGonigle claimed that the crime rate in Pittsburgh had risen 61 percent during Lawrence's tenure as mayor. On the tax issue, McGonigle warned that his opponent would hasten the move toward a statewide wage or income tax. "Sock-the-wage-earner is the keystone of the Democrats' fiscal policy," he warned. Attempting to deflect the GOP charges, Lawrence said that the formation of a tax study commission for the Commonwealth without a wage levy would be high on his agenda.

McGonigle also promised to return sound government to Harrisburg, taking on what he described as the "boss politics" of the Democratic administration. Before a crowd at a GOP ox-roast rally in Williamsport, he attacked his rival for hitching "Tammany Hall tactics to a massive propaganda assault, financed by the biggest slush fund in the history of Pennsylvania." The next day, speaking to a crowd in Gallitzin, Cambria County, Lawrence countered that the Republicans were conducting a "campaign without any sense of direction," with GOP candidates "jumping from charge to charge and from issue to issue." Addressing an overflow crowd of 1,800, he asserted that his opponents had been "lured into a trap" to conduct their campaign on the basis of "smear and innuendo."

At his party's traditional end-of-the-campaign rally in Pittsburgh's Northside Carnegie Hall, Lawrence also raised the specter of national politics: "It is of course true that our opposition is not at its best. Nationally, they seem to be divided between "modern Republicans" and "stone age" Republicans. Strangely enough, it is the "modern" Republicans who are becoming extinct. The "stone age" boys have had a great triumph—they have captured the White House speech writers." President Eisenhower, who came in to campaign for the GOP ticket before returning to his Gettysburg home to cast his ballot, undoubtedly took note of Lawrence's remarks.

The mood across the country during President Eisenhower's second midterm greatly favored the Democrats. Nationally, the party ended up gaining a record 13 seats in the United States Senate and 48 in the House of Representatives. Despite Lawrence's victory, however, the results in Pennsylvania for the Democrats fell short of expectations. Hugh Scott would best former Governor George Leader in his bid for the senate, a defeat which many would blame on Lawrence for "cutting" Leader from the ticket.

Statewide, Lawrence won by only 76,000 votes, also a disappointment considering the edge he held over his opponent in experience and name recognition, as well as the national circumstances. Only in the Philadelphia region did the new governor exceed Leader's vote totals from 1954. The state's largest city, where Democrats had overtaken Republicans in the number of registered voters, gave Lawrence a 196,000-vote advantage. McGonigle offset some of that in the suburbs, winning the four counties surrounding Philadelphia by just under 100,000 votes.

While Lawrence carried northeastern Pennsylvania by 31,000 votes, that total was far shy of Leader's totals from 1954—and disappointing in that the Democrats had increased their share of registered voters by 6 percentage points during the intervening four years. McGonigle ran well in the Republican counties of central Pennsylvania, an area where Republicans had fared poorly during the previous election. This time the GOP would reclaim domination in the region with a convincing 164,000-vote plurality.

The biggest disappointment for the Democrats occurred in southwestern Pennsylvania. It wasn't poor enough to sink Lawrence (though it sank Leader's Senate bid), but the Pittsburgh mayor performed quite poorly in his own area. Although Lawrence carried his hometown by a satisfactory 65,000 votes, he lost its suburbs and captured Allegheny County by just 53,000 votes. Although he carried the region by 94,000 votes (55 percent), this was considerably less than what was expected and what Leader had accomplished in 1954.

In actuality, it was voters in the southeast, specifically Philadelphia, who would deliver the narrow 2-point victory to the Democrats. This despite the fact that they had watched as their region's candidate, Richardson Dilworth was pushed aside for Lawrence. True, Democrats had been elected to the state's highest office consecutively for the first time in more than 100 years, but it was far from the knockout victory that they had hoped for and that Republicans had feared.

1962: SCRANTON/DILWORTH

Dilworth would get another chance to run for the job he had always dreamed of, and his race against first-term Congressman William W. Scranton would go down as one of the classic slugfests in Pennsylvania political history. The contest pitted two candidates of such nobility that each had a Pennsylvania town that bore his family's name (Dilworthtown in Chester County and Scranton in Lackawanna County). Their lineages, however, didn't deter the candidates from waging a ferocious battle. According to Pennsylvanian historian Paul Beers, Thatcher Longstreth, who had run against Dilworth in the 1955 Philadelphia mayoral race, once referred to the Democrat as "the last of the bar-knuckled aristocrats."

The 1962 race was essentially a referendum on Dilworth, one of the most controversial figures in Pennsylvania political history. He had served as both Philadelphia's treasurer and district attorney before resigning from his position as mayor in the spring of 1962 to run for governor. He had narrowly lost the race for governor 12 years earlier. The phrase "born with a silver foot in his mouth" was ascribed to Dilworth long it became better known nationally.

Conversely, Scranton, who didn't run for public office until he was 43 years old, was largely an unknown outside his home area.

Scranton's inexperience made him vulnerable to Dilworth's attacks that he was a puppet of the GOP establishment. Speaking in the Republican's hometown of Scranton, he declared that Wilbur H. Hamilton, chairman of the Philadelphia Republican organization, and Hamilton's colleague William A. Meehan, were "two of the most discredited and corrupt politicians that you could find anywhere." Dilworth charged that they, along with Delaware County Republican leader and former State Senator John J. McClure and others, including lobbyists for oil interests, the Pennsylvania Railroad, and the Pennsylvania Manufacturers Association had dictated the selection of Scranton, "That's the crew," Dilworth said, "that met in the weird old house of the weird old man, Senator McClure, in Delaware County and slated this man for Governor."

GOP leader Hamilton made clear in his response that the Dilworth's personality was indeed the focal point of their campaign, arguing, "we will win because of the protest feeling against Dilworth. There is a bitter resentment against him personally, and against his tactics in this campaign." Scranton responded to criticisms that he was inexperienced by turning the tables on Dilworth: "He never finished a job in the political field without resigning. He quit as City Treasurer. He quit as District Attorney. He quit as Mayor."

Dilworth was hurt politically during the campaign by the possibility of a grand jury probe of his own administration in Philadelphia. Scranton derided Dilworth's announced support for such a probe a few days before the election as a "stumbling, senseless, desperate hypocritical" attempt to win votes. Speaking in Philadelphia before a crowd estimated at 10,000, Scranton said that his opponent had "wept and cried before the courts" when the probe was first discussed.

But perhaps the lowest point of the bitter campaign revolved around questions of racial and religious prejudice. Dilworth initiated the argument by charging that Scranton was responsible for a restrictive clause against blacks and Jews in the deed to his home at Hobe Sound, Florida. Scranton responded that his opponent had clearly harmed himself by "his willingness to stoop into any gutter as the desperate realization dawns that he is about to lose this election." As to the charge itself, Scranton contended that in Florida, a state traditionally controlled by the Democrats, there was no remedy for him and his sisters (who had inherited the property) to remove such a clause because they were passed from owner to owner.

Another round of volleys ensued after Scranton charged that Dilworth belonged to clubs in Philadelphia, New York, and Florida that discriminated. Announcing that Dilworth's "hypocrisy deserved to be exposed," he declared: "My opponent is a member of the Racquet Club of Philadelphia and for a period he lived in residence there. It has no Jewish members. It has no Negro members. He is a member of the Philadelphia Club. It has no Jewish members. It has no Negro members. You need a pedigree five miles long to become a member."

Clearly, Dilworth's hopes for victory were pinned on getting an extremely large number in his hometown. Two years earlier, it had delivered a 331,000-vote plurality for John F. Kennedy in the presidential election, and while that figure might be unrealistic in a midterm election for governor, Dilworth needed to approach it. But even in Philadelphia, questions about Richardson Dilworth's personality were front and center. In arguing on Dilworth's behalf, Democratic city leader of Philadelphia Bill Green, Jr., stated, "I wondered at the beginning of the year whether we should take a chance on someone controversial in preference to someone who wasn't. But remember that Dilworth won the city three years ago by 209,000 votes."

Several factors ultimately undermined Dilworth's efforts in his hometown. First, Green had opposed Dilworth's candidacy at the outset, and although he ultimately came around, it was not soon forgotten. Second, came the corruption charges and Dilworth's about-face on ordering such a probe. Third, although Dilworth's numbers held strong in the city's black wards, they fell in areas of South Philadelphia where he had tried, and failed, to impose a $40 parking permit fee for residents. When the votes were counted, Dilworth had registered a 107,000 plurality, far short of what was necessary to counter the GOP trends elsewhere in the state.

In the suburbs surrounding Philadelphia, the Democratic candidate was unpopular. The corruption issues were one thing, but even more damaging were failed attempts by the Democratic organization to pick up four communities in a reapportionment of the city, in order to save all six of its Congressional seats. The term "Green Grab" became a virtual GOP slogan. Dilworth's tongue, however, did him the most harm. He once said that it wouldn't do any harm if "a few Main Liners got mugged once in a while because it might teach them a way of life." While he may have meant that suburbanites don't understand the problems of city life, the statement antagonized many to whom it was directed. He also conceived the phrase "the white noose around the city," again raising integration issues many in his party wanted to avoid. Scranton scored big in the Philadelphia suburbs, winning by 173,000 votes—a remarkable 64 percent—which easily offset the city numbers. The southeast region gave Scranton a 66,000-vote plurality.

Even less kind to Dilworth was Democratic southwestern Pennsylvania. He carried only three of the nine counties in the region, losing by 74,000 votes. Scranton even carried Allegheny County, by 54,000 votes. Not surprisingly, Scranton's base in northeastern Pennsylvania also delivered for him, providing a 21,000-vote advantage. The only county there that Scranton failed to carry was his own, solidly Democratic Lackawanna, which he lost by 1,000 votes. Central Pennsylvania delivered an even stronger than usual GOP plurality: Scranton emerged with a startling 325,000-vote edge. Dilworth failed to carry any county in the region.

It was a devastating defeat for both Dilworth and the Democrats, especially considering that it was an open-seat race. When it was over, Scranton had carried all but 5 of the state's 67 counties. His 486,000-vote victory amounted to

56-44 percent split. In the aftermath of this battle of Pennsylvania bluebloods, Dilworth was sent into political retirement and practiced law. Scranton would find an immediate place on the national stage, with calls coming soon after the election that he might be either a presidential or a vice-presidential contender.

1966: SHAFER/SHAPP

Scranton's presence and popularity were both a blessing and a curse four years later, when his Lieutenant Governor, Raymond P. Shafer, of Meadville, Crawford County, became the Republican nominee to succeed him. During the campaign, Shafer was forced to respond to charges that he would be under Scranton's control. "I'm nobody's man," Shafer replied to a caller during a radio call-in program. "I've never been under the control of Governor Scranton or anybody else." Like the previous contest, this would be a bitter battle.

Shafer's Democratic opponent was Milton J. Shapp, a millionaire businessman who had founded Jerrold Electronics, from Lower Merion, Montgomery County (Jerrold was his middle name). Shapp had survived a bruising primary with State Senator Robert P. Casey, the choice of the party establishment, in a contest in which Shapp spent $1.4 million of his own money. Calling himself "the man against the machine," Shapp overwhelmed Casey by almost 50,000 votes. Casey, who raised only $170,000, replied that he was battling the "man with the money machine." Democrats attempted to present a united front throughout the fall campaign, and Casey himself spoke out forcefully for Shapp, but clearly the party rift was far from healed.

Shapp used populist rhetoric throughout, promising increased aid for education, a "people's lobby" with himself as "chief lobbyist." He also promised to fight insurance companies, milk dealers, and the Pennsylvania Railroad. But his most ambitious plan was for what he called a "Pennsylvania GI Bill of Rights" for college and vocational students. Under such a plan, the state would make payments to eligible students, who in turn, would pay their tuition to colleges or technical schools. Shafer derided the program as a "giveaway" that would cost Pennsylvania taxpayers more than $600 million annually in interest alone. He dubbed Shapp as the most radical inflationist in American political history. Shafer, who had served in the State Senate before his stint as lieutenant governor, ran on a moderately progressive platform and on the achievements of the Scranton Administration. He promised to continue progress made in employment, education, and highway construction. Unlike his opponent, he had faced minimal opposition in the primary, from perennial candidate Harold E. Stassen. This allowed him to husband his financial resources for the fall campaign against the wealthy Shapp.

Like the campaign four years before, this one took a nasty turn when questions of bigotry once again appeared. They centered on Shapp's religious background—he was the first Jewish candidate ever nominated for governor by a major party in Pennsylvania. Appearing at a live call-in television show in Pittsburgh, Shapp claimed that there had been some anti-Semitism and that smear literature had been distributed throughout Pennsylvania. He later told reporters that he had copies of letters from Republican county organizations saying "Milton Shapiro is running ... if any other reasons are needed." Shapp, who had changed his name in 1939, singled out Republican State Senator John T. Van Sant of Lehigh County for referring to him only as "Shapiro." Shapp did make clear, however, that he absolved Shafer of any blame.

Soon after Shapp leveled his charges, the roles were reversed. The Citizens for Shafer Committee charged the Democrat with injecting racism into the campaign by distributing leaflets saying that Shafer had a restrictive clause in the deed of his Meadville home. The Shafer campaign strongly denied any such claim, adding that brochures that restricted the sale of the house to "anyone except persons of Caucasian race" had been distributed in carefully selected, predominantly minority communities several days before the election.

Shapp suspended campaigning several days before the election out of respect for former Governor David Lawrence, who was in a coma and near death from a heart attack that he had suffered while campaigning for Shapp (Lawrence died 17 days later, on November 21). Meanwhile, Shafer, in a pre-election sweep of the state, campaigned in seven cities, including an appearance with former President Dwight D. Eisenhower in Harrisburg. At a campaign rally in Philadelphia one day before the election, Senator Hugh Scott charged Shapp with using "filthy last-minute tactics" and "appealing to racism." This, Scott said, "is the man who is going to be repudiated by the voters of this State tomorrow." Adding that Shapp was "indecent and unfit," Scott said the rally marked "the burial and end of Milton Shapp."

When the votes were counted, the GOP had had a successful day. Shafer's 242,000-vote victory (53 percent) was so decisive that he carried with him the entire Republican statewide ticket, including lieutenant governor, secretary of internal affairs (the last time the two positions were elected), and two Superior Court judges. The Republicans also retook control of the State House of Representatives. Much of the Democrats' hand wringing afterward focused on Philadelphia. The city failed to deliver the votes expected for Shapp, who carried it by only 100,000 votes. Senator Joseph Clark placed the blame on the shoulders of the city's Democratic chair, Francis R. Smith (longtime head William Green had died) and demanded that he be replaced. Republicans, who had previously held only 1 seat in the city's 35-member delegation in the state House of Representatives, increased the number to 6. Shapp's tally in the city fell far short of the 342,000-vote majority that Shafer rolled up in the suburbs. In his home county of Montgomery, Shapp managed an anemic 27 percent of the vote.

Shapp didn't fare well in the southwest either. He carried Allegheny County by 36,000 votes and the region by 73,000, but both were far off normal Democratic efforts. Shapp also trailed Shafer by 5,000 votes in the six counties of northeastern Pennsylvania. In Casey's Lackawanna County home, voters remembered the bruising primary; Shapp survived with less than a 1,000-vote advantage in this strongly Democratic region. Central Pennsylvania gave Shafer a huge 248,000-vote edge, with only Elk and Erie counties going for Shapp.

1970: SHAPP/BRODERICK

After Shapp lost to Shafer, few would have predicted that a candidate defeated so decisively would return to fight another day. But his opponents in both parties seriously underestimated his persistence and his eagerness to become governor. Shapp was determined to press his energy and, if necessary, his fortune to accomplish the task. Once again, he had to survive a tough primary battle with the by-then–state Auditor General Robert P. Casey.

Although Casey again had the support of the party organization, a personal dispute Casey had with Philadelphia Mayor James H. J. Tate meant an open primary in the city. Tate had joked that he would support the auditor general "if he behaved himself," which prompted Casey to say that he "was no one's man." Casey predicted a 20,000-vote margin in Philadelphia, but the open primary enabled Shapp to carry the city by 27,000 votes. That was most of the difference as Shapp topped his challenger again, this time by only 38,000 votes statewide. After a long list of prospective Republican candidates bowed out, the party settled on Lieutenant Governor Ray Broderick of Philadelphia. Unlike Shafer, however, Broderick had the unenviable task of attempting to succeed a widely unpopular governor, which Shafer had become by the end of his term.

It was also the first time that the candidates for lieutenant governor ran with the gubernatorial candidates as a slate, and Shapp benefited by having State Senate minority leader Ernest P. Kline as his running mate. Kline, a Catholic, helped the ticket blunt the abortion issue (Shapp was pro-choice) that had threatened to hurt the Democratic effort. Kline had been Casey's running mate in the primary (Shapp ran alone), but his presence on the ticket helped forge a much stronger relationship with the Democratic establishment for Shapp. Broderick's running mate was Ralph F. Scalera, an obscure judge from Beaver County. Significantly, this was also the first election in the state's history that did not include a Protestant on either ticket (with three Catholics and the Jewish Shapp).

Shapp led in the polls throughout the campaign. His lead was so solid that he turned his attention to making calls for other Democratic candidates. At every stop, he urged his audiences to give him a Democratic House and Senate so that he could carry out his campaign promises. Broderick focused his candidacy on two main issues, promising not to raise taxes and tough law and order. Campaigning with President Richard M. Nixon and Vice President Spiro T. Agnew, he took a page out of their law-and-order playbook, charging that Shapp had marched with protestors during the 1968 Democratic National Convention in Chicago (they were allegations that Shapp later denied). A controversial Republican cartoon showing Shapp marching with yippies toting a Vietcong flag proved to be a major miscalculation for the party. Sensing that it would backfire,

Shapp chose not to respond but simply called it a smear. Most voters apparently agreed with him.

The tax issue also found little interest among voters. Broderick vowed never to raise taxes, but with a deficit estimated as high as $450 million, his claim that the budget could be balanced through savings realized by massively restructuring government rang hollow. Shapp had been on record as calling for an income tax, which he termed the fairest measure for the state's citizens. More than anything, however, Broderick couldn't escape the unpopularity of the Shafer Administration.

Shapp's political comeback was not only complete; it was devastating to the Republican Party. He defeated Broderick by an astonishing 500,000 votes, or 57 percent, remarkable for an open-seat race. He piled up an 180,000-vote margin in the Philadelphia along. Most impressive was how well he did in Philadelphia suburbs, where four years earlier he had been trounced by Shafer. He carried Bucks County by more than 12,000 votes (56 percent) and even carried Montgomery County, by more than 5,000. He narrowly lost Chester and Delaware counties, but narrowly, and held Broderick to a slim 2,000-vote margin in the region, quite an accomplishment for any Democrat at the time.

Southwestern Pennsylvania also contributed huge numbers for Shapp. He carried every county, taking Allegheny by 126,000 votes and the region by 244,000. He also carried all six counties in the northeast region, including huge pluralities in the normally competitive Lehigh Valley. In the region as a whole, he recorded a 71,000-vote advantage (60 percent). Astonishingly, the liberal Democrat even carried central Pennsylvania, by more than 6,000 votes. He not only tallied 59 percent of the vote in Erie County and 59 percent in Cambria County, two Democratic areas; he also swept Republican strongholds such as Clinton County (60 percent) and Crawford County (54 percent). The Democratic sweep netted them both houses of the State Legislature for the first time in 32 years. If ever there was a wrong candidate at the wrong time, it was Lieutenant Governor Ray Broderick.

1974: SHAPP/LEWIS

Because gubernatorial succession had been outlawed in the Constitution of 1874, the 1974 contest was the first time a governor was able to succeed himself (although several others served nonconsecutive terms). This was a subdued affair by Pennsylvania standards. Certainly, it lacked some of the nasty racial and religious allegations that had marred recent campaigns. Credit for this should go to the challenger, Drew Lewis, a Montgomery County businessman, who became the nominee after most of the heavy hitters in the party bowed out. Lewis, like Arthur McGonigle back in 1958, was taking his first stab at elected office. His campaign must have realized that it faced an uphill fight from the start, but it never stooped to the gutter.

Shapp had been a relatively popular figure at the end of his first term. Although he had successfully led the fight for a state income tax, voters generally bought his argument that he had to "bite the bullet." He successfully portrayed the tax as an act of courageousness; necessary because of the bankrupt state finances he had inherited from the Shafer regime. Shapp based his campaign on a simple theme: "running on my record." Undoubtedly, his principal achievement was a myriad of programs designed to help the elderly thanks to a windfall of money brought about by the newly established lottery.

The Democratic incumbent did offer some goals for a second term, such as cost controls on health care and working to change the state's constitution in order to institute a graduated income tax. Other, even more controversial proposals included turning over responsibility for the rehabilitation of prisoners to the State Education Department and using local schools in rural areas to provide a state-supported system of transportation for the elderly. He also proposed using idle state-owned land to construct housing for low-and middle-income groups. Shapp was an unabashed liberal, truly the first to occupy the Pennsylvania governor's mansion. For their part, Lewis and his running mate, former state House Speaker Ken Lee, attacked Shapp on his spending proposals and promised to trim welfare rolls while pledging to eradicate waste and cut costs in the state's patronage-laden Highway Department and Liquor Control Board.

Shapp had faced a test during his first term from a four-month investigation by a GOP-controlled House investigative panel headed by Representative Patrick A. Gleason (Cambria) over alleged corruption in the awarding of state contracts. By voluntarily appearing for three days before the panel, however, he had successfully blunted the charges. Later, in fact, he said that exposing the political motivation and arrogance of the Gleason Committee was the high point of his campaign. But perhaps Shapp's greatest stroke of luck was running for reelection in the Watergate year of 1974, arguably the best Democratic election cycle in history.

Shapp easily became the first governor to succeed himself in 99 years, winning by almost 300,000 votes statewide (54 percent). He carried Philadelphia by 223,000 votes, a then-record 70 percent for a Democrat. He also carried Bucks County by 12,000 while barely losing Delaware and Montgomery counties. The Democrat also pulled off the rare feat (particularly at that time) of winning the combined suburban Philadelphia vote—by slightly more than 1,000 votes. in the southwest, Shapp's numbers dropped considerably from his 1970 totals; he carried the region by just under 100,000 votes. Ordinarily, that would be respectable, but, it was a 145,000-vote drop and an 8 percent difference. Shapp's numbers in the northeast also lagged a bit, although he carried the region by 45,000 votes (57 percent). The results were similar in central Pennsylvania. Whereas he had carried the region in 1970, this time he ran 69,000 votes behind his Republican opponent. Shapp's 47 percent in the region is still far higher than Democrats normally reach.

1978: THORNBURGH/FLAHERTY

After dominating state politics for roughly a decade, surviving two tough primary battles and three general election battles, and serving two terms as governor, along with a failed presidential bid in 1976, Milton Shapp retired from the political scene as the 1978 campaign drew near. The contestants created a rarity in that both were from Allegheny County: District Attorney Richard Thornburgh for the Republicans and former Pittsburgh Mayor Pete Flaherty for the Democrats. Both had survived primary battles in a crowded field that had seven Republicans and four Democrats. On the Republican side, geography became Thornburgh's biggest ally; topped a field of rivals from the eastern part of the state who ended up splitting their base. They included Arlen Specter, House Republican leader Robert Butera of Montgomery County, and David W. Marston, a federal prosecutor whose dismissal by the Carter Administration had become highly controversial, as well as Senate Minority Leader Henry Hager of Lycoming County. Thornburgh's running mate was William W. Scranton III, son of the former governor, who in his first attempt at public office defeated five other Republicans, most prominently Faith Ryan Whittlesey, a former state representative who was then the chair of Delaware County's Board of Commissioners.

On the Democratic side, Robert P. Casey was back, along with Lieutenant Governor Ernie Kline. Although Casey was the favorite, he was hurt by the candidacy of another Robert P. Casey in the lieutenant governor's contest. That Casey, no relation to the "real" Bob Casey, was a 48-year-old biology teacher from Allegheny County. Apparently, enough voters thought that he was the "real" Bob Casey and that they could get both Flaherty and Casey on the same ticket. While the former auditor general lost by 130,000 votes to Flaherty, the "fake" Bob Casey won the lieutenant governor's race over a 14-person field. Not surprisingly, that Bob Casey proved to be a liability to the Flaherty campaign in the fall.

The turn of events left the "real" Bob Casey embittered, and reluctant to help the ticket as he had in the past. Refusing to appear at a Lackawanna County dinner, he called Flaherty's running mate a fraud and said he wouldn't lift a finger to help Casey's campaign for lieutenant governor.

Nevertheless, Flaherty began the campaign with a considerable advantage. Soon after his primary victory, some polls showed him leading by more than 30 points. One Gallup Poll had him leading by 12 points a little over one month before the election. But as the campaign drew near, so did Thornburgh. With a little over a week before voting began, a new Gallup Poll indicated that the lead had been reduced to just 4 points. Thornburgh spent much of his time in the Philadelphia area, introducing himself to Republican leaders and voters, the majority of whom had supported Specter in the primary.

Thornburgh successfully courted black voters across the state. He received the endorsements of two newspapers that had predominantly black readership in Philadelphia and Pittsburgh and won the support of three Philadelphia unions with largely black membership—the city employees union, the hospital workers, and the longshoremen. Earl Stout, a black who was the labor leader for the city workers, complained that Flaherty wouldn't even sit down to speak with him. Thornburgh also cut into other unions that traditionally supported Democrats, winning the endorsements of the Philadelphia Building and Trades Council, the Western Pennsylvania Carpenters Union, and the powerful Pennsylvania State Education Association (PSEA). Although Flaherty was able to wrest the support of the state AFL-CIO, Thornburgh's efforts had severely undercut the traditional Democratic base.

Even the Reverend Jesse Jackson endorsed Thornburgh, accusing the Democrat Flaherty of creating racial animosity when he was mayor of Pittsburgh. "Reject a man who rejected us," Reverend Jackson said of Flaherty in a radio ad run on stations serving predominantly black audiences. The GOP candidate also received support from several prominent members of the black clergy in Philadelphia.

The selection of the "other" Bob Casey also proved problematic to the Flaherty effort. It was clear that this Casey, a Pittsburgh biology teacher, had run solely to confuse voters who might think he was the former auditor general. Casey spent much of the campaign in his classroom, and when he did hit the trail, he created some embarrassing moments for the Democratic ticket. At one stop, reporters asked him to respond to Thornburgh's accusations that he was an "impostor" trying to hide his identity and to allegations that he had failed to include a Baskin-Robbins ice cream store franchise in a financial statement. Before Casey was able to speak, a campaign worker grabbed him and whisked him away. In addition, the political neophyte made a damaging gaffe when he proposed doing away with educational programs for the deaf.

Flaherty himself was described as being aloof, and he campaigned independently of the party, convinced that he could bypass traditional political support systems and take his message directly to the voters. Philadelphia's powerful mayor, Frank Rizzo, who was busy with his (ultimately unsuccessful) attempt to change the city's charter to allow him to run for a third consecutive term, was openly critical of Flaherty's refusal to attend a Democratic City Committee dinner. Although any talk in the Democratic camp of officially "cutting" Flaherty was summarily dismissed, the candidate had alienated enough of his party's leaders to damage his chances significantly.

While all this might suggest that Flaherty had little chance, it must be noted that 1978 was the high-water mark for Democratic registration in the state. The party held an advantage of 903,000 registered voters, a 58-42 percent split in the two-party ratio. Despite that, Flaherty clearly squandered the opportunity, losing to Thornburgh in a tremendous upset by 228,000 votes, a 6-point margin. The Republican's efforts to court Democratic voters in Philadelphia paid off; he lost the city by just 35,000 votes, the most successful GOP effort there in decades. In the Philadelphia suburbs, Thornburgh mended fences with voters who had opposed him in the primary. Bucks County, where the Democrats were briefly the majority party, reverted to its past voting practices and delivered a 21,000-

vote margin to Thornburgh. Overall, the southeast suburban vote gave Thornburgh a margin of 164,000 votes. The region as a whole, including Philadelphia, gave him a margin of 129,000. That was the difference in the race. Had Flaherty put up numbers in the southeast comparable to what Shapp had done, he would have been governor. His 10-point loss in the southeast was the second poorest showing of any Democratic candidate in the past 54 years (eclipsed only by Ivan Itkin's paltry 41 percent in 1998).

Flaherty prevailed in southwestern Pennsylvania, the home to both candidates, running far ahead of his opponent and winning it by 136,000 votes. But in his home of Allegheny County, which he won by only 17,000 votes, Flaherty's support was lukewarm at best. Thornburgh trounced Flaherty in the northeast by 34,000 votes, despite a Democratic advantage of 142,000 registered voters in the region. Tellingly, the Republican even carried Democratic Lackawanna County—home of the "real" Bob Casey—by more than 8,000 votes. Central Pennsylvania provided its usual contribution to GOP efforts, delivering a 200,000-vote plurality for Thornburgh.

1982: THORNBURGH/ERTEL

In the aftermath of the 1980 "Reagan Revolution," the Republicans appeared headed toward an easy reelection. In addition, the Democrats' first choice, Philadelphia District Attorney Ed Rendell, decided to pass. Although the party eventually rallied behind Congressman Allen Ertel of Lycoming County, his central Pennsylvania roots gave him little in the form of a traditional Democratic base for a statewide election. Ertel also had difficulty keeping pace with Thornburgh financially, with the incumbent raising $3.4 million, more than enough to let him run a high-profile media campaign.

As the campaign unfolded, however, what was thought to be a difficult political environment for a Democrat suddenly began to change. Amid a national recession, and a sluggish economy in the state, Ertel and his running mate, State Senator James R. Lloyd of Philadelphia, tried to frame the race entirely as a referendum on President Reagan. Referring to the state's high unemployment rate and Thornburgh's support of "Reaganomics," Ertel characterized Thornburgh as being cold and callous to the struggling. Appropriately, Ertel's last campaign stop was at a northeast Philadelphia forklift plant that employed just 27 workers, down significantly from the 1,900 who had worked there two years earlier.

Meanwhile, the Thornburgh campaign tried to deflect the Democrats' charges by asking voters to remain focused on his record and accomplishments. Although Thornburgh tried to distance himself from the Reagan Administration, he did defend it by stating that the economic problems that Reagan inherited couldn't be solved overnight. For the most part, however, Thornburgh spent most of the campaign simply trying to ignore Ertel, so as not to grant the challenger any credibility.

Thornburgh refused to debate, however, and he committed perhaps the biggest strategic mistake of the campaign when he walked out of a NAACP conference in Camp Hill just ten days before the election rather than stand with Ertel and answer questions. Thornburgh, whom the NAACP had endorsed in 1978, was already having trouble in the black community. Many had complained that the governor was balancing the budget on the backs of poor people and kicking thousands of able-bodied people off welfare, or "workfare," as it was known. In this 1982 election, Thornburgh also lost the support of many of the state's most powerful labor unions, such as the Pennsylvania State Education Association (PSEA), which had helped him immensely in his first election.

Ertel's campaign was also beset by misjudgments. He declared, for instance, that George Banks, an accused killer and state prison guard, had been "armed and trained" by Thornburgh. Ertel also accused Thornburgh of exploiting his 22-year-old-son, Peter, by using him in a commercial that highlighted the governor's support for special education. (Peter Thornburgh had suffered brain damage as the result of a car accident when he was a child.) Perhaps Ertel's most serious lapse of judgment, however, was refusing to release any of his income tax returns from the previous seven years. The problem wasn't so much that he refused, but the reason he provided: that he didn't want to be "whipsawed" by charities.

Despite polls showing him with a rather comfortable lead, Thornburgh prevailed by slightly more than 100,000 votes and a winning margin of less than 3 percent. Thornburgh ran 150,000 votes behind Ertel in Philadelphia, a significant decline from his 1978 performance, although he made it up in the suburbs with a 200,000-vote cushion, an improvement on his prior performance. Thornburgh also saw his support drop in the northeast, an area that he carried rather handily four years earlier. The vote in the northeast, which is usually fairly consistent across the six counties, varied widely in 1982. Ertel ran strong in Lackawanna and Luzerne counties in the far north (which were also relatively close to his Montoursville home), winning with 57 percent in each. He also won lightly populated Carbon County with 58 percent. Thornburgh, however, helped his cause by carrying the Lehigh Valley, winning Lehigh and Northampton counties by 14 and 4 points, respectively. The governor also won Monroe County quite easily.

While it's unusual for the Democrats to field a candidate from central Pennsylvania in a statewide race, Ertel demonstrated its utility by holding Thornburgh's advantage to 109,000 votes in the "T," well below the usual Republican margin. The Democrat won such unlikely counties as Clearfield, Columbia, Dauphin, as well as his home, Lycoming. Throughout the region, Ertel won ten counties, quite high for a Democrat. He also fell a few hundred votes short of taking such unusual battlegrounds as Juniata, Montour, and Somerset counties. His high vote total in central Pennsylvania was in Northumberland County, where he took 63 percent of the vote, exceptional numbers for a Democrat.

Ertel's performance in central Pennsylvania placed the possibility of victory well within his grasp. All that remained was to run up the usual Democratic numbers in the southwest. Unfortunately for him, however, Thornburgh took advantage of his roots, winning Allegheny County by 6,000 votes. In 1978 Flaherty had defeated Thornburgh handily in the southwest, but the absence of an opponent from there in 1982 let Thornburgh hold Ertel to just a 44,000-vote plurality, short of what the Democrat needed to win the election.

Ertel's roots in central Pennsylvania raise an interesting question: whether Democratic candidates from that region might sometimes fare better than those who hail from the usual areas of Philadelphia and Pittsburgh. Had he been able to raise more money and expand his advertising campaign in those larger media markets, the outcome might have been different. Of course, coming from a rural area is likely to cause fundraising problems for any Democrat, because he or she would probably be unknown to many big-city donors.

Of the four governors who have sought reelection since the one-term rule was lifted in the late 1960s, Thornburgh was the only one who encountered strong opposition, although it is fair to state that he was the only one forced to run in an unsympathetic political environment. In his victory speech, Thornburgh commented that while he often used the expression "swimming against the tide," he didn't realize until then "how tough a swim" and "how rough a ride" he would face.

1986: CASEY/SCRANTON

The open-seat race of 1986 provided the best opportunity for ending the eight-year partisan swap that has highlighted gubernatorial elections for the past fifty years. Republicans were optimistic that their candidate, Lieutenant Governor William W. Scranton III, could maintain the keys to the executive mansion. Democrats were equally optimistic that the political return of Robert P. Casey (the "real" Bob Casey) would net them victory. What would ensue was a campaign of almost mythic proportions, a street fight between two men whose last names were virtually synonymous with Pennsylvania politics. In the end, the race would be determined by the political equivalent of a nuclear bomb—a 30-second television ad that would long be remembered as the most famous in Pennsylvania political history.

Casey, 54, the former auditor general, was taking one last swipe at the governorship after failing to win his party's nomination in three previous attempts. This time he fought off a challenge from Philadelphia District Attorney Ed Rendell, whom some hadn't forgiven for not running in 1982, when he probably could have won. Casey beat Rendell by 164,000 votes, and although the primary race turned nasty, the general election promised to be much worse. A fourth defeat for Casey would surely consign him to the role of ultimate bridesmaid. Waiting for him was Scranton, a young, attractive candidate who had earned high marks as lieutenant governor the previous eight years. A victory in this race would thrust the Scranton, a 39-year-old moderate, into the national spotlight. In essence, it was a battle between two men presumably headed in different political directions. Each candidate selected a state senator to be his running mate. Mark Singel of Cambria County was Casey's choice, while Scranton tapped Mike Fisher of Allegheny County.

Scranton began the fall with a slight lead in the polls, but by late September a series of ads attacking Scranton's experience enabled Casey to pull even. For the next several weeks, neither candidate appeared able to break away. Then, on October 20, the Scranton campaign launched a brilliant political strategy that would change the dynamics of the contest. Disappointed that the race had developed into a "back-alley brawl," the lieutenant governor announced in front of Independence Hall that he would unilaterally cease all negative advertising.

The candidates squared off in a debate several days later that underscored their differing approaches toward some of the most important issues facing the state. Casey opposed abortion rights, while Scranton was generally pro-choice. Casey wanted to maintain the State Store system while Scranton vowed to eliminate it. Casey wanted to keep the state's system of electing judges, and Scranton wanted to scrap it in favor of a merit system.

By this time, one thing appeared clear, however, that Scranton's pledge to halt negative advertising, along with his position on abortion rights, had enabled him to pull ahead among women voters. Scranton's pledge had also seemingly inoculated him against Casey's attacks, and this in turn undercut the central theme of the Democrat's campaign. With ten days to go, Casey's own polls indicated that he had fallen 7 points behind, and pessimism gripped the Casey camp.

Two events then shaped the outcome. Unbeknownst to Scranton, a direct-mail firm sent out about 600,000 letters to registered Republicans across the state with a note from the candidate's father, former Governor William W. Scranton, urging their support for his son. The piece also included seven paragraphs that not only were critical of Casey but attempted to link him to the "corrupt Shapp administration." Furthermore, it stated erroneously that Casey had made "$100,000 a year moonlighting as a private attorney while he was auditor general." In actuality, Casey had averaged about $30,000 a year. Casey took full advantage of what even Scranton aides would later admit to being a big mistake. Casey called it "one of the most negative hit pieces ever circulated by a candidate in Pennsylvania." He stoked the fire a few days later by refusing to appear at a scheduled joint appearance before the Pittsburgh Post-Gazette editorial board in protest of the Republicans "malicious" attack.

Aware that Scranton had made serious inroads among women, Casey's campaign also launched an attack designed for men voters that questioned his opponent's very masculinity. He proclaimed that the Republican administration had taken a "pantywaist" approach to problems and that Scranton wasn't man enough to be governor. Now introduced as the "Fightin' Irishman" at rallies, Casey railed, "He's never fought for anything in his life. And we need a fighter. We're not picking the president of the fraternity at Yale University [Scranton's alma mater]. We're picking a governor!" At a rally in Waynesburg, Casey referred to his own failed attempts. "I've been knocked down a couple of times myself along the way, but I didn't run around and whine like a crybaby. I fought back. The next governor of Pennsylvania had better be a pretty tough individual."

With the campaign neck and neck heading into the homestretch, Casey, who had come so close before only to be denied, decided to roll the dice. He ran what would become the most famous political advertisement in the Pennsylvania history. Aired on the final weekend—giving Scranton little time to respond—it featured the sound of sitar music, a picture of the Maharishi Mahesh Yogi, and photographs of a 24-year-old Scranton meditating with long hair and a beard. Dubbed the "guru ad," it was followed by a Mailgram sent out by the Democratic campaign to 50,000 Republicans in central Pennsylvania. The letter, signed by one Raymond Mong, a Republican from Venango County, asked: "What message would it send to our young people if someone with Bill Scranton's values and character got to be governor?"

Although the ad may not have demonstrated finesse and perhaps lacked sophistication, it was successful. Casey had delivered a knockout blow straight to the heart of the Republican's socially conservative base. Scranton ended up carrying central Pennsylvania, but his 93,000-vote plurality was far short of what he needed. In the senatorial race on the same day, Arlen Specter defeated Bob Edgar by 309,000 votes in central Pennsylvania. Casey outpolled Scranton in 11 central Pennsylvania counties. Most impressively were the 70 percent plurality he received in Cambria County and the 61 percent in Elk County. He also defeated Scranton in traditional GOP strongholds such as Columbia, Indiana, Montour, and Somerset counties. Scranton managed a slight advantage in the Democratic county of Erie. The final tally statewide gave Casey a 79,000-vote victory, the closest gubernatorial race since Lawrence-McGonigle in 1958.

Voting trends elsewhere in the state were fairly typical, making Casey's inroads in central Pennsylvania all the more important. He carried Philadelphia by 134,000 votes or 64 percent, respectable but not an especially strong showing for a Democrat. In the Philadelphia suburbs, Scranton did very well, taking 63 percent of the vote and amassing a plurality of 159,000, which outstripped Casey's city numbers in the city. The highest percentage Casey achieved in the four counties was a weak 40 percent in both Bucks and Delaware counties.

Casey comfortably carried the southwest but not with numbers that would automatically ensure victory. He won the region by 144,000 votes, or 59 percent. A similar situation ensued in the northeast, which was the base for both candidates. Casey won the region by 53,000 votes, but Scranton easily defeated him in Lehigh and Monroe counties. Only big victories in Lackawanna and Luzerne counties (68 and 64 percent, respectively) enabled Casey to win the region—by a comfortable 16 percent.

Pennsylvania had had close elections that would leave observers wondering what if. Surely Democrats felt that way when George Leader lost his Senate bid in 1958. They must have wondered in 1964, when Genevieve Blatt lost an excruciatingly close battle for the same Senate seat. Bill Green's political ambitions were stymied in his failed quest for that seat 12 years later. Any of those individuals could have gone on to become a major national political figure, but each was cut short.

The 1986 election is one instance when the tables were turned on the GOP. Scranton's defeat was a tremendous blow to the party, sapping them of some of the confidence they may have felt from years of winning the close ones. More important, though, it would deprive the party, and especially moderates, of a man who might have affected national politics even more than his father. In this one election, when the Democrats finally won a close race, their victory was largely attributable to a highly unlikely source, voters in central Pennsylvania.

1990: CASEY/HAFER

Governor Casey's reelection in 1990 will be remembered for several things. First, it was one of the biggest landslides in state history. Second, in a case of role reversals, it was a campaign in which Casey's Republican challenger, Auditor General Barbara Hafer, ran to his left on several issues, including taxes. Finally, the candidates' vocal dispute over abortion rights placed the state at the center of a national debate on the subject. When the votes were tallied, the incumbent's record-breaking 1.08 million-vote triumph, the largest numerically in state history until then, will be the way most people remember the election. Casey took 68 percent of the overall vote, the second-best showing in the 20th century.

Perhaps even more impressive is that Casey came within a mere 586 votes in one county, Montgomery, of doing the unthinkable—running the table statewide. The abortion issue played a huge role in the county, the wealthiest and most liberal of the four in the Philadelphia suburbs. For the most part, the Republican Party machinery in Montgomery County favored abortion rights, and their state lawmakers were the first to endorse Hafer's candidacy. The issue also helped Hafer among a few Democratic leaders in the region. In one municipality, Casey's name had even been ripped off the sample ballots produced by the party to be distributed on election day. But although the abortion rights issue may cut differently at different times, in this instance the Democrat reaped the big rewards across the Commonwealth.

In heavily Roman Catholic Delaware County, for example, Republican Party leaders distanced themselves from their candidate, and Hafer lost by 16,000 votes, or 10 percent. She also lost by 18 percent in Bucks County. In Philadelphia, Hafer tried to hit the governor on both the abortion issue and on whether or not Casey was planning to bail the city out of its ongoing financial woes, but it was to little avail. She lost the city by 162,000 votes. The governor carried Hafer's geographic base of southwestern Pennsylvania by 338,000 votes, racking up 75 percent in Westmoreland County and 72 percent in Allegheny. He also reached an astonishingly 83 percent in Fayette County. Not surprisingly, Casey built enormously high pluralities in his northeastern Pennsylvania base, taking 82 and 81 percent in Lackawanna and Luzerne counties, respectively.

Without question, however, Casey's clean sweep through central Pennsylvania, the first Democrat to do so since the Civil War, was most startling. Not only did he carry all 47 counties, he received more than 60 percent in 40 of them. In Cambria County, he netted his high, 80 percent. And no Democrat is likely to match his 42,000-vote victory in the "capital" of central Pennsylvania, Lancaster County, any time soon. Overall, Casey scored a plurality of just under 400,000 votes across the vast region. Given the saliency of the abortion issue during this campaign, it's not surprising that Hafer ran poorer in central Pennsylvania than in the more socially liberal areas of the southeast.

Some of Hafer's problems were clearly her own doing. In one highly publicized moment, she referred to the governor as a "redneck Irishman," apparently alienating two groups at the same time. Hafer and her running mate, State Senator Harold F. Mowery, Jr., of Cumberland County, had difficulty raising money, particularly after narrowly surviving a primary challenger from anti-abortion activist Marguerite "Peg" Luksik in the spring. Casey ran the textbook race for an incumbent, acting gubernatorial and staying positive. He had no reason to do otherwise.

Outside of the abortion issues, Hafer had built much of her campaign around the notion that Casey (who hadn't raised taxes in his first term) had fudged the state budget and would need to enact a hike after the election. Casey responded that Hafer was the most tax-happy candidate ever to run for governor of Pennsylvania. When the Casey Administration raised taxes in its second term, Hafer could take some comfort in being vindicated. Her reputation restored, she later went on to win several other statewide races, serving another term as auditor general and two as state treasurer.

1994: RIDGE/SINGEL

Wisely rebuffing pleas by many in the GOP to run against the popular Casey in 1990, Congressman Tom Ridge of Erie wasted little time entering the 1994 race. Declaring his candidacy in February 1993, almost two years before the election, the 49-year-old decorated Vietnam veteran became the first of six Republicans who eventually made up the field. From the far northwest corner of the state, Ridge was unknown in much of the state. His big break came in the primary, when the presumed front-runner, Pennsylvania Attorney General Ernie Preate, Jr., found himself the target of a federal investigation. Ridge won the nomination by 57,000 votes over Preate and a group of others, which included Mike Fisher and Philadelphian Sam Katz, who later ran unsuccessful races for mayor of the city. The party did agree that Mark S. Schweiker, a Bucks County commissioner, would serve as running mate no matter who was the candidate.

Although the race was technically an open seat, Ridge's Democratic opponent, 41-year-old Lieutenant Governor Mark Singel, had served six months the year before as acting governor while Casey recuperated from hear-and liver-transplant surgery. Singel had been damaged politically two years earlier, when he was upset in the Democratic Party primary by Lynn Yeakel for the right to oppose Arlen Specter. In a crowded field that included Yeakel, State Treasurer Catherine Baker Knoll, House Speaker Robert O'Donnell, and State Representative Dwight Evans (who finished second), Singel prevailed. His running mate was Tom Foley, who topped a field of eight candidates vying for the job, the most prominent being William Lloyd, who would be defeated by Arlen Specter in the 1998 senate contest. Foley, originally of Montgomery County, had served the previous several years as secretary of labor in the Casey Administration.

Singel had received good marks as acting governor, and he tried to make the most of it during the campaign, stressing the executive experience that he possessed and his opponent lacked. His campaign slogan, "Ready Right Now," highlighted that strategy. Although Singel seemed to enjoy an advantage through the early part of the fall campaign, there was one important thing he didn't have—a strong endorsement from Governor Casey. The relationship between the two had severely frayed over the years. Casey had advised Singel not to run for Specter's seat in 1992, but perhaps most damaging was the lieutenant governor's decision to break from his boss and announce during that ill-fated Senate primary campaign that he was now pro-choice.

Unlike other out-party candidates, who usually can't refrain from attacking the incumbent administration, Ridge was wise to avoid criticizing Casey, who not only remained immensely popular but had become a sympathetic and courageous figure in light of his health problems. Despite Casey's noncommittal approach, it still appeared that Singel would be able to ride both his experience and the party's registration edge to victory. The race lacked some of the sizzle and bitterness of previous ones. Singel ran a cautious campaign, as if he was the incumbent, and Ridge portrayed himself as not just a moderate, but an ambiguous one at that, refusing to be pinned down on issues such as riverboat gambling, abortion rights, and the banning of assault rifles.

That all changed on October 7, one month before the election, when a man named Reginald McFadden affected the course of events. News reports revealed that McFadden had been arrested in response to a series of murder and rape cases in New York City. He was now Singel's problem, because Singel, as lieutenant governor, had served on the state Board of Pardons and had voted to release the convicted killer. The Democrat admitted to the voters that it was the biggest mistake of his life. It was further damaging because Ridge had made crime a centerpiece of his campaign, so it lent more credence to his arguments. The rest of the campaign would find Singel defending himself on the crime issue, and that was obviously not his strength.

Ridge was forced to contend with a serious challenge from the right when Peg Luksik, who had almost upset Hafer four years earlier, entered the race as the candidate of the Constitutional Party. Luksik's primary issue was her vehement opposition to abortion rights, and she took direct aim at the Republican nominee. Ridge had a history of supporting a woman's right to choose, although he pleased many within the party by promising to uphold the abortion restrictions that Casey had recently signed into law. The former Republican Luksik, who, like Singel, hailed from Johnstown, ran remarkably well for a third-party challenger in a state that has a strong two-party system. She received more than 460,000 votes (13 percent), which probably would have tipped the election to Singel had the McFadden story not broken.

As it was, however, the Democrat never completely recovered from the McFadden episode. In addition, 1994 had developed into one of the best GOP years of the century. Ridge, who was chided for being someone "nobody ever heard of, from a town nobody ever visited," prevailed by 198,000 votes, defeating Singel by 5 percentage points, 46 to 41 percent. Luksik's strong finish meant that Ridge would be the first to win the governorship with less than a majority of the vote since another Republican, John K. Tener, did so in 1910.

Singel ran respectably in Philadelphia, carrying the city by 170,000 votes. But low morale among many Democratic voters that year brought down the overall turnout, which limited its impact. Ridge offset a good deal of this in the suburbs, where he topped Singel by 112,000. Singel trailed by double digits in each county, his best showing being in Montgomery, which he lost by 11 percentage points.

Unlike Casey, Singel failed to hold his own in the central "T," losing the region by 275,000 votes. Some wondered whether the results there would have been different had Singel not strayed from Casey's position on abortion. Certainly, a greater degree of support from Casey couldn't have hurt. Both candidates did extremely well within their base, Ridge in Erie (75 percent) and Singel in Cambria (69 percent). For the Democrat, however, Cambria was the only of the 47 counties in central Pennsylvania that he carried.

The rift with Casey was most acutely damaging in the governor's base of northeastern Pennsylvania. Singel managed wins in Lackawanna and Luzerne, but they were less than what he needed. In other areas south, Ridge thumped the Democrat, winning handily in the key Lehigh Valley, an impressive showing for a non-incumbent Republican. In southwestern Pennsylvania, Singel underperformed in populous Allegheny and Westmoreland counties, winning narrowly in each. In the battle between two candidates who hailed from areas just outside the Pittsburgh metropolitan area, Ridge held Singel's overall margin to just over 29,000 votes (52 percent), much less than what the Democrat expected. Although his 46 percent of the statewide vote was far short of a majority, that didn't matter to either Ridge or his party, which again held the governor's mansion and both U.S. Senate seats.

1998: RIDGE/ITKIN

Although 1994 was an election nightmare for Democrats in Pennsylvania, the gubernatorial and senate elections of 1998 probably didn't seem much better. Their candidates—Ivan Itkin and Bill Lloyd, respectively—were so overwhelmed and under-funded that few can even remember what took place. Democrats had a difficult a time finding a top-tier candidate to run against Ridge and settled on the 62-year-old Itkin, who was seeking to be the first state legislator to run directly from his position and capture the governorship since George Leader. Even after Itkin volunteered to be the sacrificial lamb, a group of party leaders enlisted former Auditor General Don Bailey to enter the race, forcing Itkin to compete for a nomination few thought was worth anything from the start. Although Itkin prevailed by 55,000 votes in the primary, it was about the last thing that went well for him and his running mate, former Congresswoman Marjorie Margolies-Mezvinsky of Montgomery County.

Working with a Republican-controlled legislature had allowed Ridge to chalk up some impressive legislative achievements during his first term. Most visibly, he made good on his word to focus on the crime issue by pushing several initiatives through the legislature. Itkin tried to attack Ridge on such matters as doing nothing to slow the flow of out-of-state trash, and he said Ridge had hurt working families with a decision to raise the gasoline tax at a time of a huge budget surplus. But Itkin's financial inability to mount a media campaign prevented him from reaching anyone with his message. Ridge had the luxury of simply ignoring his challenger and running on an entirely feel-good reelection theme. The one time when Itkin broke free and made headlines was one that he would have preferred not to have. Trying to sympathize with the plight of exploited workers, he had inadvertently angered Latinos by using the term "wetbacks." Widespread criticism and an apology soon followed, as did "Latinos for Ridge" buttons.

Peg Luksik was again on the ballot heading the Constitutional Party, but nothing was going to prevent Ridge from getting a majority this time. He received 58 percent of the vote, which amounted to a 27-point victory over Itkin, who finished with just 31 percent. Some Democrats actually fretted that Luksik might actually outperform their candidate, but she fell off to 10 percent. She did, however, outpoll the Democrat in five counties: Blair, Butler, Cameron, Clarion, and Perry. Itkin's nadir came in Perry County, where he collected only 15 percent of the vote.

Ridge dominated every county in the state—except Philadelphia, which had become so reliably Democratic that even Itkin carried it by 75,000 votes. Unlike Bill Lloyd's quest for Senate, however, the 26-year House veteran was unable to carry even his home county, losing Allegheny by 41,000 votes. His final total was less than any major-party candidate's since Democrat Eugene C. Bonniwell managed only 365,000 votes in 1926. Itkin, who was well respected in the legislature (like Lloyd), had given up a safe seat to help his party, only to be cut off entirely by those who had recruited him. Even Ridge tipped his hat to the challenger for "slugging it out," adding that it was obvious that Itkin lacked the slightest kind of organizational or financial support from his party. If there was any solace for Itkin, it might have been that his margin of defeat didn't approach what Barbara Hafer's had been eight years earlier. (In that campaign, though, at least it can be said that the public was paying attention.)

2002: RENDELL/FISHER

Democrats had no trouble finding candidates for the open-seat race of 2002. The party's two political "stars," former Philadelphia Mayor Ed Rendell and State Auditor General Robert Casey, Jr. (son of the late former governor), were both eager to run. Both had eyed the contest for years. It was also an opportunity to renew a rivalry that had begun back in the 1986 primary, when Casey's father had defeated Rendell, then Philadelphia district attorney. This time, despite organized labor's near-unanimous support for Casey, Rendell won by a surprising 13 percent and advanced to the general election. The primary campaign was as intense as the previous battle, and it helped Rendell politically—by allowing him to deliver his message to voters and winning with such surprising ease that he appeared somewhat invincible.

Rendell's running mate was former State Treasurer Catherine Baker Knoll, who had parlayed her strong name identification to victory in a nine-person field. The list included State Senator Jack Wagner, who was Casey's choice for lieutenant governor; State Senator Allen Kukovich of Westmoreland County; State Representative Thaddeus Kirkland of Delaware County; and State Representative John Lawless of Montgomery County, a former Republican and now a Democrat. For his part, Rendell ran alone in the primary and stayed out of the contest for the second slot.

The Republicans had an opportunity to field an incumbent in Mark Schweiker, who had been elevated to governor on October 5, 2001, after Tom Ridge accepted a position in the Bush Administration as secretary of homeland security. Although Schweiker had generally won high marks for his job performance, many in the party thought he lacked the reputation to lead them to victory in the general election. Instead, they threw their support behind state Attorney General Mike Fisher for governor and State Senator Jane Earll of Erie County for lieutenant governor. Tapping Fisher may have been a costly mistake, however, because in July, just months before the election, Schweiker's popularity soared in light of the way he handled a crisis involving nine trapped coal miners in Somerset County. The decision to anoint Fisher as the candidate also infuriated State Treasurer Barbara Hafer, who was interested in running once again. Not only did she endorse the Democratic ticket; she later switched parties.

During his tenure as mayor, Rendell had built his reputation by reviving Philadelphia, both economically and culturally. The cultural revival was especially important for suburbanites, who could witness the downtown renaissance firsthand when visiting the theaters, museums, and restaurants that populate the area. Rendell hosted a cable sports talk show, which furthered his appeal. His visibility across the region was so high that it was almost as if he had been the mayor of southeastern Pennsylvania. And Rendell's visibility wasn't limited to the five southeast counties. He also became well known in the Lehigh Valley, which is also a part of the Philadelphia media market. Rendell raised more than $38 million, double what Fisher managed, which was a rare feat for a Democratic candidate statewide.

Fisher's campaign promised a continuation of the past eight years of Republican rule in Harrisburg. It charged that Rendell would need to raise taxes in order to fulfill his promises. But the anti-Philadelphia theme that Fisher trumpeted across the rest of the state backfired not only in the city but also in the Republican-dominated suburbs, which saw in Rendell a strong executive and someone who was one of their own. In Delaware County, home to one of the strongest GOP machines in the nation, Rendell won nearly two to one, taking 66 percent of the two-party vote while capturing all 49 municipalities. In Montgomery County he won even more convincingly, with 68 percent, and in Bucks County he reached 65 percent. Even the usually GOP-loyal Chester County provided Rendell with a 23,000-vote plurality, or 58 percent.

As expected, the former mayor dominated his hometown, earning a 280,000-vote advantage—a startling 85 percent of the vote. Any candidate able to amass a 515,000-vote advantage in the southeast would need to flop completely in the state's other 62 counties to be denied victory. Rendell had no such problem in the northeast, where he rolled to a 50,000-vote advantage, reaching 60 percent or more in Lackawanna (Casey's home) and Northampton counties. The only county Mike Fisher carried in the northeast was Monroe, which he won by less than 1,000 votes.

Fisher kept the overall margin respectable by running strong in central Pennsylvania. He carried every county there except Berks (which is also in the Philadelphia media market), even Democratic ones such as Cambria and Erie, where he posted double-digit leads. The Republican's strongest showings were in Potter and Tioga counties, where he reached 72 percent.

Additionally, Fisher ran stronger than expected in his southwestern Pennsylvania home. Pre-election surveys indicated that he trailed badly in the southwest, although many voters were undecided. Apparently, many of those voters followed their regional hearts when pulling the lever, as Fisher held Rendell's advantage to only 26,000 votes, a 4-percentage-point difference. Traditionally Democratic Westmoreland County was particularly kind to Fisher, giving him an 8-point win. Generally, a Democrat who wins the southwest by just 4 percent is headed for defeat.

The numbers Rendell had in the southeast, especially the suburban counties, however, were far too much for Fisher to overcome. Statewide, Rendell won by 324,000 votes, a 9-point margin, which was comfortable, but not quite the landslide expected. For Rendell, who had served as Democratic national party chairman in 2000, the returns in southwestern Pennsylvania sent a cautionary message: that he would need to expand beyond his base or risk a more competitive challenge in 2006; also, he would need to maintain his solid grip on the Republican suburbanites outside Philadelphia. The colorful Rendell became the first Philadelphian to win the governorship since Republican Martin G. Brumbaugh in 1914. Perhaps more accurately, one might say that he became the first person from "Southeastern County" ever elected to the state's highest executive post.

2006: RENDELL/SWANN

With President Bush's approval ratings in sharp decline, Republican leaders in Pennsylvania and elsewhere found themselves in a desperate political situation. Faced with the task of upending a popular, well financed governor in Pennsylvania provided further headaches. In nominating former Pittsburgh Steelers wide receiver Lynn Swann to be their nominee for Governor in 2006, the Pennsylvania Republican Party threw what was the political equivalent of a "Hail Mary." Prior to Swann being coaxed into running, the frontrunner for the party's nomination to take on Governor Ed Rendell was former Lieutenant Governor Bill Scranton, III., son of the popular governor and one time nominee of the party for this very post, when he narrowly was defeated by Bob Casey in 1986.

However, it had been forty years since Scranton's father lived in the executive mansion, and half that time since he was a candidate in his own right. Apparently, the leadership within the party felt that was too long, especially considering the fact that he had spent much of the prior decades living in California, and decided to press Swann into politics. After Scranton's calls for an open primary were rebuffed and Swann received the party endorsement, he along with another prospective candidate, State Senator Jeffrey Piccola, withdrew from the race leaving the former football star unopposed.

As for the incumbent, despite a rocky relationship with the Republican-controlled legislature, Governor Rendell was eager to claim that he had accomplished most of what he had set out to do in his first term. The highlight was passage of a property-tax-relief program, the first in nearly three decades in the state. It was largely funded through the revenue generated by what was arguably his toughest legislative challenge, the legalization of gambling, and in particular, slot machines in licensed casinos across the state. Other accomplishments that he cited throughout the campaign were increases in education funding, which came after he boldly struck $4 billion in school funding shortly after taking office, in an effort to extract budget concessions from GOP leaders in the legislature.

Swann, who helped lead the Pittsburgh Steelers to four Super Bowl rings before heading off to the Pro Football Hall of Fame after he retired in 1982, had spent the previous 26 years doing work for ABC Sports, mostly as a sideline reporter for college football telecasts. He was also recently appointed chairman of the President's Council on Physical Fitness and Sports. His attacks on Rendell focused mainly on the property tax relief bill, which though enacted, fell short of producing the 30 percent reduction that the governor had promised during the battle over legalizing gambling. There was also the specter of an early morning legislative pay raise that infuriated many voters and cast a pall over anyone associated with Harrisburg. Rendell who later admitted that signing the raise was a mistake, argued that it was necessary for him in order to obtain the support he needed for his legislative priorities.

However, Swann's campaign was also beset by blunders and inexperience right from the outset. He may have spoken of property tax reform and establishing a more business-friendly climate, but his rhetoric lacked specifics. More than anything he simply criticized his opponent. It also didn't help matters when it was reported that he rarely made the effort to cast a ballot himself on election day. Perhaps the most curious aspect of his campaign was his decision to downplay race throughout the contest. While he would remind voters that they had a chance to make history by electing the first African-American to the state's chief executive office, that's as far as he ever went. He never made clear attempt to go after African-American voters specifically, especially in Philadelphia, were he might have made inroads within this traditionally-Democratic constituency.

There was already resentment among many rank and file Republicans for the way in which the party leadership had cleared the primary field for Swann and his mistakes only exacerbated those feelings. By the time the fall rolled around, many of those in the GOP establishment had deserted him as well, such as the 13 GOP mayors throughout the state who would endorse Rendell. In fact, exit polls indicated that the incumbent Democrat attracted about one-quarter of all Republican votes and about three-quarters of self-described independents.

Rendell's ability to amass a considerable war chest also provided him with a distinct advantage in the race. Swann raised only about one-third of the $30 million that Rendell would, which allowed the Democrat to launch an aggressive television ad campaign to define the campaign long before Swann could even begin to respond. The race never became competitive, with some polls revealing that Rendell's lead was more than twenty points with the election drawing near. It even allowed the governor the ability to pour several million dollars of his own money into state legislative races, where the Democrats would ultimately capture the eight seats they would need to retake the lower house.

Given these forces, it wasn't surprising that Rendell won in even more impressive fashion than he had four years earlier. His margin of just slightly under 850,000 votes enabled him to reach the 60 percent mark statewide, five points higher than he managed against Mike Fisher. It was also slightly higher than the percentage that Bob Casey received in his senate race trouncing of Rick Santorum on the same night. Not surprisingly, Rendell's numbers improved throughout the state. He took an astounding 89 percent in his home city, where the African-American candidate Swann could only muster a measly 45,000 votes. He also took 70 percent in each of the suburban counties, except Chester (where he still grabbed 65 percent) en route to 71 percent overall in those four counties.

In the southwest, where he struggled a bit four years earlier, the incumbent won six of the nine counties and 55 percent overall, three points higher than 2002. He also dominated the pivotal northeast, winning each of the six counties by at least 60 percent, which amounted to 66 percent overall in the region, a nine point improvement from that earlier effort. Throughout the vast central Pennsylvania region, the Democrat was able to reach 47 percent, eight points higher than 2002. Also, in contrast to the two counties he carried of the 47 in the region four year earlier, this time he took 13, carrying places like Clearfield, Susquehanna, Warren, Wayne, and Wyoming, rarities for Democrats.

In retrospect, given the overall political environment, it's highly doubtful that Scranton would have been successful either if in fact the GOP had rallied around him rather than the political neophyte. However, a strong case can be made that he would have run a professional campaign and made an overall more respectable effort. Perhaps he would have prevented the destruction that occurred for the GOP further down on the ballot, which included not just the loss of the statehouse but also the loss of five congressional seats statewide. In politics, just like football, throwing a "Hail Mary" out of desperation is not a strategy one should pursue, only rarely are they successful.

2010: CORBETT/ONORATO

With a much more sympathetic political environment awaiting them in 2010, Republicans had little difficulty finding a strong candidate this time around. With Congressman Jim Gerlach of Pennsylvania's 6th Congressional District (mainly Chester County) and State Senate Majority Leader Dominic Pileggi (mainly Delaware County) withdrawing from the contest in early spring, the race was cleared for state Attorney General Tom Corbett to be their nominee. Corbett nurtured a reputation as a corruption fighter during his stint as the state's top prosecutor where he won the conviction of a number of elected officials who used their office to conduct political activity. Though State Representative Sam Rohrer of Berks County did mount a primary challenge, his support was narrowly limited to the most ideologically conservative voters within the GOP, and Corbett easily brushed it aside, taking 68 percent in the primary. Along with the party's handpicked candidate for Lieutenant Governor Jim Cawley, a Bucks County Commissioner, the GOP ticket was set.

The Democrats, however, did have a competitive primary. First, former Congressman and onetime nominee for US Senate Joe Hoeffel entered the contest. Hoeffel had also originally intended to challenge Catherine Baker Knoll for the Lieutenant Governor's race back in 2006, but backed down after being persuaded by Rendell himself that it might hurt his reelection having two candidates from the southeast on the ticket. He would probably come to regret that decision to withdraw, since this time, he was unable to raise sufficient resources.

One candidate who was well-financed was State Senator Anthony Williams from Philadelphia. However, the manner in which he raised the money; drawing heavily from several large donors closely associated with charter schools alienated large segments of the Democratic Party electorate. He ended up finishing third. Perhaps most surprisingly, however, was the disappointing campaign conducted by the current Auditor General Jack Wagner. Wagner had just come off two impressive victories statewide, had developed a solid reputation while holding that office, and seemed to possess the type of personal resume, including a strong military record that potentially should have broad appeal throughout the electorate. However, inexplicably, he was unable to raise even as much money as Hoeffel. His campaign never left the ground, and he finished a distance second.

There seemed to be a consensus among many within the party that after eight years of Rendell, the best candidate would be someone from the southwest. With Wagner unable to cash in, almost by default the nominee was Allegheny County Executive Dan Onorato. While he didn't have the same financial resources as Williams, he did raise enough to be competitive, and with the assistance of many who were part of the Rendell operation, Onorato was able to easily claim the nomination with 45 percent of the vote, over twenty points greater than Wagner, his nearest rival. Onorato's running mate was State Representative Scott Conklin, who defeated Philadelphia City Controller Jonathan Seidel by just slightly over 3,000 in the May primary.

However, just like Pat Toomey in the senate race in 2010, the Republican nominee Tom Corbett emerged from the primary season as the clear favorite. And while Joe Sestak was able to make that race a competitive one, Onorato was not. Ultimately, the GOP tide which had washed over much of the nation would crush any chance that Onorato and the Democrats may have had to hold onto the Governor's mansion.

Throughout the campaign, Corbett also proved to be an elusive target for the Democrats. His promise not to raise taxes may have been ridiculed by Onorato, but with the national economy in recession, the voters certainly seemed to appreciate it. In addition, Pennsylvanian's were constantly reminded that it was Corbett, as state attorney general, which had led the successful prosecutions of legislators and staffers in the State Capitol for engaging in electioneering while on public time. It also appeared that an element of fatigue had set in among a number of Democratic allied groups, especially labor, which had fought so hard in the 2008 presidential election, and no longer had the energy necessary to complete against the revitalized GOP.

On the issues, the Republicans assailed Onorato for job losses which had occurred in the Pittsburg area, blaming it on his decision to raise taxes. For instance, one ad faulted him for US Airways' decision to move their operating hub out of state, even though it was made prior to his term as county executive. The most memorable charge, however, and perhaps the most damaging was one that blamed his excessive tax increases for contributing to 21,000 more people being added to the unemployment rolls in the county. This placed Onorato on the defensive and his response that it was below both the state and national average failed to persuade the public. The ad also gave the impression that he had raised property taxes, when in fact, he had not. Instead, the "excessive tax increases" actually referred to a levy Onorato had signed which imposed a 7 percent tax on drinks in bars in order to help fund mass transit within Allegheny County.

Outside of the city of Philadelphia, where Onorato was able to receive 83 percent, Corbett's scored a convincing victory. He fought back the growing Democratic tide in the southeast suburbs, winning Bucks and Chester County, while taking 51 percent overall. He also carried all but Lackawanna County in the northeast, and became the first Republican to carry this region in a statewide contest since Arlen Specter in 2004. Corbett also carried every county in Central Pennsylvania, even Erie went for the Republican by a little less than 200 votes. Overall his share in the "T" was 67 percent, 13 points greater than the GOP registration advantage in the region. The battle in the southwest where both candidates resided, and considered to be the battleground was also a mismatch. Corbett carried every county in the region on his way to 57 percent overall. Even Allegheny County fell to the Republicans by a little less than 500 votes.

The final totals were devastating. Corbett carried 63 of the state's 67 counties en route to a victory just shy of 10 percentage points. For an open seat contest in a state where his party was at a registration disadvantage of over 1 million voters, it was an incredible showing for Corbett, testament to both the political advantages he possessed and also the larger advantage that Republicans overall possessed in the political environment that was 2010.

Unlike a number of other states, Pennsylvanians had never sent, what is often the thought the second most important state official, attorney general, to the governor's mansion. Corbett's victory was the first time since it was an elected position in forty years that someone from that office accomplished this fete. Finally, the Republican's victory also continued the peculiar string that had now become the hallmark of Pennsylvania Gubernatorial elections since 1954. That year, beginning with the election of George Leader, control of Pennsylvania's chief executive office had switched between the two parties every eight years. Someday this streak is bound to end as well.

CHAPTER FOUR

PENNSYLVANIA ROW OFFICE ELECTIONS

When the period of this study began, in 1950, Pennsylvania had a pair of statewide row offices that no longer exist. In addition, it would be several decades before the state's voters got the opportunity to elect the attorney general. This chapter examines the contests for all five of those positions.

Beyond the importance that the offices have from a governing standpoint, they also are relevant from an electoral perspective. First, they serve as a prime proving ground for individuals who have higher political ambitions. Unlike members of Congress, who are usually little known outside their home areas, state row officers have the same constituents as governors and United States senators. From a scholarly perspective, they can provide insights into voters' behavior. Because the offices typically involve candidates who are not as well-known as those who run for senator, governor, or president, personalities are less a factor. With a decreased emphasis on individual characteristics, voters are more apt to revert to partisan instincts. Elections for row offices can show how voters view the two parties at any particular time.

LIEUTENANT GOVERNOR

Technically, the office of Lieutenant Governor may not qualify as a row office, because it is housed in the executive branch of government. Before the state's 1968 constitutional convention, which created the team gubernatorial ticket, however, the position was independently elected.

From 1950 to 1966, the years covered in this study, the results of the elections for lieutenant governor closely matched those of the gubernatorial races (Table 4.1 through 4.4). (Of course, their elections were held concurrently and the candidates generally ran together, even though they were elected separately.) Victorious candidates for governor were able to provide the coattails necessary to lift their parties' nominees for lieutenant governor to victory. Interestingly, though, a few voting inconsistencies arose.

Table 4.1 Democratic Share of Two-Party Vote for Lieutenant Governor, Southeastern Pennsylvania

	1950	1954	1958	1962	1966
Philadelphia	54%	58%	61%	60%	58%
Bucks	40%	48%	47%	43%	43%
Chester	34%	39%	38%	34%	33%
Delaware	37%	40%	40%	39%	34%
Montgomery	33%	37%	37%	35%	33%
Suburban Totals	**36%**	**40%**	**40%**	**36%**	**35%**
Southeast Totals	**48%**	**53%**	**53%**	**50%**	**48%**
State Totals	**48%**	**53%**	**51%**	**48%**	**49%**
Winning Party	**R**	**D**	**D**	**R**	**R**

Table 4.2 Democratic Share of Two-Party Vote for Lieutenant Governor, Southwestern Pennsylvania

	1950	1954	1958	1962	1966
Allegheny	55%	57%	52%	52%	60%
Armstrong	45%	51%	45%	45%	50%
Beaver	54%	60%	56%	55%	62%
Butler	37%	45%	40%	40%	46%
Fayette	58%	67%	63%	59%	61%
Greene	63%	73%	64%	62%	62%
Lawrence	47%	53%	52%	48%	49%
Washington	60%	65%	61%	57%	63%
Westmoreland	56%	64%	59%	55%	62%
Southwest Totals	**55%**	**59%**	**54%**	**52%**	**58%**
State Totals	**48%**	**53%**	**51%**	**48%**	**49%**
Winning Party	**R**	**D**	**D**	**R**	**R**

Table 4.3 Democratic Share of Two-Party Vote for Lieutenant Governor, Northeastern Pennsylvania

	1950	1954	1958	1962	1966
Carbon	51%	52%	53%	49%	49%
Lackawanna	55%	57%	59%	54%	53%
Lehigh	45%	51%	50%	45%	46%
Luzerne	47%	51%	52%	53%	52%
Monroe	48%	54%	52%	45%	46%
Northampton	53%	60%	57%	54%	56%
Northeast Totals	**50%**	**55%**	**54%**	**52%**	**51%**
State Totals	**48%**	**53%**	**51%**	**48%**	**49%**
Winning Party	**R**	**D**	**D**	**R**	**R**

Table 4.4 Democratic Share of Two-Party Vote for Lieutenant Governor, Central Pennsylvania

	1950	1954	1958	1962	1966
Adams	41%	48%	45%	42%	39%
Bedford	41%	49%	44%	39%	39%
Berks	53%	61%	55%	50%	52%
Blair	35%	46%	42%	37%	39%
Bradford	29%	37%	35%	33%	30%
Cambria	54%	62%	57%	53%	51%
Cameron	36%	41%	38%	39%	38%
Centre	36%	46%	43%	36%	41%
Clarion	46%	48%	43%	41%	44%
Clearfield	49%	55%	51%	46%	47%
Clinton	43%	52%	48%	44%	45%
Columbia	51%	56%	52%	45%	45%
Crawford	40%	44%	43%	36%	41%
Cumberland	41%	46%	43%	35%	34%
Dauphin	35%	41%	42%	35%	32%
Elk	54%	55%	53%	51%	54%
Erie	47%	53%	48%	49%	53%

Forest	36%	44%	40%	42%	37%
Franklin	38%	45%	47%	41%	41%
Fulton	52%	57%	52%	45%	47%
Huntingdon	33%	42%	41%	36%	36%
Indiana	44%	48%	45%	42%	44%
Jefferson	40%	43%	43%	40%	42%
Juniata	46%	52%	48%	44%	43%
Lancaster	32%	40%	36%	30%	29%
Lebanon	37%	44%	40%	33%	35%
Lycoming	46%	52%	45%	40%	42%
McKean	30%	32%	36%	37%	36%
Mercer	43%	50%	49%	46%	49%
Mifflin	44%	50%	44%	40%	41%
Montour	46%	52%	45%	44%	43%
Northumberland	42%	50%	46%	43%	42%
Perry	36%	43%	42%	37%	37%
Pike	35%	36%	37%	34%	30%
Potter	37%	44%	40%	36%	34%
Schuylkill	42%	45%	47%	45%	44%
Snyder	26%	34%	29%	27%	27%
Somerset	44%	50%	47%	42%	43%
Sullivan	43%	50%	45%	44%	40%
Susquehanna	31%	37%	37%	37%	35%
Tioga	26%	32%	32%	32%	30%
Union	27%	34%	28%	25%	27%
Venango	30%	37%	34%	35%	40%
Warren	32%	37%	37%	37%	39%
Wayne	25%	29%	33%	31%	28%
Wyoming	31%	37%	36%	31%	29%
York	50%	60%	56%	46%	46%
Central Totals	**42%**	**49%**	**45%**	**41%**	**42%**
State Totals	**48%**	**53%**	**51%**	**48%**	**49%**
Winning Party	**R**	**D**	**D**	**R**	**R**

In the three contests beginning in 1950, the victorious gubernatorial candidates ran slightly stronger than the lieutenant governor candidates. In the 1962 election, however, Democratic candidate Stephen McCann of Greene County received 129,000 more votes than Richardson Dilworth in Dilworth's ill-fated second bid for governor. McCann's statewide total was 4 percentage points higher than Dilworth's. Only 414 votes in Crawford County prevented McCann from running ahead of Dilworth in every county in the state. Evidence of how poorly Dilworth ran in 1962 is that McCann finished 172,000 votes behind Republican Lieutenant Governor Ray Shafer.

Four years later, in 1966, a bizarre development almost occurred. Democrat Leonard Staisey, a native of Allegheny County, came within 61,000 votes of defeating Raymond Broderick and becoming lieutenant governor. In contrast, the Democratic candidate for governor, Milton Shapp, lost by 242,000 votes. Thus, the last independently held election for lieutenant governor almost became its most historic. Governor Ray Shafer came close to heading what would have been the state's first Republican-Democratic split administration. The governing dynamics could have presented a fascinating study. And they most likely would have changed the political environment for both parties. It is doubtful that Broderick could have salvaged his political career had he lost the lieutenant governor's race. The GOP would almost certainly have chosen someone else to run for governor in 1970. Broderick went on to lose the 1970 general election anyway, to Shapp. The 1966 outcome probably affected the Democratic choice for governor in 1970, too: Staisey, an interesting politician who had been blind since the age of seven, would probably have been the nominee rather than Shapp, who won the Democratic nomination and the election.

INTERNAL AFFAIRS

In the five elections held between 1950 and 1968 to determine the secretary of internal affairs, Democrats held a three-to-two advantage (Table 4.5 through 4.8). This position, abolished in the state's constitutional convention of 1968, had diverse responsibilities, from topography and geological survey to publicity and information. Unlike the other statewide positions, the office of Internal Affairs was not term limited. Competition in those under publicized races was extremely fierce, both regionally and statewide.

Table 4.5 Democratic Share of Two-Party Vote for Internal Affairs, Southeastern Pennsylvania

	1950	1954	1958	1962	1966
Philadelphia	54%	57%	61%	60%	59%
Bucks	41%	47%	47%	45%	45%
Chester	34%	37%	38%	36%	36%

Delaware	37%	40%	39%	39%	36%
Montgomery	34%	37%	37%	36%	35%
Suburban Totals	**36%**	**39%**	**40%**	**38%**	**37%**
Southeast Totals	**49%**	**51%**	**53%**	**50%**	**49%**
State Totals	**47%**	**52%**	**52%**	**51%**	**49%**
Winning Party	**R**	**D**	**D**	**D**	**R**

Table 4.6 Democratic Share of Two-Party Vote for Internal Affairs, Southwestern Pennsylvania

	1950	1954	1958	1962	1966
Allegheny	51%	57%	56%	56%	55%
Armstrong	42%	49%	48%	47%	47%
Beaver	49%	59%	57%	58%	58%
Butler	34%	42%	44%	43%	44%
Fayette	57%	66%	62%	60%	57%
Greene	62%	69%	64%	61%	59%
Lawrence	43%	51%	52%	50%	49%
Washington	57%	63%	62%	61%	57%
Westmoreland	53%	63%	60%	59%	57%
Southwest Totals	**52%**	**58%**	**57%**	**56%**	**54%**
State Totals	**47%**	**52%**	**52%**	**51%**	**49%**
Winning Party	**R**	**D**	**D**	**D**	**R**

Table 4.7 Democratic Share of Two-Party Vote for Internal Affairs, Northeastern Pennsylvania

	1950	1954	1958	1962	1966
Carbon	50%	52%	53%	52%	52%
Lackawanna	54%	57%	59%	55%	50%
Lehigh	45%	51%	51%	48%	51%
Luzerne	46%	51%	52%	54%	53%
Monroe	49%	54%	52%	48%	50%
Northampton	54%	60%	58%	57%	61%

Northeast Totals	46%	54%	55%	53%	53%
State Totals	47%	52%	52%	51%	49%
Winning Party	R	D	D	D	R

Table 4.8 Democratic Share of Two-Party Vote for Internal Affairs, Central Pennsylvania

	1950	1954	1958	1962	1966
Adams	41%	47%	45%	43%	43%
Bedford	41%	48%	44%	40%	39%
Berks	57%	61%	56%	52%	55%
Blair	35%	44%	42%	39%	40%
Bradford	29%	35%	35%	34%	36%
Cambria	53%	61%	59%	54%	53%
Cameron	34%	39%	39%	44%	41%
Centre	35%	45%	45%	41%	41%
Clarion	45%	47%	46%	43%	46%
Clearfield	48%	53%	49%	48%	46%
Clinton	42%	50%	48%	47%	47%
Columbia	51%	55%	52%	48%	48%
Crawford	38%	42%	43%	41%	43%
Cumberland	42%	45%	44%	38%	36%
Dauphin	35%	41%	43%	38%	34%
Elk	52%	56%	56%	57%	59%
Erie	46%	52%	49%	53%	52%
Forest	34%	42%	41%	44%	40%
Franklin	38%	44%	47%	42%	43%
Fulton	52%	56%	52%	46%	48%
Huntingdon	33%	41%	41%	38%	39%
Indiana	42%	46%	46%	44%	43%
Jefferson	37%	41%	43%	41%	40%
Juniata	46%	52%	48%	45%	43%
Lancaster	32%	39%	36%	31%	30%

Lebanon	38%	43%	41%	35%	36%
Lycoming	43%	49%	45%	43%	43%
McKean	29%	32%	36%	38%	39%
Mercer	41%	49%	50%	48%	50%
Mifflin	44%	49%	45%	43%	46%
Montour	45%	51%	45%	47%	47%
Northumberland	41%	48%	46%	45%	45%
Perry	37%	42%	42%	38%	38%
Pike	37%	35%	36%	35%	32%
Potter	37%	42%	41%	37%	36%
Schuylkill	42%	45%	47%	47%	45%
Snyder	26%	32%	30%	28%	29%
Somerset	44%	50%	48%	43%	42%
Sullivan	43%	49%	45%	45%	42%
Susquehanna	32%	36%	37%	35%	36%
Tioga	26%	30%	32%	33%	31%
Union	26%	32%	29%	27%	29%
Venango	29%	35%	35%	38%	40%
Warren	31%	36%	37%	38%	41%
Wayne	25%	28%	33%	32%	30%
Wyoming	31%	35%	36%	33%	32%
York	51%	58%	56%	48%	48%
Central Totals	**42%**	**48%**	**46%**	**43%**	**43%**
State Totals	**47%**	**52%**	**52%**	**51%**	**49%**
Winning Party	**R**	**D**	**D**	**D**	**R**

In the 1950 contest, Republican incumbent William S. Livengood, Jr., of Somerset County defeated State Senator Frank W. Ruth of Berks County by 183,000 votes. Because of their registration advantage then, Republicans tended to dominate the second-tier contests. Voters had little to base their selections on other than party and region, because newspapers rarely covered the elections. In those days before television became commonplace, no 30-second ads flooded the airwaves and influenced voters' minds.

Each of the four subsequent elections featured the same candidate on the Democratic side, Genevieve Blatt of Allegheny County. The Pittsburgh attorney, who had been the president of the Young Democratic Clubs of Pennsylvania, holds the distinction of being the first women ever to run for statewide office in Pennsylvania—her failed run for auditor general in 1952. Two years later, it was assured that a woman would finally hold statewide office when Blatt ran against Gaynelle Dixon, president of the Pennsylvania Council of Republican Women, for secretary of internal affairs. Blatt defeated Dixon by 154,000 votes. She won in 1958 as well, defeating Johnstown attorney Andrew J. Gleason by 141,000 votes. Blatt survived a major scare in her next campaign, when she defeated Audrey Kelly of Susquehanna County by only 1,410 votes.

In 1964, seeking Hugh Scott's Senate seat, Blatt defeated Justice Michael Musmanno, the choice of party leaders, for the Democratic nomination. The race was so close that the Pennsylvania Supreme Court had to decide it. The primary's internecine warfare helped contribute to Scott's narrow victory despite the troubles Republicans were having at the top of the ticket with Barry Goldwater. Although Democrats enjoyed an 81,000-vote registration advantage statewide, enough ill feelings remained toward Blatt to deny her a fourth term as internal-affairs chief. Her opponent, John K. Tabor, was highly regarded for his performance as secretary of commerce in the Scranton Administration. The numbers were remarkably consistent with Blatt's narrow victory in 1962, but this time, Tabor, who was also from the Pittsburgh area cut into the Democrat's margins in the southwest just enough to pull out a 67,000-vote victory. It marked the third straight race to be decided within 2 percentage points.

TREASURER

The state treasurer's responsibilities include approving expenditures of state funds and deciding which banks receive short- and long-term deposits. The treasurer's signature appears on all checks issued by the Commonwealth. The election results for these contests, by region, are contained in Tables 4.9 through 4.12.

Table 4.9 Democratic Share of Two-Party Vote for Treasurer, Southeastern Pennsylvania

	1952	1956	1960	1964	1968	1972	1976	1980
Philadelphia	59%	58%	67%	69%	65%	63%	70%	66%
Bucks	38%	44%	46%	53%	45%	46%	48%	42%
Chester	35%	33%	36%	####	39%	41%	35%	34%
Delaware	38%	38%	47%	47%	41%	41%	45%	40%
Montgomery	34%	34%	38%	45%	38%	40%	42%	37%
Suburban Totals	**36%**	**37%**	**42%**	**47%**	**41%**	**42%**	**43%**	**39%**
Southeast Totals	**51%**	**50%**	**57%**	**59%**	**53%**	**52%**	**55%**	**51%**

State Totals	48%	48%	51%	56%	52%	53%	53%	49%
Winning Party	**R**	**R**	**D**	**D**	**D**	**D**	**D**	**R**

	1984	1988	1992	1996	2000	2004	2008	2012
Philadelphia	67%	72%	80%	75%	79%	85%	84%	87%
Bucks	39%	47%	56%	42%	46%	55%	52%	50%
Chester	29%	39%	52%	37%	38%	54%	48%	48%
Delaware	36%	41%	52%	43%	48%	59%	55%	58%
Montgomery	34%	41%	55%	41%	47%	60%	55%	57%
Suburban Totals	35%	42%	54%	41%	45%	57%	53%	54%
Southeast Totals	**50%**	**55%**	**64%**	**54%**	**57%**	**67%**	**64%**	**65%**
State Totals	**46%**	**57%**	**65%**	**49%**	**49%**	**63%**	**56%**	**54%**
Winning Party	**R**	**D**	**D**	**R**	**R**	**D**	**D**	**D**

Table 4.10 Democratic Share of Two-Party Vote for Treasurer, Southwestern Pennsylvania

	1952	1956	1960	1964	1968	1972	1976	1980
Allegheny	52%	50%	55%	55%	58%	58%	55%	57%
Armstrong	44%	44%	45%	51%	54%	58%	54%	52%
Beaver	55%	54%	55%	63%	62%	61%	63%	61%
Butler	39%	44%	39%	49%	51%	52%	48%	45%
Fayette	62%	62%	62%	69%	64%	62%	64%	66%
Greene	63%	65%	62%	70%	67%	68%	70%	69%
Lawrence	47%	49%	51%	54%	54%	57%	59%	54%
Washington	62%	61%	60%	64%	66%	65%	62%	64%
Westmoreland	58%	58%	57%	62%	62%	62%	59%	58%
Southwest Totals	**53%**	**52%**	**53%**	**57%**	**60%**	**59%**	**57%**	**58%**
State Totals	**48%**	**48%**	**51%**	**56%**	**52%**	**53%**	**53%**	**49%**
Winning Party	**R**	**R**	**D**	**D**	**D**	**D**	**D**	**R**

	1984	1988	1992	1996	2000	2004	2008	2012
Allegheny	55%	71%	76%	51%	53%	70%	63%	61%

Armstrong	50%	68%	72%	45%	45%	62%	46%	39%
Beaver	62%	76%	80%	54%	57%	71%	58%	53%
Butler	40%	58%	67%	39%	40%	55%	38%	36%
Fayette	66%	76%	79%	60%	60%	74%	64%	56%
Greene	66%	80%	84%	59%	61%	72%	62%	52%
Lawrence	55%	69%	73%	52%	55%	69%	56%	51%
Washington	59%	75%	80%	52%	54%	69%	57%	45%
Westmoreland	54%	69%	71%	47%	49%	64%	51%	45%
Southwest Totals	**55%**	**71%**	**69%**	**50%**	**52%**	**68%**	**58%**	**54%**
State Totals	**46%**	**57%**	**65%**	**49%**	**49%**	**63%**	**56%**	**54%**
Winning Party	**R**	**D**	**D**	**R**	**R**	**D**	**D**	**D**

Table 4.11 Democratic Share of Two-Party Vote for Treasurer, Northeastern Pennsylvania

	1952	1956	1960	1964	1968	1972	1976	1980
Carbon	47%	48%	50%	59%	52%	56%	56%	54%
Lackawanna	52%	50%	60%	66%	56%	59%	51%	55%
Lehigh	43%	42%	44%	56%	52%	54%	52%	45%
Luzerne	45%	45%	58%	63%	58%	56%	56%	55%
Monroe	42%	43%	44%	58%	47%	49%	49%	44%
Northampton	51%	51%	53%	66%	60%	58%	60%	51%
Northeast Totals	**48%**	**47%**	**54%**	**63%**	**56%**	**56%**	**54%**	**52%**
State Totals	**48%**	**48%**	**51%**	**56%**	**52%**	**53%**	**53%**	**49%**
Winning Party	**R**	**R**	**D**	**D**	**D**	**D**	**D**	**R**

	1984	1988	1992	1996	2000	2004	2008	2012
Carbon	55%	58%	68%	55%	51%	62%	57%	51%
Lackawanna	57%	59%	72%	64%	62%	75%	70%	69%
Lehigh	45%	50%	62%	42%	46%	60%	54%	55%
Luzerne	56%	56%	67%	59%	53%	67%	61%	58%
Monroe	41%	44%	56%	48%	45%	57%	59%	57%

Northampton	53%	55%	63%	46%	49%	60%	56%	53%
Northeast Totals	**48%**	**54%**	**65%**	**52%**	**52%**	**64%**	**59%**	**57%**
State Totals	**46%**	**57%**	**65%**	**49%**	**49%**	**63%**	**56%**	**54%**
Winning Party	**R**	**D**	**D**	**R**	**R**	**D**	**D**	**D**

Table 4.12 Democratic Share of Two-Party Vote for Treasurer, Central Pennsylvania

	1952	1956	1960	1964	1968	1972	1976	1980
Adams	38%	41%	40%	47%	40%	48%	46%	42%
Bedford	38%	40%	37%	45%	36%	43%	46%	40%
Berks	49%	49%	49%	62%	55%	54%	56%	51%
Blair	35%	40%	35%	42%	39%	46%	45%	43%
Bradford	24%	31%	31%	38%	36%	41%	36%	34%
Cambria	57%	55%	55%	59%	49%	61%	68%	64%
Cameron	31%	33%	37%	43%	42%	53%	52%	44%
Centre	37%	39%	34%	44%	42%	55%	48%	44%
Clarion	40%	42%	44%	48%	57%	61%	49%	46%
Clearfield	47%	49%	45%	53%	49%	53%	54%	50%
Clinton	42%	45%	43%	51%	47%	60%	54%	50%
Columbia	45%	47%	43%	53%	49%	60%	49%	52%
Crawford	35%	36%	40%	48%	47%	52%	48%	23%
Cumberland	35%	36%	34%	44%	37%	41%	39%	34%
Dauphin	36%	37%	37%	42%	36%	42%	41%	39%
Elk	48%	47%	54%	58%	55%	63%	59%	57%
Erie	44%	44%	51%	58%	55%	59%	49%	42%
Forest	31%	36%	41%	42%	45%	51%	47%	41%
Franklin	37%	43%	39%	51%	43%	48%	50%	42%
Fulton	48%	49%	46%	50%	46%	52%	52%	46%
Huntingdon	31%	36%	32%	39%	39%	49%	44%	42%
Indiana	41%	43%	42%	45%	45%	55%	53%	52%
Jefferson	35%	40%	38%	44%	46%	54%	52%	45%
Juniata	43%	46%	40%	49%	42%	50%	46%	43%

Lancaster	32%	31%	30%	42%	31%	30%	34%	28%
Lebanon	36%	37%	32%	41%	34%	35%	37%	33%
Lycoming	40%	41%	41%	47%	48%	53%	45%	42%
McKean	26%	28%	36%	44%	38%	42%	39%	35%
Mercer	45%	45%	47%	54%	51%	53%	54%	32%
Mifflin	43%	42%	35%	52%	48%	56%	47%	41%
Montour	41%	42%	41%	49%	46%	57%	46%	47%
Northumberland	39%	43%	45%	50%	46%	54%	49%	49%
Perry	33%	38%	33%	42%	39%	46%	41%	36%
Pike	28%	30%	32%	41%	31%	34%	40%	33%
Potter	29%	36%	36%	41%	36%	45%	46%	39%
Schuylkill	40%	42%	48%	53%	47%	56%	53%	48%
Snyder	21%	26%	23%	33%	28%	37%	32%	29%
Somerset	42%	44%	43%	47%	42%	48%	52%	48%
Sullivan	40%	44%	46%	45%	42%	47%	47%	46%
Susquehanna	26%	33%	35%	40%	34%	41%	38%	38%
Tioga	22%	26%	28%	37%	31%	38%	38%	33%
Union	22%	26%	23%	31%	29%	45%	34%	31%
Venango	28%	29%	34%	41%	48%	53%	42%	38%
Warren	29%	30%	37%	47%	42%	47%	45%	36%
Wayne	22%	29%	31%	36%	29%	34%	36%	30%
Wyoming	25%	30%	33%	36%	34%	43%	33%	36%
York	54%	48%	44%	57%	44%	47%	44%	37%
Central Totals	**40%**	**41%**	**41%**	**49%**	**44%**	**49%**	**47%**	**41%**
State Totals	**48%**	**48%**	**51%**	**56%**	**52%**	**53%**	**53%**	**49%**
Winning Party	**R**	**R**	**D**	**D**	**D**	**D**	**D**	**R**

	1984	1988	1992	1996	2000	2004	2008	2012
Adams	34%	47%	58%	38%	35%	51%	40%	37%
Bedford	34%	44%	57%	38%	33%	52%	34%	28%
Berks	41%	50%	62%	40%	43%	60%	53%	50%
Blair	65%	45%	61%	41%	36%	58%	39%	36%
Bradford	27%	38%	50%	36%	30%	46%	38%	34%

Cambria	55%	67%	78%	60%	59%	77%	62%	53%
Cameron	37%	44%	60%	43%	43%	58%	46%	40%
Centre	35%	50%	64%	48%	42%	63%	54%	51%
Clarion	39%	59%	66%	38%	40%	58%	44%	38%
Clearfield	43%	58%	70%	51%	47%	66%	52%	42%
Clinton	40%	58%	69%	54%	45%	62%	52%	47%
Columbia	44%	56%	67%	54%	42%	62%	51%	46%
Crawford	23%	45%	60%	42%	44%	52%	46%	41%
Cumberland	26%	40%	50%	37%	28%	54%	43%	43%
Dauphin	35%	47%	59%	43%	35%	62%	55%	55%
Elk	49%	62%	74%	54%	56%	72%	59%	49%
Erie	52%	45%	72%	47%	57%	60%	58%	60%
Forest	38%	55%	68%	40%	39%	56%	46%	41%
Franklin	33%	39%	51%	34%	31%	44%	34%	31%
Fulton	37%	49%	58%	39%	32%	42%	29%	26%
Huntingdon	31%	44%	60%	42%	33%	55%	39%	34%
Indiana	43%	61%	71%	48%	47%	65%	53%	45%
Jefferson	38%	54%	63%	41%	40%	55%	41%	33%
Juniata	36%	49%	57%	40%	30%	52%	36%	33%
Lancaster	24%	31%	41%	37%	31%	44%	42%	39%
Lebanon	28%	36%	51%	38%	32%	49%	42%	37%
Lycoming	35%	44%	57%	44%	34%	45%	41%	36%
McKean	32%	36%	48%	36%	32%	43%	41%	36%
Mercer	40%	57%	62%	51%	50%	61%	53%	50%
Mifflin	34%	49%	60%	43%	31%	47%	37%	32%
Montour	37%	51%	62%	48%	37%	56%	45%	41%
Northumberland	42%	51%	61%	51%	41%	56%	48%	43%
Perry	26%	43%	54%	33%	26%	51%	37%	35%
Pike	30%	34%	46%	44%	42%	45%	48%	44%
Potter	33%	39%	48%	32%	31%	41%	32%	28%
Schuylkill	44%	53%	64%	50%	42%	64%	54%	50%
Snyder	21%	35%	48%	34%	28%	46%	34%	31%
Somerset	44%	58%	67%	47%	45%	63%	45%	36%

Sullivan	38%	47%	56%	45%	35%	51%	45%	39%
Susquehanna	32%	40%	55%	43%	37%	54%	43%	38%
Tioga	28%	35%	47%	31%	29%	43%	34%	30%
Union	25%	40%	53%	38%	31%	49%	41%	39%
Venango	38%	50%	63%	40%	44%	55%	42%	39%
Warren	34%	46%	60%	40%	43%	52%	47%	42%
Wayne	25%	34%	50%	46%	36%	49%	44%	41%
Wyoming	29%	37%	55%	42%	36%	55%	46%	42%
York	32%	41%	56%	40%	34%	47%	44%	40%
Central Totals	**37%**	**46%**	**59%**	**43%**	**39%**	**55%**	**47%**	**43%**
State Totals	**46%**	**57%**	**65%**	**49%**	**49%**	**63%**	**56%**	**54%**
Winning Party	**R**	**D**	**D**	**R**	**R**	**D**	**D**	**D**

1952: HEYBURN/LEADER

The two row offices that were at stake in the 1952 election are interesting from a historical standpoint in that both defeated candidates went on to have much more successful careers in Pennsylvania politics than their victorious rivals.

Because each was limited to one term, the two Republicans who had been elected state treasurer and auditor general in 1948 decided to switch jobs. In the 1952 contest for treasurer, incumbent Auditor General Weldon B. Heyburn defeated Democrat George M. Leader, a poultry farmer from York County, by more than 180,000 votes. Two years later, Leader was elected governor. In the 1952 race for auditor general, Charles R. Barber defeated Genevieve Blatt by 214,000 votes. Blatt's candidacy marked the first time that either major party had nominated a woman to statewide office. Two years later, Blatt became the first woman to win, when she was elected secretary of internal affairs.

1956: KENT/KNOX

In the open-seat race for treasurer in 1956, Republican State Representative Robert F. Kent of Crawford County defeated the Democratic candidate, Allegheny County Controller James W. Knox, by 220,000 votes. The statewide voting patterns were quite similar to those of the 1952 contest, which Heyburn won. Both Kent and Heyburn offset a large Democratic vote in Philadelphia by comfortably winning the southeast suburbs. Predictably, the Republicans earned small margins in the northeast, where they had a slight registration edge, and huge margins in the central "T." Both Democrats—Leader in 1952 and Knox in 1956—fell short in their efforts to score the huge margins in southwestern

Pennsylvania that they needed to have any chance at victory. In fact, in the 1956 contest, Knox carried his southwest base by just 55,000 votes, about 200,000 votes shy of the Democratic Party registration edge there. Either Democrat might have prevailed if he had taken advantage of his party's base. With a registration edge of more than 400,000 voters, the GOP needed to do little in order to win the lower-profile races.

1960: SLOAN/SMITH

In 1960, the Republican row officers, Kent and Auditor General Charles Smith, again attempted to switch offices. By then, however, the advantage that the Republican Party had enjoyed for generations had dissipated. The Democrats were now the majority party, albeit by a margin of slightly less than 3,000 voters. Momentum in the state was clearly on their side, and with John F. Kennedy leading the way at the top of the ballot, the party made a clean sweep in statewide races, deposing both Republicans in the process.

The Democratic candidate for treasurer, Grace Sloan, the president of the Pennsylvania Federation of Democratic Clubs, would become a fixture in row office politics for the better part of the next two decades. Sloan ran stronger in the southwest than her two predecessors for the office, carrying it by 136,000 votes. Combined with Philadelphia, which also had had a change in voting patterns, this proved to be the difference. Just four years earlier, the GOP still maintained a 30,000-voter registration advantage. Now, however, the Democrats had a 178,000-voter edge, a swing of 208,000 registered voters in just four years. Although voting patterns had begun changing much earlier, the influence of party identification is high in these lightly publicized contests. Sloan, who came from Clarion County, defeated Smith in his home of Philadelphia by 314,000 votes. Those figures and her solid southwest totals created a margin that was difficult for the Republican to overcome.

Party registration in the northeast had also dramatically changed to the Democrats' advantage. They held a 44,000-vote registration edge in the six counties; compared with the miniscule 255-vote margin they had just four years earlier. Sloan's 44,000-vote victory over Smith in the northeast, which exactly matched her party's registration numbers, was therefore not surprising. Smith built a 274,000-vote margin in central Pennsylvania, a 27,000-vote increase from the Republican share in the 1956 treasurer's race. Although it was enough to make the race close, it was short of the margin Smith needed to prevent Sloan from becoming state treasurer. Sloan eked out a 116,000-vote, 2-point victory and became the second woman to occupy a state row office.

1964: MINEHART/FLEMING

In the elections of 1964, the two Democratic fiscal officers, Sloan and Auditor General Thomas Minehart, accomplished what had eluded the GOP four years earlier, successfully swapping fiscal offices. It didn't hurt that President Lyndon B. Johnson was leading the Democratic Party to a record-breaking victory at the top of the ticket. Minehart defeated his Republican opponent, Robert Fleming, by 542,000 votes.

Fleming, a state senator from Pittsburgh, carried only Butler County in southwestern Pennsylvania, a region he lost by 186,000 votes. He ran behind Minehart by 75,000 votes in his home county of Allegheny. Minehart reaped a 314,000-vote windfall in Philadelphia. Thus the Democratic bulwarks of southwestern Pennsylvania and Philadelphia had delivered a 500,000-vote margin, usually more than enough to withstand a Republican surge elsewhere in the state.

Even in the Philadelphia suburbs, Minehart minimized his losses, and he carried Bucks County by 6 percentage points. Central Pennsylvania was relatively lukewarm in its support of Fleming. He carried the region by just 23,000 votes. Minehart piled up huge margins throughout northeastern Pennsylvania, carrying every county toward an 116,000-vote advantage. His strongest performance was in Lackawanna County, where he defeated Fleming by 32 percentage points. For a Republican conducting his first statewide campaign, the political environment of 1964 was difficult terrain.

1968: SLOAN/PASQUARILLA

In 1968, Sloan moved from her position as auditor general to win another term as state treasurer. With Hubert Humphrey carrying the state in the presidential race, it was little surprise that Sloan defeated her opponent, Frank Pasquerilla, a political newcomer from Cambria County, with relative ease. Although Sloan ran poorly in the Philadelphia suburbs, losing by 134,000 votes, she ran well enough in the city (a 232,000-vote edge) to overcome it. Sloan's advantages in the southwest (218,000) and northeast (52,000) were more than enough for her to shift back to the treasurer's office, this time by 200,000 votes.

1972: SLOAN/WILLIAMS

Grace Sloan made her last appearance on a statewide ballot in 1972, when she won her third term as state treasurer. That year was the first time an incumbent treasurer could stand for reelection. Although President Nixon was pounding Senator George McGovern at the top of the ticket, Sloan easily defeated her challenger, Glenn Williams, Jr., by 274,000 votes, an improvement on both her previous showings for treasurer.

Sloan's margin in Philadelphia was smaller this time (180,000), and she ran poorly in its suburbs, losing by 131,000 votes. But she carried the southwest (200,000) and the northeast (49,000) by margins almost identical to those of her 1968 race. The real surprise in the election, and the reason Williams fell far short of winning, was central Pennsylvania. The well-known Democratic incumbent lost the region by just 23,000 votes, a 2-point difference. In one of the best showings by a Democrat in central Pennsylvania over the past half century, Sloan ended up carrying 22 of the region's 47 counties. She won a majority in counties such as Forest, Fulton, Jefferson, and Montour (to name a few), where Democrats have rarely been competitive. Furthermore, she won more than 60 percent of the two-party vote in five counties: Cambria, Clarion (her home), Clinton, Columbia, and Elk. That the Democrat accomplished this while Nixon was winning central Pennsylvania by 36 percentage points is all the more impressive. Because the law prohibited her from running for treasurer again, Sloan retired from public office when her term ended in 1976.

1976: CASEY/CRAWFORD

Of all the elections discussed in this book, perhaps the most peculiar was the state treasurer's election of 1976. To a casual observer, things appeared normal enough, with the Republicans offering State Representative Patricia Crawford of Chester County and the Democrats Robert Casey (who had defeated future Treasurer Catherine Baker Knoll in the primary). But the Democratic candidate was Robert E. Casey, not the Robert P. Casey who had twice suffered narrow defeats in the Democratic primary for governor and whose term as state auditor general had just wound down.

We'll never know how many voters cast ballots thinking they were voting for the popular veteran politician, but one can assume that just enough of them did to elect Robert E. Casey, the Cambria County recorder of deeds, by a 254,000-vote margin. Casey, who made it no secret that he planned to benefit from the voters' confusion, ran a stealth campaign from the basement of a Harrisburg office building that had no telephones. Although Crawford argued that Casey was "running on the good reputation of another man," not enough voters seemed to notice in the midst of highly charged presidential and senatorial contests. The 57-year-old Democrat shrugged off criticism, pointing out that he had had the name longer than his younger, more famous namesake.

Despite the name confusion, it should be pointed out that Casey did have some experience in fiscal affairs—more, in fact, than his opponent. Before serving his four terms as recorder of deeds in Cambria County, he had worked in the state treasurer's office. In addition, he was twice elected president of the Pennsylvania Association of Elected County Officials. Still, it's unlikely that any future candidate will win a statewide office in Pennsylvania after spending just $700.

Casey, who had brushed aside the party organization and four opponents in the spring primary, clearly benefited from the Democrats' registration advantage of more than 765,000 voters. He registered huge majorities in the usual Democratic strongholds and held Crawford's margin in central Pennsylvania to just 85,000. Apparently, the voters in Casey's home of Cambria County were well aware of who he was and gave him a 36-point victory. Additionally, Casey won majorities in areas adjacent to his home—counties such as Clearfield, Jefferson, Indiana, and Somerset—that only rarely vote Democratic.

1980: DWYER/CASEY

Casey received generally good marks in his tenure as treasurer, but in 1980 he still found himself on the defensive from charges that he had misled voters. His opponent, R. Budd Dwyer, a 40-year-old state senator from Meadville, Crawford County, built his campaign around that theme, imploring voters not to be deceived again by the "Casey name-game."

Combined with a strong Republican vote led by presidential candidate Ronald Reagan, the message was enough to give Dwyer a 52,000-vote, 2-point margin. It was the first time the GOP had triumphed in a treasurer's race since Crawford County native Robert Kent won in 1956. Casey's 186,000-vote lead in Philadelphia was slightly less than his 1976 total, although he improved his showing in the southwest with a 151,000-vote advantage. Casey won in the northeast by just 12,000 votes, short of what he needed to keep from being overridden by Dwyer's central Pennsylvania totals. In the 47 counties of the central "T," the Republican amassed a 231,000-vote lead (including 77 percent in his home county of Crawford), just enough to spell the difference. This ended one of the most bizarre footnotes in the history of Pennsylvania politics—and the political career of one Robert E. Casey. Interestingly, when the "other" Bob Casey came out of retirement in 1986 to run for governor, he was forced in the early going to prove that he was the "real" Bob Casey.

1984: DWYER/BENEDICT

Dwyer's reelection campaign of 1984 found him pitted against a well-known Democratic challenger, two-time state Auditor General Al Benedict. Much of what Benedict and his administration had become known for, however, wasn't exactly positive; on numerous occasions, his office had been tainted by corruption charges. Benedict's principal aide had been convicted of 139 counts of bribery and related offense in a huge job-selling scandal. After Benedict managed to prevail over a multicandidate field in the Democratic Party primary with less than a third of the vote, many in the party leadership had spoken openly about forcing him to step aside.

In arguably the nastiest campaign for treasurer in the past half-century, Benedict leveled a series of attacks against Dwyer, specifically that the Republican had agreed to a $300,000 kickback in exchange for awarding a multimillion-dollar contract to a computer company that had business with the Treasury Department. When the mud cleared, the incumbent Dwyer had survived with an easy 308,000-vote victory. Benedict's image had deteriorated to such an extent that he carried only Erie County, his home—and by less than 4,000 votes (52 percent). Compare that with the 39,000-vote margin (70 percent) he had received just four years earlier, when he won reelection to the auditor general post. The headline in the Philadelphia Inquirer the next day, "With Defeat of Benedict, Both Parties Are Winners," pretty much wraps up the sentiments of not just Republican officials but also many Democrats.

The ethical questions surrounding Budd Dwyer would not go away. During his second term, Dwyer was at the center of a federal investigation concerning "pay for play" allegations within his office. Then, in one of the truly tragic moments in Pennsylvania political history, on January 22, 1987, one day before he was to be sentenced on those charges, R. Budd Dwyer fatally shot himself in front of both the state press corps and television cameras.

1988: KNOLL/ENGLISH

The 1988 elections brought two women candidates, Republican Barbara Hafer (running for auditor general) and Democrat Catherine Baker Knoll, each of whom would cast a large shadow over the state's row offices for the next decade. Knoll, 58, of McKees Rocks, where she served as executive assistant to the director of community services in Allegheny County, would fulfill a lifelong dream in winning back the treasurer's post for the Democrats. She had previously lost primary campaigns for treasurer in both 1976 and 1984. In the primary campaign of 1988, she easily defeated State Representative David Sweet of Washington County, the party's endorsed candidate, by almost two to one.

Because the interim treasurer, G. Davis Greene, Jr., appointed by Governor Casey after Dwyer's death, had chosen not to seek a full term, it was an open-seat contest. For those who support changing the state treasurer's position to an appointed one, this is a good test case: Greene, a Wharton-educated financial consultant, had far more experience for the job than either of the two candidates on the ballot. The Republican candidate, Phil English, had been serving out his first term as city controller of Erie (the position once held by Al Benedict), where he managed a staff of one.

The 32-year-old English survived a tough primary battle against another state representative, John Kennedy of Cumberland County, and Mario Mele, a former member of the state liquor control board. English had a difficult time getting his message across in the general election. He was outspent by the Democrat almost $900,000 to $200,000, itself a rarity in Pennsylvania statewide politics. To gain attention, English conducted several news conferences across the state, holding a greasy roasted duck by the neck as a way to illustrate that his opponent was "ducking" him on the issues. On issues, both candidates promised to continue some of the imaginative policies employed by the interim treasurer, Greene, while vowing to return integrity to an office that had been damaged by the Dwyer incident.

Money and an advantage in party registration gave Knoll an easy 471,000-vote victory, the largest margin to date. She rang up big numbers in Philadelphia and in her home backyard of southwestern Pennsylvania. In Allegheny County alone, she enjoyed a 222,000-vote margin. Her 8-point advantage in the northeast was also better than average for a Democrat, and she limited English's advantage in the central "T" to just over 103,000 votes. Knoll even reached 60 percent in Cambria, Elk, and most surprisingly, Indiana counties. English, it should be noted, came back from the defeat, winning Tom Ridge's former congressional seat in the 1994 midterm elections.

1992: KNOLL/HENRY

Knoll's reelection performance was even more dominating in 1992; she trounced 35-year-old Republican Lowman Henry by 1.3 million votes. Henry, of Greensburg, Westmoreland County, had served as an aide to Attorney General Ernie Preate before assuming the chairmanship of the Pennsylvania Leadership Council, a leading anti-tax group. Henry attempted to pin the Casey's administration's tax hikes on the incumbent treasurer, but Knoll brushed that aside, pointing out that her office had no impact on those decisions, which were products of negotiations between the governor and the legislature.

When the votes were counted, the Democratic incumbent had carried Philadelphia with 80 percent of the vote and won all of the southeast suburban counties, along with the entire southwestern and northeastern regions. Most impressive was Knoll's 272,000-vote plurality in central Pennsylvania, where she captured 39 of the region's 47 counties, reaching 60 percent in 23 of them.

1996: HAFER/KNOLL

Although term limits prevented Knoll from seeking the treasurer's position again, it could not prevent her from trying to keep the job in the family. So in 1996, the popular officeholder and the Democratic Party attempted to transfer support for Knoll to her daughter, Mina Baker Knoll, 42. This time, the Knoll family faced a much different opponent, two-term auditor general and former gubernatorial candidate Barbara Hafer.

Knoll's biggest challenge was fending off Hafer's charges that she was a political carpetbagger, because she had only recently returned to Pennsylvania after having lived for years in New York City. Knoll stressed her experience as a certified public accountant, charging that Hafer was a party hack, accusing her of "disgusting behavior," and repeating the Republican's "redneck Irishman" remark directed at Governor Casey in the 1990 campaign.

The Associated Press declared Knoll (and Democratic attorney general candidate Joe Kohn) the winner, but as votes from rural areas—which generally depend on paper ballots—came in, Hafer emerged triumphant, by 88,000 votes. While Knoll ran predictably well in Philadelphia, she fell short in Allegheny County, home to both her and Hafer and the place where the Republican had spent years generating goodwill among voters. Knoll carried the county by only

7,500 votes, far short of what she needed to win. In addition, Hafer limited Knoll's edge in the southwest to slightly more than 7,000 votes. Hafer took both Lehigh and Northampton counties and held her opponent to a 17,000-vote edge in the northeast. In central Pennsylvania, Hafer maximized her advantages and topped Knoll by 204,000 votes. As those late-arriving ballots began stacking up, victory slipped away for the Democrat as the Knoll family winning streak came to an end.

2000: HAFER/KNOLL

The Hafer-Knoll feud continued in 2000, with Catherine Baker Knoll attempting to regain her position by avenging her daughter's 1996 defeat. Largely unnoticed because of the presidential campaign, this was another bitter contest that saw both candidates essentially running as incumbents. And just as in 1996, a lead held for much of the evening dissipated. The results were reminiscent of the preceding election, and Hafer prevailed by 96,000 votes.

Once again, the difference was Hafer's ability to cut into the normally Democratic advantage in her own backyard. With both candidates being from Allegheny County, Knoll's 33,000-vote victory was in fact, a triumph for Hafer. Although Knoll ran better in the southwest than her daughter had in 1996, carrying it by 47,000 votes, she needed to do better in order to prevail statewide.

Both candidates made political headlines two years later. Knoll emerged from a crowded Democratic Party primary field to run as the candidate for lieutenant governor with Ed Rendell running for governor. Hafer, having been snubbed by party officials, who endorsed Attorney General Mike Fisher for the GOP nomination, later endorsed Rendell. Hafer's split with the Republican Party became permanent in 2004, when she officially became a Democrat.

2004: CASEY/PEPPER

During the 2004 campaign for treasurer, there was little doubt that Robert Casey, son of the former governor, would successfully move over from his auditor general's position. It was simply a question of how much his margin would be. His opponent, Jean Craige Pepper, 49, a financial consultant from Erie, was hopelessly under-funded in running against someone with a household name like Casey. The Democrat, however, did need to answer the question of how seriously his image had been tarnished by his disappointing gubernatorial campaign of 2002.

Apparently, the answer was "not at all." Casey won the race with a plurality of more than 1.35 million votes. Boosted by a high turnout for the presidential contest between George W. Bush and John F. Kerry, Casey's 3,353,489 votes set a record for the most ever received by a candidate at any level in Pennsylvania politics. The Democrat from Scranton carried 52 of the state's 67 counties en route to a 63- to 37-percent victory. Casey took Philadelphia by a record 85 percent, a 434,000-vote plurality. Even more impressive was his performance in central Pennsylvania, where he defeated Pepper by 186,000 votes while carrying 32 of its 47 counties. Those numbers caused Democrats throughout the state to salivate at the prospect of Casey's running for the U.S. Senate against incumbent Rick Santorum in 2006, which he decided to do in the spring of 2005.

2008: MCCORD/ELLIS

The race to succeed outgoing Treasurer Robin Wiessmann, who was appointed by Governor Rendell to fill the position after Bob Casey's elevation to the US Senate, is perhaps best remembered for the amount of money Democratic candidate Robert McCord was able to invest in his own campaign. McCord, a venture capitalist from Montgomery County, had been credited with co-founding and managing the Eastern Technology Council prior to launching his first attempt at elected office. In the spring, he surprised most observers by raising 3.5 million dollars, the majority of which was used to flood television sets across the Commonwealth with advertisements. Those commercials allowed his campaign to deftly respond to his critics who argued that there was an inherent conflict of interest since a good deal of the money he raised came from the financial managers with whom the treasurer's office interacts. Those charges were spearheaded by his two major Democratic rivals, both of whom began the campaign somewhat better known in political circles, former state house member and chair of the Bucks County Democrats, John Cordisco, and Jennifer Mann, a member of the statehouse from Lehigh County who was viewed by some as a having long-term potential in statewide politics. While the three candidates generally fought to a draw across their eastern base, McCord's financial advantage provided him a much greater ability to improve his name identification elsewhere, particularly the southwest, where he amassed huge margins. The final result wasn't even that close with McCord defeating each of the other challengers by almost twenty points each.

Not surprisingly, McCord continued to press his financial advantages in the fall campaign where he faced Republican Tom Ellis, an attorney and Montgomery County commissioner. Ellis wasn't able to match the well-financed McCord either, and with Barack Obama leading a strong Democratic wave statewide, the outcome was never really in doubt. The Democrat outspent Ellis by a rate of 15 to 1, a staggering disparity in a state were the GOP candidate usually has the financial advantage. McCord prevailed statewide by 12 points, and he carried Montgomery County, home to both candidates by almost 40,000 votes, and the southeast suburbs with 53 percent.

The numbers throughout the rest of the state followed predictable patterns, which was not surprising since neither were very familiar to the voters (though McCord's resources clearly gave him the advantage). Behind a strong showing in Allegheny County, McCord was able to carry the southwest and even held his own in central Pennsylvania, which Ellis won by only five points. This was an especially good election cycle for the Democrats across the board in Northeastern Pennsylvania and this race was no exception, with McCord capturing 59 percent of the two party vote in those six counties (even reaching 70 percent in Lackawanna). Considering his resources, it wasn't surprising that almost immediately talk began of which higher office McCord would look to next. However, first there would be the matter of a reelection campaign four years later.

2012: MCCORD/IREY VAUGHAN

The Republicans rallied around Diana Irey Vaughan as their best hope to derail McCord's political aspirations and she received the nomination without a primary challenge. She was an interesting choice who carried some potential, first as a woman from a party which had only ever elected one to statewide office, Barbara Hafer, who ironically ended her career by switching and joining the Democrats. She could also cite some political successes as a five-term Washington County commissioner, where she held the distinction of being both the youngest person and also the only woman ever elected to that post. Coming from the southwest also provided a strategic consideration, since it was both a long way from McCord's southeastern base and also an area that that had been trending toward the GOP in recent years.

Throughout the campaign, Vaughan focused on McCord's handling of the state's pension obligations, arguing that his mismanagement had allowed it to increase during his tenure. In an attempt to tie him to his previous career as a venture capitalist, at a time were the excesses of Wall Street angered many, she also accused him of making risky investments. An undercurrent of elitism was also part of this narrative as she assailed him for his Harvard-educated roots. This was presented in contrast to her modest background, proudly boasting that her family had grown up and lived in a trailer in West Virginia until she had reached the age of 15.

Beyond defending his record in the usual manner, McCord's campaign repeatedly highlighted the budgetary problems that Vaughan's own Washington County had also faced. McCord questioned whether someone of like Vaughan who never received a college diploma was well suited for the job of managing the state's financial assets. Despite all of the charges made from both sides, what ultimately prevented this race from being competitive was undoubtedly the financial contrast between the two candidates. Just a few weeks before the election, Vaughan's campaign was embarrassed to report that they had only $22,000 cash on hand in contrast to McCord's whopping $2 million.

This imbalance allowed McCord to flood the Pittsburgh and Johnstown television markets limiting Vaughan ability to fully exploit her regional roots. Vaughan's lack of resources prevented her from ever appearing in the Philadelphia media market, and she remained largely unknown as election day arrived. Though McCord's overall numbers slipped two points from his 2008 victory, 55% to 53%, much of that can be attributed to the dip that President Obama experienced at the top of the ticket. Most tellingly, McCord was able to outperform the President in Vaughan's own Washington County by two percentage points and in the southwest overall by five percent. With his successful reelection, to the surprise of no one, McCord announced his intention to challenge Governor Corbett to be the state's highest executive officeholder less than twelve months later.

AUDITOR GENERAL

Called the "watchdog of the state treasury," the auditor general is another statewide fiscal office elected by the people. The auditor general is responsible for examining all state expenditures and for determining whether money has been spent improperly and, ultimately, whether restitution or even prosecution is in order. The office is pivotal from a patronage standpoint, in that the auditor general sits on commissions, boards, and governing authorities that oversee the dispersing of bonds and contracts and the hiring of law firms to handle legal work. The results of these contests are listed in Tables 4.13 through 4.16.

Table 4.13 Democratic Share of Two-Party Vote for Auditor General, Southeastern Pennsylvania

	1952	1956	1960	1964	1968	1972	1976	1980
Philadelphia	59%	58%	68%	69%	67%	65%	71%	67%
Bucks	38%	44%	46%	53%	48%	50%	51%	44%
Chester	35%	33%	36%	42%	41%	43%	39%	34%
Delaware	38%	38%	47%	47%	44%	43%	46%	40%
Montgomery	33%	34%	41%	45%	42%	43%	43%	37%
Suburban Totals	**36%**	**37%**	**43%**	**47%**	**44%**	**44%**	**45%**	**39%**
Southeast Totals	**51%**	**50%**	**57%**	**59%**	**56%**	**54%**	**57%**	**51%**
State Totals	**48%**	**47%**	**51%**	**57%**	**55%**	**56%**	**54%**	**51%**
Winning Party	**R**	**R**	**D**	**D**	**D**	**D**	**D**	**D**

	1984	1988	1992	1996	2000	2004	2008	2012
Philadelphia	68%	66%	69%	82%	85%	82%	86%	85%
Bucks	40%	40%	48%	50%	55%	49%	55%	48%
Chester	32%	30%	35%	43%	49%	45%	52%	45%
Delaware	38%	36%	43%	52%	57%	53%	59%	56%
Montgomery	36%	35%	43%	49%	57%	53%	59%	54%

Suburban Totals	37%	35%	43%	49%	55%	51%	56%	51%
Southeast Totals	51%	48%	53%	61%	65%	62%	67%	63%
State Totals	52%	49%	47%	58%	59%	53%	61%	52%
Winning Party	D	R	R	D	D	D	D	D

Table 4.14 Democratic Share of Two-Party Vote for Auditor General, Southwestern Pennsylvania

	1952	1956	1960	1964	1968	1972	1976	1980
Allegheny	51%	49%	56%	61%	63%	56%	57%	57%
Armstrong	43%	44%	44%	50%	55%	56%	54%	54%
Beaver	55%	53%	56%	65%	66%	65%	66%	66%
Butler	38%	38%	41%	52%	55%	53%	51%	50%
Fayette	62%	61%	62%	69%	68%	63%	65%	68%
Greene	62%	64%	63%	70%	70%	69%	71%	70%
Lawrence	47%	48%	51%	57%	57%	58%	60%	58%
Washington	61%	60%	60%	67%	69%	66%	66%	64%
Westmoreland	57%	58%	57%	65%	67%	63%	58%	59%
Southwest Totals	53%	51%	54%	61%	64%	59%	59%	59%
State Totals	48%	47%	51%	57%	55%	56%	54%	51%
Winning Party	R	R	D	D	D	D	D	D

	1984	1988	1992	1996	2000	2004	2008	2012
Allegheny	62%	52%	50%	62%	65%	66%	74%	58%
Armstrong	60%	52%	43%	60%	55%	51%	58%	35%
Beaver	69%	62%	56%	68%	67%	63%	67%	51%
Butler	51%	45%	38%	52%	49%	46%	51%	33%
Fayette	72%	67%	60%	72%	70%	66%	72%	53%
Greene	76%	68%	58%	73%	72%	67%	71%	48%
Lawrence	59%	59%	51%	66%	65%	59%	63%	48%
Washington	69%	59%	53%	65%	66%	62%	66%	46%
Westmoreland	70%	57%	51%	59%	58%	56%	61%	42%
Southwest Totals	64%	55%	51%	62%	63%	62%	68%	52%

State Totals	52%	49%	47%	58%	59%	53%	61%	52%
Winning Party	D	R	R	D	D	D	D	D

Table 4.15 Democratic Share of Two-Party Vote for Auditor General, Northeastern Pennsylvania

	1952	1956	1960	1964	1968	1972	1976	1980
Carbon	46%	48%	51%	59%	53%	58%	58%	53%
Lackawanna	52%	50%	60%	64%	66%	70%	59%	59%
Lehigh	43%	42%	44%	56%	53%	54%	53%	46%
Luzerne	45%	45%	58%	64%	62%	62%	60%	57%
Monroe	43%	44%	43%	58%	48%	53%	50%	45%
Northampton	50%	51%	53%	66%	61%	60%	62%	54%
Northeast Totals	47%	47%	54%	62%	60%	62%	58%	54%
State Totals	48%	47%	51%	57%	55%	56%	54%	51%
Winning Party	R	R	D	D	D	D	D	D

	1984	1988	1992	1996	2000	2004	2008	2012
Carbon	55%	57%	49%	60%	60%	52%	59%	47%
Lackawanna	57%	60%	53%	78%	75%	47%	72%	65%
Lehigh	45%	47%	44%	47%	59%	51%	60%	52%
Luzerne	56%	61%	50%	70%	66%	52%	65%	54%
Monroe	41%	41%	44%	48%	54%	49%	61%	55%
Northampton	53%	52%	48%	47%	60%	52%	59%	50%
Northeast Totals	52%	54%	48%	59%	63%	50%	63%	54%
State Totals	52%	49%	47%	58%	59%	53%	61%	52%
Winning Party	D	R	R	D	D	D	D	D

Table 4.16 Democratic Share of Two-Party Vote for Auditor General, Central Pennsylvania

	1952	1956	1960	1964	1968	1972	1976	1980
Adams	36%	41%	41%	48%	39%	49%	46%	41%
Bedford	37%	40%	37%	46%	35%	45%	40%	36%

Berks	49%	49%	49%	61%	56%	60%	58%	53%
Blair	34%	39%	36%	42%	40%	49%	40%	40%
Bradford	24%	30%	30%	41%	34%	41%	37%	37%
Cambria	55%	55%	56%	59%	62%	67%	45%	59%
Cameron	30%	33%	37%	47%	42%	54%	45%	48%
Centre	35%	39%	34%	46%	41%	61%	47%	43%
Clarion	41%	41%	39%	57%	49%	56%	54%	52%
Clearfield	45%	49%	46%	55%	49%	54%	51%	50%
Clinton	41%	40%	42%	54%	48%	60%	54%	47%
Columbia	44%	47%	44%	54%	52%	66%	58%	52%
Crawford	34%	37%	37%	51%	46%	54%	56%	51%
Cumberland	34%	36%	34%	44%	37%	50%	39%	33%
Dauphin	36%	37%	37%	43%	36%	48%	44%	40%
Elk	49%	47%	53%	63%	60%	69%	57%	57%
Erie	46%	44%	50%	59%	43%	64%	70%	70%
Forest	30%	36%	37%	49%	40%	50%	50%	47%
Franklin	36%	42%	42%	48%	41%	49%	48%	40%
Fulton	46%	49%	46%	51%	43%	51%	50%	41%
Huntingdon	30%	36%	31%	42%	37%	50%	40%	38%
Indiana	40%	43%	41%	48%	47%	58%	47%	51%
Jefferson	34%	39%	38%	49%	45%	53%	46%	47%
Juniata	43%	45%	40%	49%	41%	51%	47%	44%
Lancaster	31%	31%	30%	42%	33%	33%	35%	30%
Lebanon	36%	37%	32%	42%	34%	39%	38%	34%
Lycoming	39%	41%	40%	48%	46%	57%	47%	42%
McKean	26%	28%	35%	48%	37%	42%	40%	37%
Mercer	44%	45%	46%	56%	52%	54%	57%	53%
Mifflin	41%	42%	36%	53%	44%	54%	46%	41%
Montour	40%	42%	41%	52%	48%	60%	50%	46%
Northumberland	38%	44%	45%	51%	46%	58%	50%	49%
Perry	32%	38%	33%	43%	38%	51%	42%	34%
Pike	27%	30%	31%	41%	27%	38%	39%	33%
Potter	29%	36%	35%	43%	35%	45%	46%	40%

Schuylkill	39%	42%	48%	54%	48%	58%	54%	49%
Snyder	21%	26%	23%	35%	27%	39%	33%	29%
Somerset	42%	44%	43%	48%	45%	50%	43%	43%
Sullivan	40%	44%	45%	47%	44%	49%	50%	48%
Susquehanna	26%	33%	35%	41%	38%	46%	41%	37%
Tioga	21%	26%	27%	39%	30%	38%	37%	32%
Union	21%	25%	24%	33%	28%	44%	37%	33%
Venango	27%	29%	32%	48%	43%	51%	46%	46%
Warren	29%	30%	36%	49%	41%	49%	49%	43%
Wayne	21%	28%	31%	36%	33%	44%	37%	35%
Wyoming	24%	30%	31%	38%	39%	52%	39%	37%
York	50%	48%	44%	57%	44%	48%	42%	41%
Central Totals	**39%**	**41%**	**41%**	**50%**	**44%**	**53%**	**48%**	**45%**
State Totals	**48%**	**47%**	**51%**	**57%**	**55%**	**56%**	**54%**	**51%**
Winning Party	**R**	**R**	**D**	**D**	**D**	**D**	**D**	**D**

1952: BARBER/BLATT

The first election within the scope of this study was the 1952 contest between State Treasurer Charles R. Barber and Pittsburgh attorney Genevieve Blatt. Although Barber, a Republican, won by a slightly larger margin than Weldon Heyburn, the previous auditor general with whom he had traded offices, the voting margins across the state were remarkably consistent with one another. This is not surprising, given the paucity of information available to the voters in those days.

Among the five southeastern counties, the voting percentages were exactly the same in four; the exception being that Barber scored 1 percent higher in Montgomery. Furthermore, in the nine counties of western Pennsylvania, the percentages were within 1 percentage point of each other. The same was true in the northeast, where three counties provided the same percentages and the other three were within 1 percentage point. Only in central Pennsylvania was there even a slight deviation in the vote for the two offices. Of the region's 47 counties, 8 deviated by more than 1 percentage point, although 7 of those differed by only 2 percentage points. The only county in the state to have a gap of more than 2 percentage points between the two elections was York. That shouldn't be surprising; in that the Democrat candidate for treasurer, George Leader, hailed from the county (he ran 4 points better than Blatt). None of the other three candidates seemed to receive any benefit from their home counties, further demonstrating the lack of attention to those races.

1956: SMITH/SMITH

The similar voting pattern was also true in the open-seat campaigns for both posts in the 1956 election. In the auditor general's contest, Republican State Representative Charles C. Smith of Philadelphia defeated State Insurance Commissioner Francis R. Smith, also of Philadelphia, by 247,000 votes, only 27,000 more than the margin that Republican Robert Kent won by in the treasurer's race. The percentages matched exactly in every southeast county, and they came within 1 percentage point of each other in all the counties of the southwest except Butler, which Charles Smith carried with 62 percent, 6 points higher than Kent had in the treasurer's contest. In the northeast, the margins were also all within 1 percentage point, as was the case in central Pennsylvania, with one exception. That was in Clinton County, which the Republican, Charles Smith, carried with 60 percent of the vote, 5 points higher than Kent.

1960: MINEHART/KENT

The successful Democratic candidate for auditor general in 1960 was Thomas Minehart, a former Philadelphia councilman who by the time of the election lived in Fort Washington, Montgomery County. Although the GOP had lost its grip on the row offices, one thing held true: Voting patterns again remained remarkably similar across the state. In the southeast, only Montgomery County deviated by more than 2 percentage points (it was 3 points) between the treasurer and auditor general contests. None of the nine counties in the southwest was outside the 2-percentage-point range either. As with the treasurer's contest, a strong Democratic vote in the northeast and the southwest largely accounted for Minehart's victory. He received 54 percent of the vote in the southwest, a 3-point increase over Francis Smith's totals in 1956.

In the northeast, Minehart's numbers were almost identical to those that Grace Sloan posted in her victorious treasurer's contest. Thus, Minehart increased the Democratic share of the vote by 7 percentage points, to 54 percent. In central Pennsylvania, the trend remained: Both Republicans took 59 percent each time, and only in three counties did the votes differ from each other by more than 2 percentage points. In fact, two of those were counties that happened to be homes to the candidates. Sloan ran 5 points better in her native Clarion County than Minehart, although she received only 44 percent. In Crawford County, Robert Kent's home, Kent beat Minehart by 3 points more than Charles Smith did in his treasurer's contest (Kent won by 20 points). The only county that deviated more than 2 percent and that did not contain a candidate was Forest, where Kent took 63 percent of the vote, 4 points higher than his GOP colleague. Forest was, and remains, the county in the state with the fewest registered voters. For instance, Democrat Thomas Minehart received only 836 votes from Forest County in the 1960 election.

1964: SLOAN/HELM

Sloan moved over to the auditor general's position in 1964, when she and Minehart successfully swapped offices. Again, both candidates won with ease, what with LBJ at the top of the ticket and the Democrats holding a majority of the state's registered voters. Sloan's margin over W. Stuart Helm was an enormous 682,000 votes, all the more impressive because Helm, a Republican from Armstrong County, was also the speaker of the state House of Representatives and relatively well known in his own right.

Although voting patterns again remained similar between the offices of treasurer and auditor general, some variation began to appear, specifically in central Pennsylvania. For a Democrat, Sloan ran especially well in the rural areas, winning by just fewer than 10,000 votes in the 47 central Pennsylvania counties. She ran more than 2 percentage points stronger than Minehart in 13 counties. In her Clarion County base, Sloan registered 57 percent of the vote, a 13-percentage-point gain from her treasurer's race four years earlier. The only Pennsylvania county in which Sloan trailed her Democratic colleague by more than 2 points was Franklin, where she received 48 percent of the vote, compared with Minehart's 51 percent.

In southwestern Pennsylvania, which Sloan carried by 22 points, her totals surpassed Minehart's by more than 2 points in five of its counties, and she led her Democratic colleague by 4 points overall. Nevertheless, in each of the southwest counties other than Allegheny, where Sloan's numbers topped Minehart's by 6 points, her totals were only 3 points greater. The Democrats' percentages were exactly the same across the five counties of southeastern Pennsylvania, with both receiving 59 percent of the vote. Both Democrats also carried northeastern Pennsylvania easily, although Minehart's 63 percent was 1 point greater. Again, none of the six counties deviated by more than 2 points between the two offices.

1968: CASEY/DEPUY

With Sloan moving back to treasury for two more terms, the 1968 contest saw the election of a man whose family continues to cast a large shadow over Pennsylvania politics. State Senator Robert P. Casey had been introduced to statewide voters two years earlier, when, despite being the choice of the Democratic Party organization, he lost in the Democratic primary to an outsider, Milton Shapp.

State Secretary of Revenue Warner Depuy, who had served in the cabinets of Republican Governors Scranton and Shafer, may have been well qualified, but he proved to be no match for Casey, who had already built a strong following across the Commonwealth. Casey posted big numbers in Philadelphia and ran well enough in its suburbs to register an 187,000-vote advantage in the southeast. The key to Casey's success, however, was the support he received from voters in southwestern Pennsylvania, hundreds of miles from his Lackawanna County home. He carried the nine counties by 312,000 votes—but more important, his 64 percent matched his party's registration edge in the region, a feat that Democratic candidates have rarely achieved. Also, for the first time during the period of this study, some significant separation occurred between the vote totals for treasurer and for auditor general in the two regions. Casey ran more than 2 percentage points stronger than Sloan in three of the five counties in the southeast and in eight of the nine in the southwest.

In the northeast, interestingly, there was little difference in voting patterns for the two offices outside of Casey's base in Lackawanna and Luzerne counties, which he carried by 10 and 4 percentage points, respectively, more than Sloan. Casey carried the northeast by 88,000 votes, a 20-point advantage. There was a disparity of more than 2 percentage points in 14 of the 47 counties in the "T," but no real trend was present, as the victorious Democrat ran ahead of his or her colleague in half of them. While Depuy ran fairly well in central Pennsylvania, carrying the region by 168,000 votes, his opponent's strengths elsewhere in the state were too much to overcome. The Republican also enjoyed strong support in his Pike County home, but having such a sparsely populated political base provides few tangible rewards. Despite taking 73 percent of the vote in the county, Depuy netted only 2,600 more votes than his opponent.

1972: CASEY/MCCORKEL

Casey demonstrated his considerable vote-getting abilities in 1972, when he won reelection by defeating Franklin McCorkel by 531,000 votes, despite George McGovern's drubbing in the presidential race. Although Casey's numbers tailed off quite a bit in Philadelphia, he ran slightly stronger in the Philadelphia suburbs (almost winning Bucks County) and emerged from the southeast with a 125,000-vote edge. And he again maximized his party's advantages in southwestern Pennsylvania, this time taking 62 percent of the vote, 4 points higher than his party's registration in the region.

Casey also continued his domination in the northeast, improving to 62 percent, a 98,000-vote advantage. His Lackawanna County base gave him an overwhelming 70 percent. The most significant development, and a portent of things to come, was Casey's showing in central Pennsylvania. The incumbent improved his share in that GOP stronghold by 9 percentage points. In fact, Casey carried the region by 70,000 votes, a rarity for a Democrat, taking 27 of its 47 counties. Only McCorkel's native Lancaster County, which McCorkel carried with 67 percent, came close to delivering the typical Republican vote. Casey's 53 percent in "T" was an astonishing 21 points higher than McGovern managed on the same day.

1976: BENEDICT/GLEASON

With term limits preventing Casey from seeking a third term, the 1976 race was an open-seat contest between Republican Patrick A. Gleason and Democrat Al Benedict. Although both candidates vowed to continue the aggressive policies of "Kamikaze Casey," each carried his own set of political baggage. Gleason, a third-term state representative from Johnstown, had gained notoriety for the heavy-handed way he had conducted himself as chairman of a committee investigating corruption in the Shapp Administration. Grilling Shapp for more than 20 hours over a three-day period during the summer of the Democrat's reelection campaign, Gleason turned the governor into a sympathetic figure, practically ensuring him of another term. In the primary, Gleason narrowly survived a challenge from Eleanor Jean Thomas, a bookkeeper and self-described "whistle-blower" from Somerset County, who became a perennial candidate for a variety of offices.

Benedict, who had served as controller for the city of Erie, promised to work closely with other Democratic Party officials, from the governor down. That was probably not the best message during a time when ethical issues touching one public official or another seemed to appear regularly. But with the Democrats possessing a 765,000-voter registration advantage statewide, and Jimmy Carter winning the presidential race, they continued their dominance of the under publicized row offices.

The degree of straight party voting among the two row offices did begin to decline. Using the 3-percentage-point-or-above measure, 30 counties deviated in their vote between this contest and the treasurer's, which Benedict's fellow Democrat, Robert E. Casey, won. Interestingly, Lackawanna County gave Benedict 59 percent of the vote, 8 points more than Casey, who many voters realized wasn't their Bob Casey, the "real" one from Scranton.

1980: BENEDICT/KNEPPER

Benedict also withstood the Republican tide of 1980, becoming the only Democrat to win statewide. He defeated State Representative James W. Knepper of Allegheny County. In what developed into an unusually bitter contest for a row office, Knepper charged that Benedict had presided over a corrupt administration, using his office as a vehicle for dispensing political favors to his friends and allies. The incumbent denied the allegations, challenging his opponent to produce the evidence. As discussed in the previous section, many of those ethical questions eventually came to light. For now, however, Benedict survived, though by a margin of only 98,000 votes, a 2-point win.

Benedict's numbers declined throughout the state except in one region, southwestern Pennsylvania, where he again took 59 percent of the vote. Knepper reduced Benedict's previous numbers by 6 points in the southeast, 4 points in the northeast, and 3 percent points in the central "T." Had Knepper performed similarly in the southwest, he probably would have won. But he lost by 80,000 votes in his native Allegheny County alone.

1984: BAILEY/SHANAMAN

In 1984 the Democrats extended their winning streak in auditor general races to seven, when Don Bailey, a former congressman from Greensburg, Westmoreland County, defeated Susan Shanaman by 153,000 votes. Shanaman, the former head of the Public Utility Commission, sought to link Bailey with the outgoing, corruption-plagued Benedict (who was running for treasurer). She had dispatched State Representative Tom Swift of Crawford County with surprising ease in the GOP primary. Bailey, who had faced a contested primary against Allegheny County Controller Frank Lucchino, withstood her charges by projecting a positive image as both a former college athlete and a Vietnam War hero. He also avoided being overcome by President Reagan's 356,000-vote coattails. The race was a polite affair, especially compared with the rancor that marked that year's treasurer (Dwyer-Benedict) and attorney general (Zimmerman-Ertel) contests.

Shanaman, a Republican from Lebanon County, ran well in central Pennsylvania, which she carried by 14 points, and in the suburbs of Philadelphia. Shanaman also ran well in northeastern Pennsylvania, losing by only 4 points. She even carried Lehigh County by 10 percentage points. Bailey, however, piled up large enough numbers in both Philadelphia and Allegheny counties (234,000- and 146,000-vote pluralities, respectively) to prevail by 4 percentage points statewide. With his victory, Bailey became one of the party's few bright spots on election night 1984 and, considering his resume, perhaps its strongest prospect for future glory.

1988: HAFER/BAILEY

The vote-getting power that Bailey showed in 1984 makes Barbara Hafer's victory over him in the 1988 contest—the first for the GOP in the auditor general's post since 1956—all the more impressive. Bailey's luster had been tarnished a bit two years earlier, when he lost a close contest with Congressman Bob Edgar in the Democratic Senate primary. Running for the Senate soon after being elected auditor general with a promise to clean up the mess left by the previous administration probably hurt Bailey in the minds of many voters. Also, he faced criticism for having raised more than $200,000 from subordinates in his office over the course of the two campaigns. Finally, Bailey had to defend himself when one of his deputies was indicted on charges of extortion and racketeering. Still, that doesn't diminish the accomplishment of Hafer, a former nurse who was unknown in much of the state before the campaign. Her victory effectively ended the political career of Bailey, who carried a biography most would envy. The Democrat was on the losing end of one of the closest statewide races in years, losing by only 36,000 votes.

Also, the Bailey-Hafer match-up was one of the nastiest battles for auditor general in memory. Besides the previously mentioned charges leveled at Bailey, Hafer was accused, when she was chair of the Allegheny County Prison Board, of being somehow responsible for the deaths of two inmates because she had been campaigning for lieutenant governor (a campaign she later abandoned). Bailey also tried to taint Hafer for her support of a construction project contracted to a firm that was later revealed to have ties to organized crime. All three commissioners (Hafer and the other two, who were Democrats) had rescinded the contract when that information came to light.

Bailey demonstrated his political strength in the northeast, which he carried by 8 percent, and in central Pennsylvania, where he held Hafer's margin to just 8 percent. But the race was lost in the state's urban centers. Even though Bailey carried Philadelphia with 66 percent, he received 72,000 fewer votes in the city than Michael Dukakis did as the presidential candidate. Consumer Party candidate Max Weiner, a Philadelphian who was also in the auditor general's race, received 34,000 votes in the city alone, much of it coming from Democrats disaffected by the more conservative Democrat. Weiner received 69,000 votes statewide, again much of it coming out of Bailey's political hide. The 69,000 constituted about half of Hafer's victory margin.

In Allegheny County, there was significant cutting on the Democratic ticket. Weiner wasn't the beneficiary there; it was Hafer herself, who as county commissioner was both well-known and popular among enough Democrats to pry away some of their votes. Hafer held Bailey's margin in Allegheny County to just 19,000 votes, a sharp drop from Dukakis's 118,000-vote margin over eventual winner George H. Bush. The results launched Hafer as a major figure in Pennsylvania politics while relegating Bailey to relative obscurity.

1992: HAFER/LEWIS

Hafer's victory in 1992 was no less impressive than her previous one, coming as it did in a tough year for Republicans—incumbent or not—in Pennsylvania. Her opponent, H. Craig Lewis, 48, was a state senator from Bucks County, who had first been elected in 1974 at the age of 30. Lewis had unsuccessfully sought the Democratic Party nomination for U.S. senator back in 1980.

Hafer had to defend herself against allegations similar to those she had accused Bailey of four years earlier, that she had forced employees in the auditor general's office to contribute to her campaign fund, an illegal practice known as "macing." Lewis had no direct proof that workers had been coerced and the amount in question, estimated at $36,000, which was far less than Bailey had collected. The most unusual development occurred in the early days of the campaign, after Hafer's Capitol office was burglarized on July 31. Hafer accused powerful Democratic State Senator Vincent Fumo of being behind the effort. Fumo, a Philadelphia State Senator, responded by calling Hafer "a very bizarre and off-the-wall public official." Lewis denied having any knowledge of the incident.

Hafer's most significant accomplishment was her ability to overcome her greatest defeat, her disastrous gubernatorial campaign two years earlier, when she suffered one of the most lopsided losses in state history. Throughout that campaign, Hafer said that Casey, who was running for reelection, had covered up a looming billion-dollar state deficit. Casey repeatedly denied Hafer's accusations, but after the election was over she had been vindicated: Casey was forced to sign a record tax increase. With her credibility restored, Hafer's image had changed overnight to that of a no-nonsense truth teller.

In much of the state, Hafer increased her margins over her 1988 victory, defeating Lewis by 272,000 votes, a 6-point win. The only exception was Philadelphia, where Lewis took 69 percent, 209,000 votes more than Hafer. Hafer ran well in Lewis's backyard—the city's suburbs—even taking his home county, Bucks, by 11,000 votes. Hafer ran especially well in the southwest, losing by just 249 votes in her home of Allegheny County, and the region overall by just 12,000 votes.

Hafer markedly improved her showing in the central "T," taking 61 percent of the vote and capturing all but Cambria and Mercer counties, which she lost by a combined 1,699 votes. She even took more than 52 percent of the vote in the northeast, a region that had given her only 27 percent of the vote in her gubernatorial campaign against the favorite son, Casey. After that embarrassment, Hafer's triumph here meant that Bill Clinton wasn't the only "comeback kid" of 1992.

1996: CASEY/NYCE

With Hafer's move to the treasurer's job, the 1996 campaign for auditor general marked the reappearance of a familiar name in Pennsylvania politics. Robert Casey, Jr., a 36-year-old attorney and son of the former governor, was the same age his father had been when elected auditor general 28 years earlier. (Bobby, as he goes by, dropped the Jr. in his campaign literature.) Unlike his father, however, he did not have the support of the party establishment in the primary campaign. That went to Tom Foley, who had been the Democratic nominee for lieutenant governor two years earlier. In a spirited contest against Foley and two others, Casey's political career got off the ground with a narrow 10,000-vote victory.

Casey's opponent, State Representative Robert Nyce, was also from northeastern Pennsylvania—although farther south, in Northampton County. Nyce had earned a solid reputation both as a legislator and a politician (he once defeated an incumbent Democrat in a strong Democratic district), but he was unable to overcome the goodwill that the Casey name possessed. Casey's win was impressive, especially for a first-time statewide candidate. In fact, he received more votes than any other candidate on the ballot in 1996, including

President Clinton, winning by 661,000 votes statewide. In the 16-point win, Casey carried 48 of the state's 67 counties. He received a gigantic 357,000-vote victory in Philadelphia, which could have been expected, and 71 percent in Elk County, which was not. Although Casey had never sought elected office before, his name had, and it was worth quite a bit, even in the Pennsylvania "T," which Casey took by 76,000 votes. An interesting question to ponder, with Bob Casey now serving his second term in the United States Senate, is how different the states politics would be if he had found himself on the wrong side of that razor-thin margin back in the primary.

2000: CASEY/TRUE

The Republicans had a difficult time finding a candidate willing to take on Bobby Casey in 2000. They finally convinced 59-year-old State Representative Katie True of Lancaster County to give up her safe legislative seat for the thankless task. The race was particularly important for Governor Tom Ridge, who believed that some highly critical "performance audits" of his administration conducted by the auditor general's office were politically motivated. Despite Ridge's fundraising assistance, True raised only a little more than $500,000, not enough to get her name out across the state.

It probably wouldn't have mattered. This time, Casey's victory margin was even larger, 789,000 votes. Casey carried fewer counties in the central "T" (37) than he had in 1996, running behind True by 4 points. But he built up larger margins elsewhere in the state—particularly the Philadelphia suburbs, which he carried by 95,000 votes. Casey was now primed for the open-seat gubernatorial race of 2002, and Katie True wound up back in the legislature, after Republicans repaid her efforts with a new legislative seat following redistricting.

2004: WAGNER/PETERS

Like most other campaigns for auditor general through the years, the 2004 race was barely noticeable amid other contests, especially the presidential race. The open-seat battle between Democrat Jack Wagner and Republican Joe Peters was similarly unpublicized. Democrats took advantage of their registration advantage in maintaining control over this watchdog position, as they had in every election since 1960 with the exception of Barbara Hafer. Wagner, a Vietnam veteran and a state senator from Allegheny County, had an advantage over his opponent in name recognition. Just two years earlier, he had received fine reviews as Casey's running mate in Casey's unsuccessful primary bid for governor against Ed Rendell. In fact, Wagner came much closer to winning a spot in the general election than Casey did.

Peters, from Lackawanna County, had an interesting background as well, having worked to fight drug trafficking in the presidential administrations of both George H. Bush and Bill Clinton. More recently, the former police officer had served as the head of the state attorney general's drug and organized crime divisions. Peters had initially expressed interest in seeking the open attorney general's position, but party officials persuaded him to run for auditor general instead.

Wagner put together the traditional Democratic coalition to win easily, by 356,000 votes, a margin of 7 percentage points. He benefited from a huge presidential vote in Philadelphia, where he ran up a 387,000-vote plurality. Presidential candidate John Kerry's strong showing in the Philadelphia suburbs also helped Wagner. Wagner carried both Delaware and Montgomery counties and took the suburbs by slightly less than 18,000 votes. Wagner also ran well in his base of southwestern Pennsylvania, building up a 271,000-vote margin. He outpolled Peters by 189,000 votes in his native Allegheny County alone.

Peters ran well in central Pennsylvania, carrying the region by 322,000 votes, and in the typically Democratic northeast, which he lost by only 3,500. Peters did especially well in his native Lackawanna County, which he won by 6 percentage points. Just as in the presidential election, however, Republican voters in the Philadelphia suburbs dashed any hopes the Republican Party had of retaking the auditor general's position.

For the Democrats, this was an important victory, in that it helped give them control of a majority of the state's row offices for the first time since 1988. Wagner was also the first Democrat in 20 years who was not named either Casey or Rendell to win a statewide election. His victory demonstrated that the party could win statewide even if its candidate didn't possess the star power of either.

2008: WAGNER/BEILER

Not only did he win reelection four years later, Jack Wagner crushed his GOP opponent Chet Beiler, a former Lancaster County party chair, in the most lopsided auditor general race of the modern era. In fact, the incumbent Democrat was able to achieve what no other victorious candidate had ever accomplished during the period of this study when he tallied over 60 percent of the statewide vote.

Wagner's impressive showing was based on a combination of factors. As a wounded Vietnam veteran, he had a personal story that was certainly inspiring. He also had considerable experience running for office, initially, as a state senator, later with a bid for Lieutenant Governor, and of course his successful race for this office four years earlier. Finally, he also developed a strong reputation as the state's fiscal watchdog, willing to confront those within his own party, as a number of conflicts with the Rendell Administration would attest.

The Republican candidate, former Lancaster County party chair, Chet Beiler, possessed an interesting and unique background as well. Professionally, with the help of neighboring Amish craftsmen, he was able to build his company, Country Gazebos, into a major national supplier, with manufacturing plants located as far away as California. However, what truly distinguished his candidacy from anyone else's who had come before, was the fact that he was the first Amish-born candidate for statewide office in Pennsylvania history. Though his parents left the faith when he was four, they did continue to reside in Lancaster County were they ran a dairy farm.

The overall numbers throughout the state are what one would expect from such a thrashing. Wagner dominated Philadelphia (of course), but also the suburbs, winning each, and getting as high as 59 percent in Delaware and Montgomery counties. He took all six counties in the northeast even more handily, the low being that same 59 percent in Carbon and Northampton, while reaching a high of 72 percent in Lackawanna County. Not surprisingly, Wagner's southwestern base provided even a higher margin, a plurality of over 400,000 votes, and 68 percent overall. Most impressively, however, was that the Allegheny County native even carried the central 'T,' becoming one of the few Democrats ever to be able to make that claim. The end result, a victory by 1.2 million votes, fanned the flames of his future ambitions.

2012: DEPASQUALE/MAHER

Term-limited, the race to succeed Jack Wagner proved far more competitive, and in fact, was the tightest statewide race of the five being contested in this presidential year. The reason was partly due to it being an open seat contest, as well as one in which both candidates shared such similar backgrounds. The Democratic candidate was three-term State Representative Eugene DePasquale,, while the Republican, John Maher, also member of the state house, first elected in a special election back in 1997. While the Democrat ran unopposed for his party's nomination, Maher, who had the support of much of the GOP establishment, easily brushed aside a challenge from retired state senate staffer Frank Pinto for his party's nomination. Pinto, whose support came largely from some of the more conservative groups in the state, criticized both DePasquale and Maher for hedging their bets by simultaneously running for their state house seats as well.

In the fall campaign, DePasquale focused his campaign on ordering an audit on how The Pennsylvania State University was spending its' state funding allocation. He also sponsored a bill in the legislature that would end the special exemption that they, plus the three other state-related universities (University of Pittsburgh, Temple University, and Lincoln University) enjoy. His campaign also hammered away on the issue of Marcellus Shale. He promised to order an audit of all the water protection programs in the state in order to determine whether they were protecting drinking water from the natural-gas extraction. Both messages had appeal across party lines.

In addition, he contended that he would be better able to check Governor Corbett's administration, a claim routinely made by candidates for this office from those of the opposition party. Maher dismissed that notion and also responded that monitoring the Marcellus Shale would also be a priority for him. However, for the most part, he centered his campaign on his own personal background. As a certified public accountant, he argued that he was more qualified for the job and would be better suited to ferret out waste in state government. In addition, he brought with him a degree of business experience as a founder of the accounting firm, Maher Duessel CPAs, that he felt his opponent lacked.

The election returns were what one would expect from a closely matched, but relatively unnoticed political campaign in this state. DePasquale carried Philadelphia with 85 percent and also took Delaware and Montgomery counties with 56 and 54 percent, respectively. Meanwhile, the Republican carried Bucks (52 percent) and Chester counties (55 percent). A good indicator of what you would expect to find in a "normal" election at this point in the southeast. The same is mostly true in the southwest, although Maher's Allegheny County roots probably helped him gain a larger share in this region than a Republican ordinarily would. In fact, he carried all but two of the nine counties overall in the region, though the large Democratic bloc in Allegheny allowed DePasquale the ability to carry it by four points overall.

Maher also held his own in the northeast, losing it 54-46 percent, a respectable showing for a Republican from outside the region. He was able to take Carbon County and came within 400 votes of almost capturing Northampton County as well. DePasquale didn't do particularly well in his native central Pennsylvania. In fact, he only received a majority in two of the 47 counties (Dauphin and Erie) located here. Even in his home of York County he was held to only 42 percent. Nevertheless, DePasquale was probably able to minimized his losses in central Pennsylvania just enough, receiving 40 percent overall, to seal the victory.

The Democrat's overall margin of victory was slightly over 180,000 votes, a difference of just slightly over three percentage points, and probably an accurate reflection of what a "normal election" looks like in 2012 Pennsylvania. Although it was the closest of the statewide contests held this particularly year, it effectively elevated the 41-year old DePasquale to a position which may also launch him towards even higher office down the road. Though defeated, Maher could perhaps seek solace in the fact that he once again was reelected to the state house, this time unopposed.

ATTORNEY GENERAL

Governors appointed the attorney general until 1978, when Pennsylvania voters ratified a constitutional amendment requiring that the attorney general be elected. Because of the broad powers to investigate and prosecute crime in inherent in this position, it provides a highly visible platform for people who have even higher political ambitions. As an example, the last three individuals who have held the post later ran for governor.

As discussed in Chapter Two, the Republican Party's historical domination of U.S. Senate seats was one of the hallmarks of Pennsylvania politics. But even that could not match what the Republicans accomplished in races for state attorney general until recently. Prior to Kathleen Kane's victory in 2012, the GOP was able to roll up a perfect streak, winning all seven prevsious elections. The results for all eight contests are contained in Tables 4.17 through 4.20.

Table 4.17 Democratic Share of Two-Party Vote for Attorney General, Southeastern Pennsylvania

	1980	1984	1988	1992	1996	2000	2004	2008	2012
Philadelphia	63%	63%	67%	70%	80%	79%	81%	80%	87%
Bucks	43%	40%	42%	44%	46%	45%	49%	47%	53%
Chester	33%	33%	33%	41%	40%	36%	44%	43%	52%
Delaware	41%	38%	38%	42%	48%	46%	53%	50%	61%
Montgomery	36%	37%	39%	44%	48%	45%	52%	50%	58%
Suburban Totals	**39%**	**37%**	**38%**	**43%**	**46%**	**44%**	**50%**	**48%**	**56%**
Southeast Totals	**50%**	**49%**	**50%**	**53%**	**59%**	**56%**	**61%**	**59%**	**67%**
State Totals	**49%**	**49%**	**48%**	**49%**	**49%**	**44%**	**49%**	**47%**	**57%**
Winning Party	**R**	**R**	**R**	**R**	**R**	**R**	**R**	**R**	**D**

Table 4.18 Democratic Share of Two-Party Vote for Attorney General, Southwestern Pennsylvania

	1980	1984	1988	1992	1996	2000	2004	2008	2012
Allegheny	56%	59%	56%	57%	50%	47%	54%	47%	63%
Armstrong	52%	54%	55%	51%	47%	37%	40%	32%	45%
Beaver	61%	64%	64%	61%	55%	50%	53%	43%	56%
Butler	46%	49%	45%	48%	38%	31%	34%	28%	41%
Fayette	64%	65%	66%	65%	61%	56%	55%	48%	59%
Greene	63%	64%	66%	68%	62%	55%	55%	44%	57%
Lawrence	56%	58%	58%	56%	55%	49%	48%	43%	53%
Washington	61%	62%	63%	64%	47%	47%	51%	40%	53%
Westmoreland	57%	59%	57%	56%	47%	42%	43%	35%	49%
Southwest Totals	**57%**	**60%**	**57%**	**58%**	**50%**	**46%**	**50%**	**43%**	**57%**

State Totals	49%	49%	48%	49%	49%	44%	49%	47%	57%
Winning Party	R	R	R	R	R	R	R	R	D

Table 4.19 Democratic Share of Two-Party Vote for Attorney General, Northeastern Pennsylvania

	1980	1984	1988	1992	1996	2000	2004	2008	2012
Carbon	49%	52%	50%	45%	53%	47%	49%	47%	55%
Lackawanna	54%	52%	41%	31%	57%	49%	49%	48%	74%
Lehigh	47%	46%	44%	47%	48%	44%	50	58%	59
Luzerne	53%	55%	43%	35%	57%	45%	49%	46%	61%
Monroe	43%	38%	40%	41%	44%	41%	47%	53%	57%
Northampton	53%	52%	51%	51%	52%	48%	50%	62%	56%
Northeast Totals	**51%**	**50%**	**44%**	**41%**	**52%**	**46%**	**49%**	**54%**	**61%**
State Totals	**49%**	**49%**	**48%**	**49%**	**49%**	**44%**	**49%**	**47%**	**57%**
Winning Party	**R**	**R**	**R**	**R**	**R**	**R**	**R**	**R**	**D**

Table 4.20 Democratic Share of Two-Party Vote for Attorney General, Central Pennsylvania

	1980	1984	1988	1992	1996	2000	2004	2008	2012
Adams	36%	36%	39%	44%	34%	29%	35%	28%	43%
Bedford	35%	37%	40%	38%	31%	26%	29%	23%	35%
Berks	60%	44%	44%	45%	43%	40%	46%	46%	54%
Blair	39%	42%	41%	40%	33%	32%	32%	27%	43%
Bradford	31%	32%	32%	29%	33%	28%	30%	30%	42%
Cambria	57%	61%	59%	51%	55%	45%	51%	44%	59%
Cameron	38%	40%	39%	43%	34%	35%	36%	33%	46%
Centre	42%	44%	45%	45%	40%	34%	46%	44%	59%
Clarion	44%	45%	47%	46%	40%	33%	36%	41%	43%
Clearfield	46%	50%	51%	50%	42%	36%	43%	35%	49%
Clinton	44%	51%	50%	46%	48%	40%	43%	42%	55%
Columbia	45%	49%	42%	38%	46%	36%	40%	39%	52%
Crawford	41%	41%	43%	39%	38%	32%	35%	33%	43%

Cumberland	29%	36%	34%	36%	34%	27%	34%	28%	42%
Dauphin	30%	44%	40%	40%	42%	34%	44%	39%	56%
Elk	50%	49%	54%	49%	48%	42%	49%	43%	53%
Erie	53%	56%	49%	43%	48%	40%	44%	46%	59%
Forest	38%	42%	46%	41%	41%	34%	39%	35%	48%
Franklin	35%	32%	35%	38%	31%	28%	30%	27%	38%
Fulton	41%	39%	42%	44%	33%	28%	29%	25%	29%
Huntingdon	36%	34%	38%	39%	32%	26%	33%	28%	42%
Indiana	46%	51%	52%	50%	47%	39%	44%	37%	50%
Jefferson	41%	42%	44%	45%	39%	32%	32%	27%	40%
Juniata	37%	42%	39%	37%	36%	27%	30%	21%	39%
Lancaster	29%	28%	29%	34%	29%	25%	31%	31%	45%
Lebanon	32%	38%	33%	36%	35%	28%	31%	28%	41%
Lycoming	41%	50%	39%	34%	35%	27%	31%	31%	42%
McKean	33%	34%	34%	38%	36%	32%	33%	35%	39%
Mercer	48%	52%	53%	52%	50%	47%	48%	47%	53%
Mifflin	39%	41%	40%	42%	36%	26%	28%	23%	40%
Montour	42%	48%	40%	34%	43%	32%	35%	33%	47%
Northumberland	44%	57%	45%	40%	45%	36%	36%	32%	48%
Perry	30%	36%	32%	35%	30%	22%	29%	20%	37%
Pike	33%	32%	32%	38%	40%	39%	39%	44%	46%
Potter	33%	33%	35%	37%	31%	30%	29%	28%	31%
Schuylkill	47%	47%	47%	41%	46%	38%	43%	38%	53%
Snyder	25%	39%	28%	28%	27%	19%	26%	23%	38%
Somerset	44%	49%	49%	45%	42%	34%	40%	31%	44%
Sullivan	41%	43%	42%	36%	39%	31%	35%	31%	44%
Susquehanna	34%	33%	32%	30%	36%	30%	35%	34%	46%
Tioga	31%	35%	32%	33%	31%	29%	30%	30%	34%
Union	29%	48%	32%	33%	32%	25%	33%	32%	43%
Venango	38%	43%	43%	42%	41%	39%	35%	31%	44%
Warren	36%	40%	41%	40%	40%	38%	37%	38%	44%
Wayne	33%	28%	26%	28%	37%	29%	33%	33%	48%
Wyoming	32%	33%	27%	23%	35%	26%	32%	31%	49%

York	37%	37%	36%	42%	38%	29%	34%	32%	45%
Central Totals	**41%**	**43%**	**41%**	**41%**	**39%**	**33%**	**37%**	**35%**	**48%**
State Totals	**49%**	**49%**	**48%**	**49%**	**49%**	**44%**	**49%**	**47%**	**57%**
Winning Party	**R**	**R**	**R**	**R**	**R**	**R**	**R**	**R**	**D**

1980: ZIMMERMAN/O'PAKE

The contest of 1980, between Republican LeRoy S. Zimmerman and Democrat Michael O'Pake, was emblematic of how almost all elected attorney general contests would unfold. The debate would be rancorous, the vote totals would be close, and (despite several instances in which the media projected otherwise) the Republican would win.

Zimmerman had gained such a strong reputation as a prosecutor in Dauphin County that he received the endorsement of both political parties the last two times he was elected there. O'Pake, a state senator from Berks County who chaired the Judiciary Committee, was running for attorney general and simultaneously seeking reelection to his legislative seat (which he said he would resign if elected attorney general). That approach became a central issue in the attorney general's race, with Zimmerman accusing O'Pake of hedging his bets. In a campaign that generally receives little attention, it was an issue voters could identify with, and it may have cost O'Pake the bigger prize.

O'Pake appeared to be the winner until late returns came in on Wednesday morning. When all the votes were counted, the Republican had pulled out a 120,000-vote, 3-point victory. Zimmerman benefited from Ronald Reagan's coattails at the top of the ticket, offsetting the Democrats' registration advantage. Voting patterns were generally predictable, with O'Pake underperforming just enough in many key Democratic regions to come up short.

For instance, while O'Pake received 63 percent of the vote in Philadelphia (the same percentage as President Carter), that total was less than what the party's two other row office candidates got. This was surprising, because O'Pake's home of Berks County was part of the Philadelphia media market. In addition, Zimmerman ran well in the Philadelphia suburbs, where O'Pake may have expected to do better because of proximity.

Predictably, Zimmerman won convincingly in central Pennsylvania, with 59 percent, although O'Pake did carry his Berks County base by 20 points. O'Pake failed to maximize the Democratic vote in the northeast, taking just 51 percent of the vote in the six counties. He even lost Lehigh County by 6 percentage points, surprising given its proximity to his Berks County home. In southwestern Pennsylvania, O'Pake also came up just shy of expectations, taking 57 percent of the vote across the nine counties, where the Democrats claimed 69 percent of the two-party registration. It wasn't dramatic, but Zimmerman held down O'Pake's percentages just enough to overcome the GOP statewide disadvantage in registration and emerge victorious. For the Democrats, coming up a little short was a taste of things to come.

1984: ZIMMERMAN/ERTEL

As tough as the first campaign for Pennsylvania's elected attorney general was, it paled in comparison with the next one. Zimmerman's battle to win another term, this time against Democrat Allen Ertel, was a street fight that left both candidates clutching for their integrity as election day drew near. Rather than focusing on crime and punishment, the candidates went after each other on personal matters. Ertel hammered the incumbent for delaying an investigation into an alleged bribe offered to his press secretary. Its existence wasn't disclosed until two weeks before the election, as the result of a federal indictment. Zimmerman's main line of attack was on his opponent's tax returns. Ertel had reported owing nothing on his federal income taxes in both 1980 and 1981 because of heavy business deductions.

Financially, Zimmerman had a clear advantage, raising well over $1 million, roughly double the amount he had collected four years earlier. Ertel was not as fortunate; he was still in debt from his 1982 gubernatorial campaign, and his fundraising was much less prolific. To purchase additional television time, he was forced late in the campaign to mortgage his farm and put up his investment portfolio as security for bank loans.

Voting patterns across the state were similar to those of Zimmerman's victory over O'Pake in 1980, but this time the results were even closer. Of more than 4.6 million votes cast, Zimmerman won by less than 29,000, a margin of 0.63 percent. The numbers in Philadelphia were nearly identical to those of 1980, although Zimmerman did slightly better this time in the suburbs. His numbers declined, however, in both southwestern and central Pennsylvania.

Ertel, who was from Lycoming County, took advantage of his base in north central Pennsylvania by winning there and posting respectable numbers elsewhere in the region. One of the keys to Zimmerman's close victory was his showing in the northeast, where he held Ertel's advantage to less than 4,000 votes. But Berks County proved to be the difference. In this county alone—Mike O'Pake's political base—Zimmerman improved his performance by over 35,000 votes, more than enough to account for his victory margin. He was off to another term, and for Alan Ertel it was the second narrow defeat in a row and the end of his political career.

1988: PREATE/MEZVINSKY

The open-seat contest of 1988 continued the trend established for the newly elected office. It was contentious and close, and the Republican emerged victorious. This time it was Ernie Preate, district attorney of Lackawanna County, defeating Ed Mezvinsky, the former chair of the state Democratic Party.

Mezvinsky had served as a member of the United States Congress from Iowa before moving to Montgomery County a decade earlier. Unlike previous Democratic candidates for attorney general, however, Mezvinsky was not going to be outspent. A multimillionaire, he reportedly dumped more than $1 million of his own money into the campaign. His finances were certainly an asset in his surprise primary victory over Turnpike Commissioner Jim Dodaro, the choice of the Democratic Party organization.

Which candidate could do a better job cracking down on illegal drug use was the central issue in much of the campaign. As November drew near, personal accusations began to be tossed about, and the enmity was unusually strong. Preate charged that Mezvinsky had participated in a failed grain deal with a group of individuals that included an Iowa man named Eugene H. Pietsch. Pietsch had recently been convicted of possession with intent to deliver several hundred pounds of marijuana. Mezvinsky responded that others had brought Pietsch into the deal and that he had no knowledge of Pietsch's conviction, but the incident reflected poorly on a candidate seeking to become the state's top law enforcement official.

Preate was also forced to defend himself against charges; specifically that he had accepted more than $10,000 in contributions from people mentioned in a Pennsylvania Crime Commission report. In addition, he had accepted money from several people named in court documents for their involvement in a state police raid on illegal video poker machines in Lackawanna County. By far, the most serious charge was that Preate had knowingly leaked information about an impending raid after the State Police had made him aware of it.

The defining moment of the campaign, however, occurred the weekend before the election. Mezvinsky began airing a television ad that accused Preate of violating his pledge never to plea bargain with drug dealers. The spot contended that as district attorney, Preate had offered a plea bargain to an alleged heroin dealer. The charge backfired, however, when the Preate campaign quickly responded with an ad featuring Philadelphia District Attorney Ronald D. Castille. Castille, a Republican and a Preate supporter, called Mezvinsky a liar who had jeopardized an ongoing drug investigation.

The victory margin for Preate was 142,000 votes statewide. He ran well in the traditional Republican areas and added a strong showing in the northeast, his political base, which he won by more than 46,000 votes. It was a 12-point victory there, rare for a Republican. Mezvinsky failed to cut into his opponent's margins in the Republican suburbs of Philadelphia, where he was now living and that also hurt his chances. His efforts also came up short in southwestern Pennsylvania, where his winning margins were less than what a Democrat generally needs in order to be successful.

Although this was the last campaign for Mezvinsky, it was not the last for the Mezvinsky family. Four years later, his wife, former television news reporter Marjorie Margolies Mezvinsky, became the first Democrat to win the Montgomery County congressional seat in almost one hundred years. Their son, Marc Mezvinsky would also marry former first daughter Chelsea Clinton in

2010. However, sadly and ironically, both of these individuals seeking the office of the state's highest law enforcement officer in this 1988 election eventually served time in prison.

1992: PREATE/KOHN

In Preate's reelection campaign of 1992, he faced Democratic challenger Joe Kohn of Devon, Chester County. Kohn, 35, was seeking his first major office after having worked as a private practice attorney specializing in consumer and environmental cases. Largely unknown in the state, he raised more than $2 million from within his own family to make the race competitive.

On issues, the contest presented a real contrast in both ideology and in how each candidate perceived the responsibilities of the attorney general's office. The candidates differed on their view of the state's recently enacted Pennsylvania Abortion Control Act. Preate had argued in favor of it before the United States Supreme Court, which Kohn said he would not have done. Also, while Preate had focused much of his attention on the war on drugs, Kohn proposed mandatory drug treatment for offenders and suggested alternative sentencing for nonviolent criminals. The personal attacks that had by then become customary centered on Preate's charges that his opponent was a wealthy, inexperienced attorney who was only dabbling in politics after landing a job in his father's prestigious Philadelphia law firm. Kohn shot back that Preate was using his office to beef up his image for a future gubernatorial run.

In Philadelphia, Kohn piled up a 214,000-vote margin, benefiting enormously from Bill Clinton's performance at the top of the ticket. But although Kohn improved on Mezvinsky's 1988 numbers in the Philadelphia suburbs (which was Kohn's home as well as Mezvinsky's), he still lagged 124,000 votes behind Preate in those four counties. Preate pulled in the Republican typical margins in central Pennsylvania, which he won with 59 percent. And in the northeast, Preate's home base, he rolled over Kohn. Improving on his 1988 effort, the incumbent defeated Kohn by 18 points, an 82,000-vote advantage in this swing area. Lackawanna, Preate's native county and usually a reliable Democratic area, gave the Republican a 35,000-vote, 38-point advantage. Although Kohn ran well in the southwest, winning by 16 points, it wasn't enough to keep Preate from winning by 126,000 votes. Overall, it was a respectable effort by Kohn given his inexperience against the incumbent Preate. It also set him up well for another try four years later, when the seat would be vacant.

1996: FISHER/KOHN

Kohn did run again in 1996, and for a brief time he appeared to be the state's new attorney general. That was at 10:18 P.M. on election night, when the Associated Press declared him the winner. About an hour and a half later, Kohn happily gave his victory speech in front of supporters at his campaign headquarters. A few minutes later, Governor Ridge called to offer his congratulations. It appeared that the Democrats had won an attorney general's race at last.

The Associated Press, however, had jumped the gun (as it did in the state treasurer's race, too). As often happens in Pennsylvania elections, the later returns—coming largely from rural areas, where ballots are transported long distances to be tabulated at county courthouses—overwhelmingly favor Republicans. This election was no exception, and Democrats again watched as victory slowly but inexorably slipped away.

The winner was declared after midnight and long after most television sets had been turned off. When all the votes were counted, Republican Mike Fisher, a state senator from suburban Pittsburgh, had prevailed by 62,000 votes. It was not all that close, considering the call by the Associated Press, and it was double the 1984 margin. Kohn ran amazingly well in both Philadelphia and its suburbs. In Philadelphia, he piled up a 290,000-vote edge—80 percent—and in the suburbs he seemed to benefit this time from his local roots, holding Fisher to a 66,000-vote advantage. Kohn won in the northeast by 4 percentage points, and although he was roundly defeated in central Pennsylvania (as expected), that wasn't what made the difference.

The reason for Fisher's victory was easy to find. The state senator, who had been the 1986 Republican nominee for lieutenant governor in a losing cause, took full advantage of the years he had spent representing southwestern Pennsylvania. Voters rewarded the Republican with a 5,000-vote victory in that Democratic area. In his Allegheny County base, Fisher came within 3,000 votes of beating his opponent, an unusually strong showing for a member of his party. Fisher also carried the populous neighboring counties of Washington and Westmoreland by 6 percentage points each, both impressive achievements. It all added up to a pleasant surprise for Fisher, considering how the results appeared to be heading. For Kohn and the Democrats, it would be another heartache, with more on the way.

2000: FISHER/EISENHOWER

The 2000 race was relatively mild compared with many of the others. Mike Fisher was a solid bet to win reelection over Democrat Jim Eisenhower, a former federal prosecutor from Philadelphia. Eisenhower attacked Fisher for not taking as active a role as other state attorney generals had in a multistate settlement with tobacco companies. He also accused Fisher of selecting law firms that he was connected with to negotiate the settlement rather than opening up the selection for bidding. But the race never seeped into the public consciousness, being overshadowed by other contests, particularly the year's hotly contested presidential race.

After five consecutive races that had been close, this one was never in doubt. Fisher won reelection by more than 500,000 votes. In Philadelphia, Eisenhower rode the coattails of presidential candidate Al Gore to a 289,000-

vote margin, but he was crushed in much of the rest of the state. Fisher rolled up a 540,000-vote lead in central Pennsylvania, a 34-point advantage. He also improved his numbers in the northeast, carrying all six counties and outpolling Eisenhower by 9,000 votes.

Fisher again enjoyed strong support in his southwest base, carrying six of the nine counties for an 89,000-vote advantage. Particularly impressive was the 58 percent he received in Westmoreland County. Fisher's strong showing throughout the state boosted him toward an inevitable run for governor in 2002. He would lose, but President Bush later selected him to fill a federal judgeship.

2004: CORBETT/EISENHOWER

The 2004 contest followed the pattern that by now had become familiar. In fact, it produced a sense of déjà vu for anyone who had been around eight years earlier, when Joe Kohn squared off against Mike Fisher. In each election, the Democrats nominated a candidate from suburban Philadelphia who had lost in his first try against an incumbent and who was now running in an open-seat race. In both cases, the candidates improved on their earlier efforts. And both Kohn and Eisenhower thought they were headed to the victory circle several hours after the vote counting began. Again, though, for the seventh straight time, it would be the Republican with his hand raised triumphantly.

This time the winner was Tom Corbett, a former state and federal prosecutor from Pittsburgh. Corbett had served as the state attorney general in 1995–96 after Governor Ridge appointed him to fill the last 15 months of Ernie Preate's term. (Preate had been forced to resign after pleading guilty to mail fraud.) Corbett had pledged not to run for a new term in the 1996 election, a common concession in such situations.

The 2004 race focused not just on specific legal issues but also on how each candidate perceived the role of attorney general. Corbett maintained a traditional crime-fighting posture, but Eisenhower charged that the Republicans had behaved passively in the office, and he promised to take a more activist role. His role model, New York Attorney General Eliot Spitzer, had recently received national attention by vigorously pursuing legal action against firms that had avoided federal governmental regulation in consumer and environmental matters.

Corbett was forced to defend himself for the four years he had spent working for Waste Management, Inc., after leaving his interim job as attorney general. Critics charged that he would be soft on environmental polluters after having been employed by the company, the state's largest landfill operator. It wasn't just Eisenhower and the Democrats making the claim; a Republican, Montgomery County District Attorney Bruce Castor, had attacked Corbett relentlessly in an unusually bitter GOP primary battle. Corbett responded by stressing his record of successfully convicting polluters in several high-profile cases. He also ran on his record of restoring credibility in the state's justice department after the Preate affair had left it in shambles.

The final twist of the campaign came shortly before the election, when it was revealed that Corbett, trailing both in money and in the polls, had received $480,000 from a national fundraising group known as the Republican State Leadership Committee. The committee, funded largely by the tobacco and insurance industries, qualifies as a 527 group (the section of the federal tax code which now allows corporate donations in light of the McCain-Feingold Campaign Reform Act). The problem, however, is that Pennsylvania law prohibits corporations from donating money to political campaigns. The Republican's campaign argued that the committee had received contributions from individuals and partnerships (such as law firms and political action committees), which is legal. Less than a week before the campaign ended, a Philadelphia judge gave Corbett twelve hours to disclose the sources of the contribution—or he wouldn't be able to use the money. Corbett insisted that the gift was legal; and although he admitted that he couldn't identify every person or organization, most of the money had already been spent to purchase valuable advertising time.

Like previous Democratic candidates for attorney general, Eisenhower appeared to be the winner early in the evening. The early returns favored precincts reporting from the southeast. Not only did Eisenhower win Philadelphia by an immense 384,000 votes; he also came within less than 6,000 votes of carrying the Philadelphia suburban vote. As it was, he topped Corbett in both Delaware and Montgomery counties.

Again, however, regionalism played a major role in southwestern Pennsylvania. Corbett made the most of his favorite-son status, defeating Eisenhower by a little more than 1,000 votes in the heart of the Democratic base. Most impressive was his 14-point victory in Westmoreland County. Northeastern Pennsylvania, the state's best predictor, also went narrowly for Corbett. Surprisingly, the Republican won every county in that traditionally Democratic area. Despite Eisenhower's strong showing in the southeast, his weaker performances in the southwest and northeast made him vulnerable.

Then, as had happened so many times before, the late-arriving ballots from central Pennsylvania put the Republican over the top. Corbett took full advantage of a huge turnout in central Pennsylvania (due to the presidential contest) and recorded a 476,000-vote advantage in the region, more than enough to give him a statewide victory of almost 100,000 votes. For more than a month, Eisenhower refused to concede; first pressing for a recount, although it was later determined that Corbett's margin was outside the 0.5 percent that would warrant such action. Also, Eisenhower continued to assert that Corbett had been the beneficiary of the illegal campaign contribution, suing his opponent to force disclosure. All was in vain, however, and Corbett was ultimately sworn in as the fourth elected attorney general—all Republicans—in Pennsylvania.

2008: CORBETT/MORGANELLI

The campaign theme for Tom Corbett's reelection was simple; focus on his record and tout his accomplishments of the previous four years. With that established, there was very little his Democratic opponent Northampton County District Attorney John Morganelli could do to counterattack. Without a doubt, the incumbent had been the most visible attorney general to hold that office since it became an elective one in 1980. In particular, his 18-month investigation, commonly known as "Bonusgate," would engulf both politicians inside the capital and the public at large, ultimately becoming the biggest corruption scandal to hit the Commonwealth since the 1970s.

Along with a number of staffers, the "Bonusgate" probe netted the conviction of Democratic Majority Leader William deWeese and Democratic Whip Mike Veon, primarily for awarding taxpayer-funded bonuses to staffers for doing campaign-related work. In 2006 alone, the total doled out amounted to well over $1 million. Over on the Senate side, former Democratic Leader Robert Mellow pled guilty and also eventually went to prison for using staffers to do political fund-raising and campaign work. Remarkably, some of this activity even took place while his colleagues on the other side of the aisle were already being prosecuted for roughly the same exact crime. Over on the GOP side, former Speaker of the House John Perzel and several others were also convicted and served time for spending millions in public funds on computer software that was primarily used to support their party's slate of candidates.

The only institution in the capital that was spared was the Republican state senate caucus, a fact that did not go unnoticed by Corbett's critics. Morganelli argued that the Attorney General had botched the initial probe by authorizing a raid of the House Democratic offices which, in effect, also tipped off others allowing them to destroy potential evidence and elude the investigators. At minimum, the challenger argued that an independent prosecutor should have been called in to handle the investigations right from the start. Corbett fired back, defending his record and maintaining that there was evidence that it was only the House Democrats who were destroying documents, thus precipitating the search.

Morganelli himself was no stranger to statewide politics. First elected District Attorney in 1991 at the age of 35, he had narrowly lost twice to David Eisenhower in the Democratic primary for this same office the previous two election cycles. He also had the distinction of being one of the few statewide candidates to come from the Lehigh Valley in over a half century. Only Until Pat Toomey's successful US Senate bid two years later, only State Representative Bob Nyce's unsuccessful run for auditor general back in 1996 had ever made it even this far. With a surge in Democratic voter registration of almost 500,000, and their presidential nominee, Barack Obama, dominating the headlines at the top of the ticket, some wondered whether the time was finally ripe for a Democrat to capture this seat. But that was not the case at all. While generally favored (there is a paucity of polling available for these statewide races, so it's not all that clear), Corbett's victory margin of almost 400,000 votes far exceeded the expectations of just about every observer.

It wasn't just the overall numbers but the impressive level of support he received stretching across the entire Commonwealth, again, this was especially impressive in the face of Obama's resounding presidential victory. Although Philadelphia was predictably strong for the Democrat, Corbett more than held his own in the suburbs, carrying Bucks and Chester counties, while essentially fighting Morganelli to a draw in Montgomery and Delaware. Overall, Morganelli won the suburban vote in the southeast by just over 50,000 votes, far short of what a Democrat normally requires in order to be competitive statewide. In fact, across the southeast, Corbett outperformed the GOP presidential candidate Senator John McCain by an astonishing 250,000 votes. He also ran stronger than McCain by about 50,000 votes in the northeast overall, where he was able to carry half of the counties, including both Lackawanna and Luzerne, a rarity for a Republican. Only in Lehigh and Northampton counties, Morganelli's political home did the Democrat meet expectations.

Corbett gave the Democrat an especially strong drubbing in central Pennsylvania, carrying every one of the regions 47 counties, on the way to a 600,000 vote plurality (65 percent), and once again, far outpacing the top of the ticket. However, perhaps the most impressive aspect of Corbett's victory was his showing in his own political home in southwestern Pennsylvania. He dominated each of these seven counties, even winning Allegheny by six percentage points. Corbett even reached as high as 72 percent in neighboring Butler County. Overall, he carried this traditionally-Democratic leaning area by 170,000 votes.

It was a resounding victory for Corbett, and a strong vote of confidence in how he had conducted himself as the attorney general in the previous four years. Rather than being a political opportunist, as his opponents had charged, the voters of Pennsylvania saw him instead as a tough, no nonsense crime fighter, intent on rooting out corruption even within the state's highest places. That image, burnished in the minds of many would serve as the model four years later when he would launch himself toward the state's highest executive office—Governor.

2012: KANE/FREED

In a state were ambitious office seekers are usually required to take a long, slow climb to get to the top of the political ladder, Kathleen Kane's sudden emergence in 2012 was the exception. Not only was she the first woman, but also the first Democrat elected to the position of state attorney general. That she accomplished both, despite being largely unknown to the general public the short time before the spring primary only further confounds. That she did all this in what ultimately was a landslide of historic proportions was only icing on the cake. No question, that in a year when the presidential campaign barely touched down in the Keystone State, it was this former assistant District Attorney from Lackawanna County who proved to be THE top political story of 2012.

But perhaps most shocking of all was the issue itself that would serve as the spark for her epic victory. It was the 46-year old Kane's repeated criticism of former Attorney General-now Governor Tom Corbett and his appointed successor Linda Kelly for their prosecution of ex-Penn State Assistant Football Coach, Jerry Sandusky in a child sex abuse scandal that shocked the nation. Although Sandusky was eventually convicted on 45 charges and sentenced to 30-60 years in prison, many seemed to agree with Kane's contention that the 33-month investigation was drawn out by Corbett so as to not interfere with his 2010 gubernatorial campaign. The tragic circumstances of the case were so unfathomable that they eventually led to the sudden retirement of legendary football coach Joe Paterno midway during the 2011 football season.

Kane's opponent was longtime prosecutor, and current Cumberland County District Attorney David Freed. Well-respected in his field, Freed possessed a resume strikingly similar to ever other Republican nominee for this office, all of whom were eventually successful. But if there was ever a politician in the wrong place, at the wrong time in this state, it was Freed. The 42-year old also had the right pedigree; he was the son-in-law of LeRoy Zimmerman, the first person elected to this same office back in 1980. Unfortunately, for him, however, it was his connection to another previous occupant of the post, Governor Corbett, that he could not escape.

Though he continually denied it, Freed was unable to shake the Democrat's charge that he was the Governor's personal, handpicked successor. And with the Sandusky story dominating the headlines, his vow to review the handling of the case failed to resonate for those who partially blamed Corbett for the events which led to the downfall of their beloved football coach. Kane herself did not hesitate to pounce on this and repeatedly promised that if she were in charge, the whole incident would not simply be reviewed, but would be investigated. From the Democrats perspective, the real opponent wasn't Freed at all—it was Corbett himself.

Kane also had a considerable financial advantage. She was able to raise over $3 million for the general election, surpassing the Republican's $2 million. Kane's financial assets, some of which were drawn from her family's warehouse and trucking company, *Kane is Able*, went a long way to propel her out of obscurity in the spring primary when she upset former Bucks County Congressman Patrick Murphy for the Democratic nomination. Elected in the Democratic wave of 2006, only to get washed away in the GOP surge four years later, the former Iraq War veteran had ambitions and was seen as a potential star within his party.

The primary battle between these two ambitious Democrats proved highly contentious, and became a national story. It ultimately served as somewhat of a proxy battle for the supporters of President Bill Clinton on one hand and the current President, Barack Obama on the hand. Kane had worked on the Hillary Clinton presidential campaign in 2008 as the volunteer coordinator for

Northeastern Pennsylvania. Meanwhile, Murphy was one of the first prominent Democrats to endorse Obama in that primary battle, despite receiving assistance from the Clinton's when he won his first term two years earlier. This no doubt jogged President Bill Clinton's memory and he thought it important enough to come into the state in order to stump for Kane.

Kane's own attacks upon Murphy focused on their differing backgrounds as she continually hammered away with the charge that the people need "A prosecutor—not a politician." In response, Murphy contended that his prosecutorial background in military courts during the Iraq War gave him the credentials needed to become an effective attorney general. With the candidates basically agreeing on the issues, this race came down to personality and Kane's appeal prevailed, not to mention the money (she spent over $2 million, much of it from her family). Ultimately, she won by about 40,000 votes statewide, a six-point victory.

In retrospective, given his ties to Corbett and the Governor's relationship to the Sandusky case, it's not farfetched to suggest that it was the primary election which determined who the next attorney general was going to be. The fact is that David Freed never really stood a chance. For an open seat race that involved two candidates both of whom were largely unknown months before the election, the final margin was unprecedented. Kane ran ahead of the entire Democratic statewide ticket, all five of whom won statewide, while receiving more votes than both Obama and Senator Casey. She totaled over 3.1 million in all, winning by 800,000, a 14 point gap over Freed.

Regionally, the Democrat easily carried the southeast, winning all five counties, including Chester (Casey was the only other Democrat on the five person statewide ticket to do so), while racking up 61 percent in Delaware County and 58 percent in Montgomery County. Kane also attracted the most votes of any Democrat in the southwest receiving 57 percent in the region, three percentage points higher than Rob McCord, who finished second among the five Democrats. Not surprisingly, she also carried her Northeastern base, with a high of 74 percent in her native Lackawanna County. Again, Kane was able to run ahead of the entire ticket in the region, four points better than Casey (also his base), and McCord.

Perhaps most surprising, however, was how this woman, the first ever elected to this office in state history performed in central Pennsylvania. In the same place where many previous Democratic nominees had watched their hopes crumble, Kane carried 10 of the 47 counties, and 48 percent overall. Prior to this, the best a Democrat had ever done for attorney general in central PA was Allen Ertel's 43 percent in 1984, and he was from Lycoming County. In fact, it had been twenty years since a Democrat had even crossed the 40 percent threshold. Perhaps most tellingly, Kane carried 15 of the 23 counties in which Penn State University has a campus presence, many of which are located within central PA. This, of course, includes the main one in State College, Centre County, and an area in which she attracted 59 percent of the vote. While Kane promised to not only serve out her term as attorney general but even wait two additional years before she might seek another office, that vow will surely be tested in the coming years. In the aftermath of this victory, it is more clearly a question of when, not if, she decides to reach for an even higher rung on the political ladder.

CHAPTER FIVE

PRESIDENTIAL ELECTIONS IN PENNSYLVANIA

1952: EISENHOWER/STEVENSON

It's not unusual for individuals or events to symbolize each passing decade. The 1960s were times when the twin forces of Civil Rights and Vietnam dominated the news. In the 1970s, it was Watergate. The 1980s were the decade of Ronald Reagan, and Bill Clinton embodied the 1990s. Arguably, however, no one individual or event has come to personify an era—not just in American politics but also in American life—as "Ike" did in the 1950s. The mere mention of Dwight D. Eisenhower's name conjures up an image of 1950s postwar baby boom and prosperity in America as none other. Among politicos, his name has even evolved into an adjective, as in an Eisenhower-type victory. No landslide, but a comfortable, relatively uneventful campaign. What's been lost over the years is that Eisenhower's first presidential triumph, in 1952, was anything but easy or preordained. Although it seems now that his being elected president was a fait accompli, it has been forgotten how close his election in 1952 was—not just in Pennsylvania but across the nation.

Forecasters had given Eisenhower a slight edge over his opponent, Democratic Governor Adlai Stevenson of Illinois, but the number of undecided voters made the contest a toss-up. In fact, a poll of Pennsylvania legislative correspondents on the eve of the election found six predicting a victory for Stevenson and five for Eisenhower. A pre-election survey, published by the *Philadelphia Inquirer*, also gave Stevenson the advantage, 215 electoral votes to 202 for Eisenhower, with 114 in doubt. Although the Republican nominee was generally favored to carry Pennsylvania, this state was one of several that would ultimately determine the outcome.

Beneath the backdrop of McCarthyism and Korea, it has also been largely forgotten how nasty and bitter the campaign became. Even President Truman interjected himself, trading barbs with Eisenhower while making an 18,000-mile whistle-stop tour on Stevenson's behalf. The acrimony between Truman and the man who would ultimately succeed him escalated so far that the incumbent President charged Eisenhower with impugning the character and patriotism of former military men by promising to speed the return of soldiers from Korea.

Of course, the race wasn't as close as predicted, with Eisenhower receiving about 53 percent of the vote both nationally and in Pennsylvania. In southeastern Pennsylvania, however, the results were split. Although the Republican received 64 percent of the vote in the four suburban counties (Table 5.1), Philadelphia was another story entirely. In what would be a harbinger of things to come, Stevenson carried the city by 160,000 votes (58 percent), even though the GOP had a 298,000-voter registration edge. Spurred on by what was described as the largest number of black voters ever to turn out in the city, the Democrats also increased their Congressional seat advantage to five of the six in Philadelphia. The sole Republican able to withstand this Democratic onslaught in the city was Congressman, and future United States Senator, Hugh Scott, who survived with a 3-point win.

Table 5.1 Democratic Share of Two-Party Vote for President, Southeastern Pennsylvania

	1952	1956	1960	1964	1968	1972	1976	1980
Philadelphia	58%	57%	68%	74%	67%	56%	67%	63%
Bucks	37%	39%	46%	61%	45%	36%	48%	37%
Chester	35%	30%	36%	54%	37%	30%	39%	32%
Delaware	38%	36%	48%	57%	44%	35%	44%	38%
Montgomery	33%	31%	39%	57%	42%	35%	42%	35%
Suburban Totals	36%	34%	43%	57%	43%	34%	44%	36%
Southeast Totals	51%	48%	57%	66%	56%	45%	55%	49%
State Totals	47%	43%	51%	65%	52%	40%	51%	46%
Winning Party	R	R	D	D	D	R	D	R

	1984	1988	1992	1996	2000	2004	2008	2012
Philadelphia	65%	67%	77%	83%	82%	81%	84%	86%
Bucks	36%	39%	51%	52%	52%	51%	54%	51%
Chester	30%	32%	45%	46%	45%	48%	55%	50%

Delaware	38%	39%	51%	56%	56%	57%	61%	61%
Montgomery	35%	39%	52%	54%	55%	56%	60%	57%
Suburban								
Totals	**36%**	**38%**	**50%**	**53%**	**53%**	**54%**	**58%**	**55%**
Southeast								
Totals	**49%**	**51%**	**61%**	**64%**	**63%**	**63%**	**67%**	**66%**
State Totals	**46%**	**49%**	**56%**	**55%**	**52%**	**51%**	**55%**	**53%**
Winning								
Party	**R**	**R**	**D**	**D**	**D**	**D**	**D**	**D**

A key to Eisenhower's success in this state was how well he did in the southwest (Table 5.2). In Allegheny County, for example, he held Stevenson's advantage to 11,000 votes despite a Democratic plurality in the county of more than 122,000. Stevenson had higher margins in some of the region' less populous areas but escaped with only a 63,000-vote edge in the nine counties. Also, Stevenson failed to produce numbers in several strong Democratic areas of the northeast (Table 5.3), such as the coal regions of Lackawanna County, where he had only a 3,000-vote edge. Eisenhower took 53 percent of the vote in the six-county northeast, a 33,000-vote advantage. He also carried all but Cambria County in the central "T," reaching 61 percent and a 314,000-vote plurality over Stevenson in this bedrock GOP region (Table 5.4).

Table 5.2 Democratic Share of Two-Party Vote for President, Southwestern Pennsylvania

	1952	**1956**	**1960**	**1964**	**1968**	**1972**	**1976**	**1980**
Allegheny	51%	45%	57%	66%	58%	43%	52%	52%
Armstrong	44%	39%	43%	67%	50%	37%	53%	50%
Beaver	55%	49%	56%	72%	62%	42%	58%	59%
Butler	38%	34%	39%	61%	47%	33%	46%	41%
Fayette	62%	58%	61%	74%	64%	45%	62%	59%
Greene	59%	57%	56%	75%	62%	42%	62%	61%
Lawrence	48%	44%	51%	65%	53%	43%	56%	51%
Washington	61%	55%	58%	72%	63%	45%	60%	58%
Westmoreland	58%	52%	55%	72%	61%	44%	56%	52%
Southwest								
Totals	**53%**	**47%**	**55%**	**68%**	**57%**	**43%**	**54%**	**53%**
State Totals	**47%**	**43%**	**51%**	**65%**	**52%**	**40%**	**51%**	**46%**
Winning								
Party	**R**	**R**	**D**	**D**	**D**	**R**	**D**	**R**

	1984	1988	1992	1996	2000	2004	2008	2012
Allegheny	57%	60%	64%	58%	58%	58%	58%	57%
Armstrong	51%	55%	59%	50%	42%	39%	38%	31%
Beaver	63%	66%	68%	60%	55%	51%	49%	47%
Butler	44%	45%	49%	41%	36%	35%	36%	32%
Fayette	62%	66%	70%	65%	58%	54%	50%	46%
Greene	59%	65%	71%	66%	55%	50%	50%	41%
Lawrence	55%	58%	63%	59%	53%	49%	47%	45%
Washington	59%	62%	68%	60%	55%	50%	48%	43%
Westmoreland	53%	56%	60%	51%	47%	44%	42%	38%
Southwest Totals	**56%**	**60%**	**63%**	**57%**	**54%**	**52%**	**51%**	**49%**
State Totals	**46%**	**49%**	**56%**	**55%**	**52%**	**51%**	**55%**	**53%**
Winning Party	**R**	**R**	**D**	**D**	**D**	**D**	**D**	**D**

Table 5.3 Democratic Share of Two-Party Vote for President, Northeastern Pennsylvania

	1952	1956	1960	1964	1968	1972	1976	1980
Carbon	46%	43%	49%	68%	52%	40%	55%	44%
Lackawanna	51%	46%	62%	74%	60%	44%	57%	51%
Lehigh	42%	49%	42%	65%	48%	36%	50%	41%
Luzerne	45%	41%	59%	71%	58%	39%	55%	47%
Monroe	38%	35%	36%	63%	42%	31%	48%	38%
Northampton	49%	44%	51%	74%	57%	44%	56%	47%
Northeast Totals	**47%**	**42%**	**54%**	**71%**	**55%**	**40%**	**54%**	**46%**
State Totals	**47%**	**43%**	**51%**	**65%**	**52%**	**40%**	**51%**	**46%**
Winning Party	**R**	**R**	**D**	**D**	**D**	**R**	**D**	**R**

	1984	1988	1992	1996	2000	2004	2008	2012
Carbon	45%	47%	56%	57%	52%	49%	51%	46%
Lackawanna	49%	52%	57%	63%	62%	57%	63%	64%
Lehigh	40%	43%	52%	52%	51%	51%	58%	54%

Luzerne	46%	50%	53%	58%	54%	52%	54%	52%
Monroe	34%	36%	48%	49%	49%	50%	58%	57%
Northampton	46%	48%	55%	55%	53%	51%	56%	52%
Northeast Totals	**44%**	**47%**	**54%**	**56%**	**54%**	**52%**	**57%**	**55%**
State Totals	**46%**	**49%**	**56%**	**55%**	**52%**	**51%**	**55%**	**53%**
Winning Party	**R**	**R**	**D**	**D**	**D**	**D**	**D**	**D**

Table 5.4 Democratic Share of Two-Party for President, Central Pennsylvania

	1952	1956	1960	1964	1968	1972	1976	1980
Adams	34%	34%	38%	56%	35%	29%	42%	35%
Bedford	36%	35%	32%	53%	31%	25%	42%	31%
Berks	47%	43%	45%	67%	50%	36%	48%	38%
Blair	34%	34%	36%	52%	35%	23%	39%	34%
Bradford	24%	26%	30%	51%	32%	26%	38%	33%
Cambria	56%	47%	59%	68%	55%	39%	54%	52%
Cameron	31%	25%	39%	58%	38%	30%	45%	38%
Centre	33%	33%	32%	64%	41%	39%	46%	44%
Clarion	36%	33%	35%	60%	40%	31%	44%	38%
Clearfield	45%	42%	43%	63%	46%	36%	50%	43%
Clinton	41%	40%	39%	70%	49%	37%	53%	44%
Columbia	42%	40%	38%	61%	40%	34%	51%	43%
Crawford	34%	33%	39%	63%	43%	34%	49%	42%
Cumberland	33%	32%	31%	53%	32%	26%	37%	32%
Dauphin	35%	32%	35%	52%	37%	29%	42%	38%
Elk	46%	38%	54%	71%	53%	37%	52%	45%
Erie	43%	38%	51%	70%	54%	41%	53%	48%
Forest	29%	29%	36%	58%	36%	27%	47%	40%
Franklin	35%	37%	35%	59%	37%	28%	42%	35%
Fulton	45%	43%	38%	56%	35%	32%	44%	33%
Huntingdon	31%	32%	30%	53%	33%	26%	41%	38%
Indiana	41%	38%	41%	60%	45%	37%	48%	47%

Jefferson	35%	34%	36%	56%	40%	30%	44%	40%
Juniata	41%	39%	35%	57%	36%	33%	44%	39%
Lancaster	30%	28%	30%	50%	30%	23%	33%	27%
Lebanon	36%	32%	32%	47%	30%	21%	36%	25%
Lycoming	38%	33%	38%	58%	41%	29%	45%	38%
McKean	26%	26%	36%	58%	38%	27%	38%	35%
Mercer	48%	41%	45%	64%	50%	39%	53%	47%
Mifflin	41%	37%	32%	59%	41%	27%	45%	41%
Montour	38%	34%	39%	59%	41%	29%	46%	40%
Northumberland	38%	37%	45%	62%	43%	35%	50%	40%
Perry	31%	32%	30%	53%	31%	25%	38%	31%
Pike	27%	23%	30%	51%	30%	23%	40%	25%
Potter	28%	30%	35%	53%	32%	28%	44%	35%
Schuylkill	40%	38%	50%	66%	48%	37%	51%	41%
Snyder	20%	22%	20%	45%	23%	20%	32%	24%
Somerset	41%	39%	42%	55%	40%	31%	46%	40%
Sullivan	38%	39%	45%	56%	39%	32%	46%	39%
Susquehanna	26%	29%	36%	54%	33%	30%	42%	34%
Tioga	21%	23%	27%	51%	27%	27%	41%	33%
Union	20%	22%	21%	46%	25%	25%	35%	28%
Venango	27%	25%	32%	57%	40%	31%	41%	40%
Warren	28%	27%	36%	64%	42%	33%	47%	38%
Wayne	21%	24%	32%	47%	29%	23%	35%	28%
Wyoming	24%	26%	31%	52%	31%	25%	39%	32%
York	47%	45%	41%	64%	39%	30%	42%	35%
Central Totals	**39%**	**36%**	**40%**	**60%**	**41%**	**32%**	**45%**	**38%**
State Totals	**47%**	**43%**	**51%**	**65%**	**52%**	**40%**	**51%**	**46%**
Winning Party	**R**	**R**	**D**	**D**	**D**	**R**	**D**	**R**

	1984	1988	1992	1996	2000	2004	2008	2012
Adams	30%	35%	41%	41%	36%	33%	40%	36%
Bedford	29%	34%	39%	37%	29%	27%	27%	22%
Berks	34%	37%	47%	47%	45%	47%	55%	49%

Blair	34%	38%	41%	41%	36%	34%	38%	33%
Bradford	27%	33%	40%	43%	35%	34%	41%	37%
Cambria	55%	60%	62%	60%	52%	49%	50%	41%
Cameron	33%	34%	41%	42%	36%	33%	40%	35%
Centre	37%	43%	51%	50%	45%	48%	56%	50%
Clarion	35%	41%	46%	46%	36%	35%	39%	32%
Clearfield	39%	46%	51%	48%	39%	40%	44%	36%
Clinton	40%	50%	55%	57%	48%	42%	49%	44%
Columbia	36%	39%	46%	50%	43%	40%	48%	43%
Crawford	39%	43%	48%	47%	41%	42%	45%	40%
Cumberland	30%	34%	38%	40%	36%	36%	43%	41%
Dauphin	38%	42%	45%	48%	45%	46%	55%	53%
Elk	39%	47%	51%	54%	44%	46%	52%	42%
Erie	48%	53%	59%	59%	55%	54%	60%	58%
Forest	36%	44%	53%	52%	38%	39%	43%	39%
Franklin	30%	31%	36%	37%	31%	28%	34%	31%
Fulton	29%	33%	38%	38%	28%	24%	25%	21%
Huntingdon	30%	35%	42%	42%	33%	33%	36%	31%
Indiana	46%	52%	58%	52%	45%	44%	46%	59%
Jefferson	34%	39%	45%	42%	33%	31%	35%	27%
Juniata	34%	37%	40%	41%	31%	28%	32%	27%
Lancaster	24%	29%	33%	35%	32%	34%	44%	40%
Lebanon	28%	33%	36%	39%	36%	33%	40%	36%
Lycoming	32%	35%	39%	39%	35%	32%	38%	33%
McKean	31%	36%	43%	45%	36%	37%	41%	36%
Mercer	50%	53%	59%	57%	51%	49%	50%	48%
Mifflin	36%	37%	44%	44%	34%	29%	33%	26%
Montour	33%	36%	41%	44%	37%	35%	42%	40%
Northumberland	38%	41%	46%	50%	43%	40%	43%	40%
Perry	28%	31%	34%	36%	29%	28%	33%	30%
Pike	28%	32%	42%	45%	44%	41%	48%	44%
Potter	26%	32%	35%	37%	30%	29%	31%	27%
Schuylkill	41%	43%	48%	52%	47%	45%	46%	43%

Snyder	21%	23%	30%	34%	28%	29%	35%	32%
Somerset	42%	45%	47%	46%	37%	35%	37%	28%
Sullivan	33%	38%	43%	44%	36%	37%	40%	36%
Susquehanna	30%	35%	42%	45%	39%	39%	44%	39%
Tioga	28%	34%	38%	40%	32%	31%	36%	32%
Union	26%	29%	36%	36%	33%	36%	43%	38%
Venango	40%	43%	51%	49%	41%	38%	42%	37%
Warren	37%	43%	51%	51%	45%	42%	47%	41%
Wayne	24%	28%	37%	42%	38%	37%	44%	39%
Wyoming	26%	30%	38%	45%	39%	39%	67%	43%
York	31%	34%	43%	43%	37%	36%	43%	39%
Central Totals	**36%**	**40%**	**45%**	**46%**	**40%**	**39%**	**46%**	**42%**
State Totals	**46%**	**49%**	**56%**	**55%**	**52%**	**51%**	**55%**	**53%**
Winning Party	**R**	**R**	**D**	**D**	**D**	**D**	**D**	**D**

1956: EISENHOWER/STEVENSON

By comparison, the 1956 rematch between Eisenhower and Stevenson was rather uneventful, with the incumbent being in firm control throughout the campaign. Of course, Eisenhower was now the incumbent and, during a time of relative prosperity, he naturally had a significant advantage. Also, international events such as the Suez crisis in the Middle East and the Soviet invasion into Hungary dominated the headlines as election day approached. As George I. Bloom, Chairman of the Republican State Committee, proclaimed: "America will never exchange the known for the unknown in these critical times as the Democrat bosses are asking the voters to do. Now that a shooting war has started in the Near East, the people more than ever want the sure, firm hand of Ike on the helm of the government in Washington."

Democrats meanwhile found themselves in the unenviable position of attacking the manner in which the prosperity had been created—never a good sign. Bloom's counterpart, Joseph M. Barr, the Democratic State Chairman, argued that the Republican prosperity was a gossamer sort of prosperity based on overextended credit buying, runaway inflation, and a complete lack of stabilizing economic factors to make good times an enduring part of America's future. As 1952, Democrats also tried to attack the bottom half of the Republican ticket. Even Bloom colorfully admitted, "If any one factor will cause Americans of all political faiths to vote against Mr. Eisenhower, it is the somber shadow of Vice-President Nixon, who is generally regarded as a political footpad in phony angel's wings."

Nationally, Ike improved on his 1952 numbers, increasing his electoral-vote total from 442 to 457. Stevenson, who had captured only nine states in his 1952 run, won only seven in 1956. The only non-Southern state that the Democratic candidate carried in either presidential bid was Missouri, which he took in 1956. Eisenhower improved his performance in Pennsylvania, more than doubling his statewide margin from 269,000 to 603,000 votes (which increased his percentages from 53 to 57 percent statewide). Even increasingly Democratic Philadelphia proved disappointing to Stevenson—his victory margin in the city declined from 160,000 to 124,000.

Stevenson had an even more difficult time in the southwest. In 1952, the Illinois native had carried the region by only 63,000 votes. Four years later, he lost it, by more than 68,000. Eisenhower carried Allegheny County alone by 69,000 votes despite a Democratic registration edge of 161,000. Aside from Nixon's 1972 landslide, this was the only time a Republican presidential candidate has carried the southwest region during the years of this study. No wonder the Democrats have never again nominated a candidate who had lost a previous presidential election.

1960: KENNEDY/NIXON

The 1960 election was anything but typical. The historical implications of John F. Kennedy's election as the first Roman Catholic president have been much discussed. From a Pennsylvania perspective, the political environment in 1960 was also noteworthy. For the first time in the 20th century, the Democratic Party had achieved majority party status in the Commonwealth, albeit by a slight 3,000-vote margin. In an election expected to be close, it is no surprise that Pennsylvania, with its 32 electoral votes, would be a major battleground.

Unlike Truman, who took an active role in trying to determine his successor, the incumbent in 1960, President Eisenhower, was reluctant to assist Vice President Richard M. Nixon. It wasn't until five days before the election that Eisenhower relented and stood side by side with Nixon in a New York City ticker-tape parade. A few days later, on the eve of the election, both Truman and Eisenhower arrived in Pittsburgh within roughly one hour of each other to campaign for their respective party's nominee.

Truman spoke at the traditional Democratic closing rally, held that year at the Northside Carnegie Hall, while Eisenhower held sway across the Allegheny River at the Hilton Hotel. Later in the evening, Eisenhower delivered a speech on network television from the same location. As evidence of how politics has changed, the Republicans had tentatively planned to charge $50 per plate to attend the dinner honoring President Eisenhower. Interest was tepid, however, and what was once a fundraiser soon turned into a financial loser when the ticket price was lowered to $10. Allegheny County Republican Chairman Edward J. Flaherty described the reduction both creatively and diplomatically when he explained that the committee simply wanted to open the dinner to the rank and file.

Kennedy's religion unquestionably played a role in the Pennsylvania outcome. It certainly helped the Democrat in areas containing a large Catholic population, foremost of which was Philadelphia. Kennedy built a 331,000-vote plurality in the city, which his opponent was hard pressed to overtake in the rest of the state. It should be remembered that in 1960, Philadelphia had 57 percent of the region's population compared with only 40 percent today. Philadelphia's importance is underscored by the fact that when Senator John Kerry carried Philadelphia by an enormous 412,000 votes on his way to capturing the state in the 2004 election, the city vote comprised just 8.5 percent of the statewide total. In 1960, Philadelphia accounted for 18 percent of the statewide vote. Thus Kennedy's margin was even more difficult for the GOP to overcome in the rest of the Commonwealth than was Kerry's.

Significantly, Kennedy also ran exceptionally well in much of the Philadelphia suburbs. In heavily Catholic-Delaware County, for instance, Kennedy lost by only 11,000 votes (earning 48 percent of the total vote) even though his party had a 21–79 percent registration disadvantage. Economic issues contributed to Kennedy's support in economically depressed areas such as the anthracite coal regions of Luzerne County, which he won by 32,000 votes (59 percent), despite its Democratic Party registration of just 42 percent. The Kennedy-Johnson ticket also took neighboring Lackawanna County, which also had a high Catholic population, by 30,000 votes, or 62 percent. Combining tough economic conditions with a large Catholic population also helped Kennedy in Allegheny County, where he enjoyed a 108,000-vote margin (57 percent). Those numbers were boosted by a 91,000-vote plurality in the city of Pittsburgh, where Kennedy carried all but 1 of the city's 32 wards.

However, Kennedy's religion cut both ways in Pennsylvania. Five heavily Protestant counties in south-central Pennsylvania—Adams, Berks, Lancaster, Lebanon, and York—combined to give Nixon an 88,000-vote margin. Those areas contain a large number of Amish and Mennonites, many of whom had registered to vote for the first time. York County, in particular, proved disappointing for the Democrats. Despite a 17,200-registration advantage, Kennedy lost to Nixon by 16,700 votes in the county. Kennedy's totals were 4 and 6 percentage points less than Stevenson had managed in his two failed presidential bids.

Undoubtedly, the real story of the 1960 election in this state was Philadelphia, and the big winner was Representative William J. Green, Jr., chairman of the city's Democratic Party. He was credited with helping Kennedy accumulate not only the greatest popular vote in the city's history but also the highest plurality. Newly elected Vice-President Lyndon B. Johnson called it the most amazing thing ever to happen in Philadelphia politics.

1964: JOHNSON–GOLDWATER

Four years later, when Johnson headed the ticket, the outcome was hardly in doubt. His 1.46 million-vote margin of victory (65 percent) was the highest ever recorded in the modern era. So lopsided was the Democratic victory that Johnson's Republican challenger, Senator Barry Goldwater, managed to carry only four of the state's 67 counties (Lebanon, Snyder, Union, and Wayne). Goldwater even failed to carry Lancaster County, losing it by slightly less than 800 votes. In the 47 counties that make up the Pennsylvania "T," Johnson received 60 percent of the vote, just five points below his statewide total. No other Democratic candidate for president has come close to carrying the region since then (President Clinton's 45 percent in 1992 ranks second). Johnson was also the only Democrat presidential candidate in the past 54 years to carry Chester County, thus making 1964 the only time the Democrats made a clean sweep of the Philadelphia suburbs. Overall, Johnson racked up a 43,000-vote plurality in the four counties.

In Philadelphia itself, the other end of Pennsylvania's political spectrum, it's no surprise that the Johnson and Humphrey ticket smashed all types of records. They amassed a 431,000-vote margin, which at the time was both the greatest popular and the highest plurality in the city's history. Within Philadelphia, the Goldwater defeat was so complete that the Republican Party would end up with only 1 of the city's 35 seats in the state house.

After the election, Republican Senator Hugh Scott, who barely held onto his seat in the face of the landslide, charged that the Goldwater campaign was the worst managed in American history. It would be hard to argue with his analysis. Scott was much less prophetic when he stated in the same radio interview that although the GOP was temporarily leaderless, someone would emerge—though assuring the audience that it would not be Richard M Nixon.

1968: NIXON/HUMPHREY

Nixon returned of course, staging one of the most remarkable comebacks in American political history when he defeated Vice President Hubert H. Humphrey in 1968. After Nixon had lost the presidential election in 1960 and the race for Governor of California in 1962, most had written him off. Nixon himself famously scolded the press after his 1962 defeat, saying that they wouldn't have him to kick around anymore. It's difficult to imagine a candidate who had lost two previous races of such magnitude ever receiving another presidential nomination. If Humphrey had begun his 1972 campaign sooner, perhaps he himself could have done it in 1972, and Al Gore would certainly have been tough to displace as his party's nominee in 2004 if he had decided to run. In any event, no other candidate since has been nominated by his party after a defeat—and again, Nixon was coming off not one but two straight losses.

In Pennsylvania, the 1968 campaign was marked by several unusual circumstances. First, the Republican Party had become the majority party for the first time since 1960. Although the Republican advantage may have been only 60,000, it is significant because the Republicans have not been in majority ever since. By 1970, they would again find themselves on the minority side, by 20,000 registered voters. In the 1930s and 1940s, Republicans Herbert Hoover and Thomas Dewey had carried the state in a losing effort, but in 1968 the situation was reversed. Nixon became the first Republican ever to win the presidency while losing Pennsylvania. That this occurred in what had been one of the most Republican states in the union just a short time earlier is evidence that politics in the Commonwealth had changed.

In contrast to 1960, this time Nixon was on the victorious end of an election-night cliffhanger in 1968. In fact, the contest was almost as close as the one eight years earlier: the 1968 results were not known until the morning after the election, when the hotly contested states of California, Illinois, and Ohio were finally called for the Republican. Nationwide, Nixon received 43.4 percent of the vote, compared with 42.3 percent for Humphrey. Nixon's electoral vote total was 301, two shy of Kennedy's in 1960. Unlike the 1960 contest, in which the third-party candidacy of Harry Byrd managed just 15 electoral votes, the candidacy of Alabama Governor George Wallace in 1968 was a much more serious, much more formidable threat.

Governor Wallace, a states-rights Democrat, received 12.9 percent of the popular vote and 46 electors (all from the deep South). He had considerable support in the Keystone State, where he received 8 percent of the vote. Although Wallace may have prevented Humphrey from carrying the South and hence the election, he took votes from both candidates in Pennsylvania, and Humphrey prevailed by 169,000 votes. Humphrey's victory was due largely to the support he received in Philadelphia, which he carried by 271,000 votes.

Governor Raymond P. Shafer cited two main reasons why Nixon was unable to carry the state. First, Wallace drew support mainly from normally Republican voters. Whether this is true remains a question. Before the election, it was presumed that Wallace would cut into his fellow Democrat's vote in blue-collar areas across the state, specifically in heavily ethnic areas such as South Philadelphia. Second, Shafer suggested that the Philadelphia suburbs also underperformed for the Republican ticket. In fact, however, Nixon's numbers in the suburbs were identical with those he had achieved against Kennedy in 1960, when he took 57 percent of the two-party vote.

The numbers in much of the rest of the state were also comparable to those of 1960. In the southwest, Humphrey ran even slightly stronger than Kennedy had, carrying the region by 185,000 votes. His percentage of the two-party vote was 57 percent, 2 points higher than Kennedy's. In the northeast region, Humphrey also surpassed Kennedy slightly, taking 55 percent of the two-party share. In central Pennsylvania, Humphrey held Nixon's advantage to 59 percent, which was 1 point less than Nixon's central Pennsylvania total in 1960.

1972: NIXON/MCGOVERN

The 1972 election, in which President Nixon squared off against the Democratic nominee, Senator George McGovern of South Dakota, had no suspense or confusion, in either the state or the nation. It wasn't the largest landslide of the 20th century (Franklin Roosevelt in 1936 and Lyndon Johnson in 1972 both received a higher percentage of the vote and Ronald Reagan won more electors in 1984), but it certainly was a landslide. The McGovern–Sargent Shriver ticket managed to win only Massachusetts and the District of Columbia and was on the losing side of a 60–37-percent margin.

Not surprisingly, the incumbent easily carried Pennsylvania—by slightly less than a million votes, for a 60–40 percent victory. McGovern won one county, Philadelphia. Even there, the Democrat's margin was only 88,000 votes, the party's smallest in the past 50 years. Nixon ran particularly strong among blue-collar white voters—particularly Catholics—both in Philadelphia and elsewhere in the state. Democratic Mayor Frank Rizzo, an outspoken supporter of Nixon, promised that he would keep McGovern's numbers below the 100,000-vote mark that the Democrat would need if he had any hopes of winning statewide. It wouldn't have mattered, because the Nixon victory was so complete beyond the city limits. For instance, the Republican won 66 percent of the suburban Philadelphia vote and won by 247,000 votes.

Allegheny County went for the GOP—the most recent time that this has happened—and Nixon won the southwest region as a whole, 57–43 percent. Nixon did even better in the ethnic swing areas of northeastern Pennsylvania, where he received 60 percent of the vote. Not surprisingly, McGovern was overwhelmed in central Pennsylvania, where he got just 32 percent of the vote. The nadir of the Democrat's effort in Pennsylvania occurred in Snyder County, where he mustered a mere 20 percent of the vote.

One aspect of Nixon's victory caused many Republican leaders to scratch their heads. Despite Nixon's huge victory, his coattails were virtually nonexistent. The Democrats swept the two statewide row office races contested and maintained control of the State Senate and a majority of the congressional delegation. The only direct impact in the Commonwealth was a switch in control of the State House to the Republicans.

Nationally, the results were similar, as the Democrats maintained solid control of both branches of Congress. Throughout the 1972 campaign, Nixon had avoided identification with GOP candidates in congressional and state races, for fear of alienating traditional Democratic blue-collar and ethnic voters. This bipartisan, personal approach angered many party officials, who felt that Nixon could have unleashed a Republican tide. Even the party's national chairman, Senator Robert Dole, quipped that although the election results were a great personal salute to the President, they could hardly be called a victory for the party.

1976: CARTER/FORD

By 1976, Nixon had resigned in the aftermath of the Watergate scandal and Gerald R. Ford, who had replaced Vice-President Spiro Agnew, was squaring off against Governor Jimmy Carter of Georgia. After the 1972 mismatch, the nation was again engaged in a highly competitive contest, and the battle for Pennsylvania was front and center. Down the stretch, both candidates spent three of their last nine days campaigning in the state. Both vice presidential candidates, Senator Robert Dole and Senator Walter F. Mondale, also traveled throughout the Commonwealth in the closing days. Pennsylvania was, as one of Carter's chief officials called it, the gateway to the northeast.

In an election virtually split right down the Mississippi River, a near sweep of the eastern United States was essential to Carter's victory, as he carried only three states in the west (Texas, Oregon, and Hawaii). Carter captured 297 electoral votes in defeating Ford, 50.1 to 48 percent. The results were tight in Pennsylvania as well, with Carter winning by 123,000 votes, a 2-point victory.

An important key to Carter's win was the support he received from Mayor Rizzo of Philadelphia. The powerful Democratic leader had rebuffed McGovern four years earlier, but this time his city machine would deliver a huge plurality. Nevertheless, the relationship was tested several days before the election, when Rizzo refused to appear with Carter at a downtown rally. The reason cited was that the mayor would have had to share the stage with some city leaders who had recently led an unsuccessful recall drive against him.

Rizzo worked his troops on election day, however, delivering a 256,000-vote margin for Carter, which allowed him to claim credit for the Democratic victory. The headline of the *Philadelphia Inquirer* the next day said it all: "Rizzo Role: Kingmaker." Rizzo's critics argued that the numbers fell short of those that the city provided for Democrats in 1960 and 1968. Additionally, as much as 40 percent of Carter's vote came from black voters, a constituency Rizzo had little control over. The fact remained, however, that the President-elect himself made sure on election night to thank the Philadelphia mayor personally for his efforts.

Many of Ford's campaign strategists thought that other factors had a greater impact on their defeat. Specifically, they cited their candidate's inability to ring up the numbers they needed in the Philadelphia suburbs and the staunchly Republican rural areas of the state. Yet although Ford simply got too few votes, he fared quite well in the Philadelphia suburbs. He won the four suburban Philadelphia counties by 105,000 votes, achieving a 56–44 percent advantage. This was slightly more than the Republican vote in the two "normal" elections of 1960 and 1968. Only Bucks County, where Ford received only 52 percent of the vote, could be considered truly disappointing for the Republicans. Otherwise, however, the GOP strategists were correct in their assessment. Apparently Carter's roots as a peanut farmer paid political dividends in some rural areas of central Pennsylvania: He held Ford's margin in the 47 counties of the "T" to 154,000 votes, a 10-point advantage. This was in stark contrast to the 1960 and 1968 elections, in which Nixon doubled that figure.

Ford's totals in northeastern Pennsylvania were consistent with those of his predecessor. He lost by 40,000 votes in the six counties, slightly worse than Nixon in 1960 but slightly better than 1968. In the traditionally Democratic southwest, the incumbent Republican President was able to hold down Carter's numbers, reaching 46 percent—far better than Nixon had achieved in his two tight contests. Carter received a plurality of only 88,000 votes in the southwest, compared with Kennedy's 152,000 and Humphrey's 185,000.

In retrospect, a variety of factors caused Ford's defeat, but more than anything else it was primarily due to his lackluster showing in central Pennsylvania. He may not have won the state if he had run only as well in the region as Nixon had in 1968, but matching Nixon's 1960 numbers in central Pennsylvania would probably have won the state for Ford.

By 1976, the Democratic Party candidate should have carried the state. What had been a strong Republican state just two decades earlier had changed considerably. This was virtually the high point of Democratic Party power in the Commonwealth (the Democrats' actual peak in registered voters came two years later, in 1978). They were unquestionably the majority party in the state, enjoying a registration advantage of 765,000 voters. In any competitive election, they would have been expected to prevail. The 1976 contest was this type of "normal" election, and the party delivered. Four years later, however, President Jimmy Carter endured a reelection campaign that followed a totally different pattern entirely.

1980: REAGAN/CARTER

Somewhat forgotten about the 1980 race is that heading into the final stretch it appeared that the nation was heading for another election-night cliffhanger. Despite having to fight off a tough primary challenge from Senator Edward M. Kennedy of Massachusetts, a rocky economy, and a hostage crisis of American diplomats in Iran, polls indicated a tight battle between President Carter and his Republican challenger, the former governor of California, Ronald Reagan.

Momentum appeared to be with Carter as the campaign came to a close. A *Newsweek* poll taken one week before the election found the race a tossup, with Reagan ahead only 44 to 43 percent. Then two events coincided dramatically to reshape the contest. First was an announcement of demands by the Iranian government ten days before the election, making it clear that there would be no release of the hostages before election day. Second, after weeks of pressing for a two-person debate (at the exclusion of moderate Republican Congressman John Anderson of Illinois), Carter finally got what he wanted. The strategy backfired when the Democratic incumbent was viewed as being soundly beaten in their only debate. Reagan's classic line—"Are you better off now than you were four years ago?"—has been appropriated by many a challenger since.

After all the votes were counted, Reagan had a landslide. He captured 50.8 percent of the vote to Carter's 41 percent. Third-party candidate Anderson trailed with 6.6 percent. The incumbent President won only six states and the District of Columbia. But that was only the beginning of a nightmarish evening for the Democrats. The Republicans captured control of the United States Senate for the first time since the 1950s. They also cut far enough into the Democrats' advantage in the House of Representatives to give the new president a working majority in the House as well. The 1980s and the Reagan Era had been launched.

The Democrats did poorly in Pennsylvania, too. Reagan carried the state by more than 327,000 votes, defeating the incumbent by approximately 7 percentage points. The numbers across the Commonwealth were like those that Eisenhower had twice put together in the 1950s. Although the Reagan victory was not quite a landslide, it had the net effect of one. In fact, Reagan provided the coattails both nationally and in the state that Republicans had hoped Nixon would deliver eight years earlier, when he won by a much larger margin than Reagan did.

1984: REAGAN/MONDALE

Reagan's success continued four years later in a race that lacked any significant suspense. His 1984 opponent, former Vice-President Walter Mondale, failed to generate excitement beyond the traditional Democratic core of unions, racial minorities, and women's rights groups. Except for a brief bounce after the Democratic National Convention that moved Mondale into a virtual tie with the president, the outcome was really never in doubt.

Even Mondale's selection of Congresswoman Geraldine Ferraro of New York, the first woman ever to run on a presidential ticket, backfired. It energized some of the party faithful and provided at least a degree of optimism for Democrats, but almost immediately, allegations concerning her husband's business interests stopped any momentum dead in its tracks. An NBC News exit poll on election night indicated that only 16 percent of voters said that the selection of Ferraro made them more likely to support the Democratic ticket, compared with 26 percent who were less likely.

Reagan's appeal was nationwide—he carried every state except Mondale's Minnesota and the District of Columbia. He carried Pennsylvania by 356,000, slightly better than his margin four years earlier. The 54–47 spread, however, was about half that of his national spread and certainly not a landslide. In fact, Pennsylvania had been viewed as a virtual tossup in the weeks before election day. Pennsylvania, which had unemployment levels much higher than the national average, would seem to have presented the Democrat with a sympathetic audience. That Mondale visited the state 16 times during the campaign helped make the state one of the more competitive ones in the nation.

Philadelphia provided the Democratic challenger with a 234,000-vote advantage over Reagan, a 57,000-vote increase over Carter's effort in 1980. Reagan, however, increased his margins in the southeast suburbs, which he took by a 254,000-vote plurality—24,000 more than in his election of 1980. Reagan also improved his numbers by 2 and 3 percent in the northeast and central regions, respectively. In southwestern Pennsylvania, though, Mondale ran 151,000 votes ahead of the incumbent, a 12-point margin. Four years earlier, Reagan had run only 61,000 votes behind Carter. Allegheny County showed the most significant difference. The former vice president carried the county by 88,000 votes, compared with Carter's 26,000.

Campaigning on the "Morning in America" theme, the Republican ran a personal campaign similar to Nixon's 1972 effort, essentially devoid of issue substance. With the nation at peace abroad and an economic recovery well underway at home, Reagan had the luxury of running a textbook incumbency campaign. As impressive as it was, however, the triumph was more a personal victory for the president than it was for his party. It certainly didn't usher in an electoral realignment, as he and some of his supporters had predicted. Rather, the Republicans lost two Senate seats, and although they picked up a few congressional seats, the gain didn't make up for what they had lost in the midterm election two years earlier and was far short of approaching a majority.

Even Congressman Robert H. Michel, the GOP House leader from Illinois, stated afterwards that he was concerned his party didn't pick up twice the number of seats that it had. For the Democrats, who had lost four of the last five campaigns, that was probably a small consolation. Once again, it was back to the drawing board, with the usual promises of reevaluation. "The Democratic Party used to be more than the sum of its parts," said one Mondale supporter. "Now it is less."

1988: BUSH/DUKAKIS

Some Democrats thought that their problem was having a northern liberal at the top of the ticket. But memories were short: In 1988, the party nominated another one, Massachusetts Governor Michael Dukakis. This time, however, at least the Democrats made an effort to balance the ticket, both regionally and ideologically, with the selection of Texas Senator Lloyd Bentsen for vice president. By the time the campaign was over, however, many felt that the order should have been reversed. The Mondale campaign may have floundered, but it never really had a chance given the political atmosphere in 1984. But against Vice President George H. Bush in 1988—a candidate who had his own share of problems—Democrats did have a chance. That was at least until the Dukakis team proceeded to run arguably the worst campaign in modern presidential history.

In Pennsylvania, for the first time since Adlai Stevenson in 1952, a candidate carried the southeast region while losing statewide. In Philadelphia, Dukakis registered a 231,000-vote margin, earning 67 percent of the vote among the five counties. Low turnout in the city, however, negated some of the impact. For instance, Dukakis ran 2 points better than Mondale had but received 52,000 less votes overall. In the suburbs, Bush carried the four counties impressively, although the 206,000-vote margin was slightly short of Reagan's two efforts.

Southwestern Pennsylvania, which continued to be beset by tough economic conditions, proved fertile ground for the Democratic message. Dukakis carried every county in the region except Butler, for an overall 200,000-vote advantage, which was a sharp improvement from party efforts four years earlier. The Democrat registered at least 60 percent of the vote in five of the nine counties, including the largest, Allegheny, where he defeated Bush by 118,000. However, in northeastern Pennsylvania, which also could have been ripe for the Democrats, Dukakis floundered. He lost the region by 22,000 votes and 6 percentage points, carrying only Lackawanna County. Bush carried the normally competitive Lehigh County by 14 percentage points. Any hope Dukakis may have had of carrying Pennsylvania faded with his weak performance in Lehigh. As expected, Bush rolled to a 307,000-vote, 20-point victory in central Pennsylvania. Only Cambria, Clinton (by just 24 votes), and Erie Counties eluded him.

The statewide numbers spelled out a 105,000-vote victory for the vice president, a slim 2-point margin. A higher turnout in Philadelphia and a slightly stronger showing in the rest of the state would have given Dukakis the state's 25 electoral votes. Delaware County Republican leader Thomas Judge, who served as Bush's campaign chair in the state, had predicted that the key to the election was the Philadelphia suburbs. "If we are able to get that 45,000 plurality [in Delaware County]," he said, "we would win the state." He was correct, as the county's 52,000-vote margin proved to be enough for George Bush. Delaware County and its fellow suburban Philadelphia counties would hold the key to the next four presidential elections in Pennsylvania—and this time it would be bad news for the GOP.

1992: CLINTON/BUSH

A year and a half before Bush's 1992 reelection campaign, it certainly didn't appear that he would face any trouble. In the aftermath of the Persian Gulf War, his job approval numbers ranged between 80 and 90 percent—among the highest a president had ever recorded since polling was developed. Many Democrats in Congress, particularly those who had voted against giving the president the authority to go to war, felt endangered. But in one of the biggest strategic errors that a modern president ever made, Bush appeared hesitant to use the considerable clout he had won. Rather than spending his political capital to build a domestic policy agenda, he opted to maintain a status quo. That may have been fine under normal conditions, but as 1991 came to a close, an economic recession had suddenly placed voters in a much more irritable mood.

Problems began to appear for Bush in the spring of 1992, when he was criticized from both sides of the political spectrum—and from the middle as well. Conservative columnist and former Nixon speechwriter Patrick J. Buchanan began hammering him from the right. A stinging speech that Buchanan made later in the year, at the Republican National Convention, largely blunted any bounce that the president might have hoped to pick up when the enclave dispersed. Additionally, a 62-year-old Texas billionaire named H. Ross Perot came at Bush from the middle, catching the public's fancy when he began to express his own presidential ambitions. Although his peculiar behavior may have prevented him from becoming a truly serious presidential threat, he was able to stir up even more anger toward the political system and those in power. From the left, Democrats took aim in their own primary battles. When it was over, they had as their nominee the 46-year-old governor of Arkansas, Bill Clinton. Clinton possessed a number of personal liabilities (which Bush would repeatedly flail at) that would have sunken most candidates, but he also exhibited an extraordinary display of campaign ability.

In early July, Clinton's selection of another young southerner, Senator Al Gore, Jr., on the eve of the Democratic National Convention in New York, and Perot's withdrawal from the race during convention week itself, irrevocably changed the dynamics of the race. Clinton, who had struggled in late spring over questions about draft dodging and womanizing, emerged as the clear alternative to the president. By the time the Democrats departed New York and headed home, their candidate had surged to a 20-point lead. Unlike Michael Dukakis, who also held a commanding midsummer lead, Clinton had the political skills to keep this one from slipping away. Even Perot's reentrance into the race months later only underscored Clinton's basic theme: that the country was headed in the wrong direction. Although President Bush had his own set of political strengths, his campaign was hard pressed to argue that he symbolized change.

Any hopes that the Bush campaign may have harbored for pulling off a surprise victory didn't even include Pennsylvania. The media as well as both camps had already written off Bush's chances in the Keystone state. Rather, Bush would need to run the table in states such as Michigan, Ohio, Wisconsin, and even New Jersey, all of which offered him a better opportunity. On election day, more voters turned out across the nation to cast their ballots than at any time since 1960. The 55 percent mark reversed a decline that had continued for decades.

Clinton ran slightly ahead of his national numbers in Pennsylvania, defeating Bush by an impressive 448,000 votes. The challenger took slightly more than 45 percent of the state vote (2 points higher than his national total), to Bush's 36 percent (2 points lower than nationally). Ross Perot received a little over 18 percent of the vote, only slightly below his national number. Although Perot won no electoral votes, his would stand as the second-highest third-party bid of the century, trailing only Theodore Roosevelt's Bull Moose effort in 1912, which netted 27 percent of the popular vote. Measuring just the share of the two-party vote, Clinton held a 56–44 percent advantage.

As expected, the Democrat ran strong in Philadelphia, building a 302,000-vote plurality. In the suburbs, a trend would emerge that would more than anything determine how Pennsylvania's electoral votes would be distributed in future elections. Clinton narrowly won three of the four traditionally Republican suburbs outside Philadelphia (all except Chester), just enough to carry the region, by 2,400 votes. Ever afterward, the GOP would be forced to find ways to bring those suburbanites back.

With these suburban defections, the only hope Republicans had of winning was to make up numbers in the traditionally Democratic but more socially conservative southwestern and northeastern areas. But Clinton also ran strong in his party's base, taking the economically depressed southwest by 245,000 votes, 63 percent of the two-party vote, which was higher than any Democrat since Lyndon Johnson in 1964. Only Butler County landed in the GOP column and only by 1,000 votes. Clinton ran well in the northeast as well, winning the region by 32,000 votes, and again losing only one county, Monroe. Clinton's 54 percent of the two-party vote was the best Democratic effort in the northeast since Jimmy Carter achieved the same mark in 1976.

Even central Pennsylvania underperformed for the Bush campaign in 1992. While he easily carried the region, he did so by only 132,000 votes, far short of what his party ordinarily needs to win statewide. In fact, Clinton won 11 counties in the region: Cambria, Centre, Clearfield, Clinton, Elk, Erie, Forest, Indiana, Mercer, Venango, and Warren. Clinton's 45 percent in central Pennsylvania against an incumbent Republican president was an exceptional performance—and, again, the best for a Democrat since 1964.

1996: CLINTON/DOLE

While the 1996 presidential campaign may not have been much fun for Republicans, it at least contained considerable excitement and color. By contrast, the 1996 campaign between the incumbent president, Bill Clinton, and veteran Republican Senator Robert Dole was hardly memorable for anything. That's fine for the party in power but bad news if you're trying to wrest control. Although Dole was widely respected by most voters in both parties, there was a general feeling that he had been selected as the nominee mostly because it was his turn. Even Ross Perot's candidacy this time seemed warmed over, offering little enthusiasm to its supporters. Not surprisingly, the national turnout dropped by 5 percentage points.

Another important change that had occurred since the previous campaign was that the Republican Party, owing to its huge victory in the midterm elections of 1994, now commanded a majority in both houses of Congress for the first time since the 1950s. Clinton used that to his political advantage, however, successfully portraying the GOP leadership—Dole in the Senate and Newt Gingrich, Speaker of the House—in an unfavorable light. That was especially true during the previous winter, when the majority of voters held the Republicans responsible for shutting down the federal government during a budget dispute with the president.

Dole's image was particularly damaged in the minds of women voters. While a "gender gap" had been developing as far back as the 1980 campaign, this time it blew the election wide open. Exit polls revealed that the two candidates fared nearly the same among men, with Dole, in fact, slightly ahead. Among women, however, Clinton enjoyed an advantage of approximately 15 percentage points, the largest on record. The result was a comfortable reelection for the president, nationally and in Pennsylvania.

The numbers Clinton posted were higher throughout much of the state than in his 1992 victory, though with one notable exception. Statewide and nationally, Clinton received just short of 50 percent of the overall vote (55 percent of the two-party share in the state), while Dole ended up with 40 percent. Perot's numbers were half of what they were in his previous effort, both statewide and nationally. The president ran slightly stronger in Philadelphia this time, amassing a 328,000-vote advantage. He also improved in the suburbs, winning the same three counties as in 1992 (Bucks, Delaware, and Montgomery), but by much higher margins. His plurality was 42,000 among the four counties.

Clinton slightly improved his numbers in central Pennsylvania, losing the region by only 125,000 votes this time. He carried 10 counties, adding Columbia and Schuylkill, while dropping Centre, Clearfield, and Venango, from his previous list. In both 1992 and 1996, Clinton's poorest showing in the entire state was in central Pennsylvania's Snyder County. Clinton also improved his performance in the northeast, taking the same five counties in building up a 49,000-vote edge. Lackawanna County, where he defeated Bush by more than 19,000 votes, gave the Democrat a 26-point margin.

In southwestern Pennsylvania, Dole lost handily, but he cut significantly into the Democratic base. Although he lost the region by 121,000 votes in 1992, that figure was half of what President Bush had lost by. Clinton experienced a drop in all nine southwestern counties, most noticeably in populated Westmoreland, which he won by 1,600 votes, a decline of 9 percentage points from 1992. In fact, Clinton ran 79,000 votes behind Michael Dukakis's numbers from 1988 and 30,000 votes behind Walter Mondale's 1984 total.

Thus, while Democrats were making major inroads among the more moderate Republican voters in the Philadelphia suburbs, they were seeing their support frayed among their more socially conservative supporters in southwestern Pennsylvania. It was an opening that the Republican Party would seek exploit in future presidential elections.

2000: BUSH/GORE

When most people think of the 2000 election, the events that unfolded in Florida come to mind first. It's hard to recall that in the days before the election, it wasn't just the Sunshine State but also Pennsylvania and Michigan that were thought to hold the key to the race. It's also easy to forget that although the post-election battle for Florida's 25 electoral votes would grip the nation's attention, the campaign itself was far from memorable. It was a rather dull contest between Vice President Al Gore and Republican Governor George W. Bush of Texas.

The vice president had clearly sought to distance himself from his boss, who had been forced to survive an impeachment proceeding. In the post-election analysis, however, most observers would regard that stance as a major mistake. Throughout the campaign, Gore had to battle both a reputation for blandness and a tendency to exaggerate. Bush, who aspired to become the first son of a former president since John Quincy Adams in 1824 to be elected president, had to deal with the image that he possessed little more than a family pedigree. The Texas governor had been accused of not being serious enough for the office, particularly when it came to his knowledge on world affairs. The truth was that the majority of the public wasn't enamored of either candidate. In an environment of general peace and prosperity, both ran fairly issueless campaigns. It's no wonder that voter turnout didn't even reached 49 percent, the lowest in modern times.

In view of how close the contest was nationally, it's surprising how large Al Gore's victory was in Pennsylvania. Although the state was considered a toss-up as voters headed to the polls, the vice president carried it by 205,000 votes, a 4-point victory. Green Party candidate Ralph Nader received 2 percent of the vote. In fact, Bush lost the state by double the amount Michael Dukakis had in 1988. Nevertheless, based on the results in Florida, George Bush would become the first president to win the electoral vote while losing the popular vote since Benjamin Harrison in 1888.

Once again, southeastern Pennsylvania proved to be the difference. Gore received numbers in Philadelphia that were unprecedented in modern presidential politics, reaping a 348,000-vote advantage over the Republican. For Bush, being able to attract only 18 percent of the two-party vote in the state's largest city made winning the state's 23 electoral votes a daunting task. Losing the suburban vote once again, however, made it next to impossible. In fact, Gore's 54,000-vote margin in these four counties was greater than Bill Clinton's two totals combined. Delaware and Montgomery counties were particularly troublesome for the Bush campaign, where it dropped them by 12 and 10 points, respectively. Only Chester County, which provided the Texas governor with a 10-point advantage, remained firmly loyal to the GOP.

The results in the northeast were quite consistent with the previous two presidential elections. In fact, Gore's 39,000-vote victory in the region was 7,000 votes more than Clinton's in 1992. Across the area, the results also closely matched previous campaigns, with Monroe County the only one to support Bush. In central Pennsylvania, however, Bush pushed back the gains Clinton had previously made, taking it by 324,000 votes, a stronger showing than his father had achieved in this region when Bush senior carried the state in 1988. Only Cambria, Erie, and Mercer counties failed to fall into the GOP column in 2000.

More significantly, however, the Bush campaign was again able to increase its level of support in the southwest. The Republican won huge margins in Armstrong and Butler counties and even added Westmoreland County (by 6 percent), which after Allegheny County is the second-most populous in the region. A decent showing by Gore in Allegheny was all that prevented Bush from carrying the southwest. Even here, however, Gore numbers were only slightly better than Mondale's were in 1984. In the final analysis, Pennsylvania's voters were not the deciding factor in this presidential contest.

For the first time since 1968, the state had thrown its electoral weight behind the defeated candidate. After one of the most controversial and bitter presidential campaign in American history, the race for the White House 2004 would begin immediately.

2004: BUSH/KERRY

Falling three electoral votes short of victory, Al Gore surprised many in December 2002, when he announced that he would not seek the presidency again. That opened the field for the Democrats, and after a short, front-loaded primary season, the party settled on a candidate, Massachusetts Senator John Kerry, who gave them what they believed was their best chance at victory. In contrast to 2000, however, the issues were serious this time, particularly because of the horrifying events of September 11, 2001.

Although the 2004 race appeared to be shaping up as close as the previous one nationally, polls showed Kerry maintaining a close but consistent lead in Pennsylvania. The contest also had a local flavor, in that the Democrat was married to Fox Chapel resident Teresa Heinz Kerry, widow of Senator John Heinz, who had died in a tragic 1991 airplane crash.

Despite the 42 trips that President Bush made to the state, the Republicans came up short in Pennsylvania for the fourth straight time. The key to the Democratic victory—southeast voters—was even clearer this time. In an election that recorded the largest turnout both nationally and statewide since the Kennedy-Nixon race in 1960, Senator Kerry carried Philadelphia by an enormous 412,000 votes. In percentage terms, the margin was just short of Democratic efforts in the two previous elections, but it surpassed all others because of the raw vote totals.

Given those figures, the Republicans needed a return to their pre–1992 presidential voting in the suburbs to have a realistic chance at carrying the state. Again they would be terribly disappointed. Not only did Kerry carry the four-county region, where the GOP enjoyed a 243,000-vote registration edge, he would carry it by 87,000 votes, easily surpassing what Al Gore had accomplished in 2000. Coming out of the southeast, the Democrat built what proved to be an insurmountable 499,000-vote advantage.

To carry the state, Bush would have needed a gigantic turnout in the rural areas of the state combined with outright victories in the traditionally Democratic southwest and northeast regions. He achieved the first, and came closer than the Democrats would have preferred in the second. Although the president's share of the two-party vote in central Pennsylvania increased by only 1 percentage point, to 61 percent, the high turnout boosted his numbers just as high turnout boosted Kerry's numbers in Philadelphia. Across the 47 counties in the "T," Kerry carried just 1 county, Erie. Cambria County went Republican for the first time since the 1972 McGovern debacle. President Bush amassed a 428,000-vote advantage in the region, a figure so high that it almost balanced out the southeast.

But the president needed to do more than limit Kerry's advantage in the southwest and northeast; he needed to carry those regions. In the northeast, he limited Kerry's advantage to just 24,000 votes, a 4-point differential. Only a 15,000-vote advantage in Lackawanna County prevented Bush from capturing the region. Elsewhere, only a few thousand votes in counties such as Lehigh, Luzerne, and Northampton separated the two candidates. Monroe County again went Republican—this time by four votes. Overall, it was a good showing in the region for Bush and would usually have been enough for a Republican to win statewide.

In southwestern Pennsylvania, Bush ran even better, carrying five of the region's nine counties. Westmoreland County gave him a 22,000-vote edge, while Greene and Lawrence counties went with the GOP for the first time since the 1972 Nixon landslide. In two other counties combined, Beaver and Washington, only 2,782 votes separated the two candidates. Only Fayette and Allegheny counties were relatively comfortable for the Democrat, who had ties to the area by virtue of his spouse. If not for Kerry's 97,000-vote plurality in Allegheny County, Bush would have carried the region easily and perhaps would have won the state as well.

Pennsylvania's status as a bellwether state, however, was dealt another blow. For the second straight time, the state had given its electoral votes to a defeated presidential candidate (although it had, of course, supported the popular-vote winner in 2000). The reason for the Democratic triumph statewide was easy to uncover: Republicans in southeastern Pennsylvania's four suburban counties received either the credit or the blame, depending on one's perspective.

Democratic declines in the southwest, however, muted any talk of an electoral lock for their party in the Keystone State. Ironically, their more liberal stances on social issues have helped Democrats attract converts in the southeastern suburbs but have begun to alienate some members of their political base in the southwest and northeast. The story of the 2004 election in Pennsylvania may have been those southeast suburbs, but Democrats are also fully aware that they need to reverse the trends some of these other areas of the state if they are going to continue to hold the edge.

2008: OBAMA/MCCAIN

Pennsylvania's role in the presidential election of 2008 will probably be best remembered not for the general election itself, but rather for the Democratic Primary battle that took place in the spring. For years, political observers in the state have lamented the fact that Pennsylvania's rather late primary date had made it a nonfactor in the presidential nominating process. Governor Rendell even attempted to have it moved it up on the schedule, but change is never easy in the Commonwealth and that effort went nowhere. You would need to go as far back as 1980, when Senator Edward Kennedy challenged President Jimmy Carter, that the state truly had an impact in the selection of one of the party's presidential nominees. Though Kennedy won the primary that year, it fell short of the convincing margin that he needed to overtake the incumbent president.

However, with a seven week gap since last the contest was held in Mississippi, the nation watched as Senator Barack Obama and Senator Hillary Clinton fought tooth and nail for the support of Pennsylvania voters all the way to primary day on April 22. With Arizona Senator John McCain already clinching the Republican nomination, the Democrats had the state all to themselves. Holding a slight lead of over 100 delegates heading into Pennsylvania, Obama may have had the momentum but the former First Lady, led by Governor Rendell and Philadelphia Mayor Michael Nutter, had the organizational muscle to make the state uncomfortable for the front-runner from Illinois.

The whole campaign in the state got off to a rollicking start when video emerged in late March that showed Obama's former pastor from Chicago, the Reverend Jeremiah Wright, making highly incendiary racial remarks from the pulpit. While Obama originally denounced the statements in question (though not Wright as a person), for many it didn't go far enough, and his opponents even took to speculating on whether Obama was sitting in the pew on the days the speeches occurred. Eventually, the issue quieted down, especially after May, when Obama officially left the church, though the Republicans would try to reignite the spark in the fall.

While neither candidate failed to miss an opportunity to bash President Bush, who's approval ratings around this time into his sixth year in office were dismal, they both aimed most of their fire at each other. The nastiness became so palpable that many wondered aloud if Clinton, now a Senator from New York, might be willing to suspend her campaign and step away from the fight. For them, the real winner in all of this was McCain.

However, the reverse proved to be true. The intensity and enthusiasm, while potentially damaging to whomever eventually took the nomination, injected a shot of adrenalin into Democratic registration efforts. More than 50,000 voters in Philadelphia joined the party, and while many were new voters, about 5,000 were also Republicans, and even more were formally unaffiliated. Likewise in Allegheny County, the Democrats enhanced their margin by about 28,000 voters. However, the change in the southeast suburbs gained the largest headlines, as for the first time in decades Democrats overtook registered Republicans in Bucks and Montgomery counties and, when grouped together with the unaffiliated, now outnumbered their rivals in Chester and Delaware counties as well.

Of course, some of these voters were already voting Democratic at the presidential level, and probably voted for John Kerry in the previous election. Studies have shown that individuals change their voting patterns before they change their registration, and many times it is a watershed event which finally prompts the move to the other party. This is what occurred in Philadelphia after the election of Joe Clark in 1951. This primary was just such an event. Statewide, the Democratic advantage over the Republicans ballooned from

638,000 in November, 2007, to over 1,014,000 by the April primary, an increase overall of slightly over 375,000 more voters.

A geographic and cultural divide was also present in the contest with Obama running strong among the younger, better educated, liberal and black voters who dominate Philadelphia, while western Pennsylvania and areas in the northeast, were prototypical Clinton strongholds, with more of an ethnic, blue-collar mix of voters. Clinton also continually reminded voters of her Pennsylvania roots, as her father, Hugh Rodham, was a Scranton native.

However, with less than two weeks to go, and polls showing Obama closing the gap, the Illinois senator would make what might be considered the biggest mistake of his political career. Speaking at a fundraiser in San Francisco, California, while he was commenting on how political leaders had abandoned the interests of working-class folks, Obama infamously stated, "And it's not surprising, then, they get bitter, they cling to guns or religion or antipathy to people who aren't like them..." For this, he was assailed by both the Clinton camp and also Republicans for being elitist, condescending, and someone who didn't understand or respect their traditional values. It also helped that Clinton had already created a narrative in recent weeks that she now captured the momentum in the race and those remarks highlighted her claim that he was out of touch and wouldn't be able to carry the key swings states in November. Without question, it would expose him in the fall campaign to those criticisms since the Republicans would make sure that the issue wasn't forgotten.

When the seven weeks were finally over, outside of the 20 million spent, enriching local television stations, just like 1980, not much had changed. Clinton's overwhelming 200,000 vote victory (55 percent), and carrying all but seven counties certainly allowed her to press on to later battles, but like Kennedy's victory in 1980, it also soon became evident that it was too little, too late for her to wrest away the nomination. However, it did give some hope to the Republicans for the fall. They reasoned that if John McCain could exploit those areas, both ideological and geographical, where Obama appeared vulnerable, it might actually give the GOP a chance to find a way back to winning back the Keystone State.

However, any hope that McCain had to carry Pennsylvania and the nation, for that matter, largely vanished when the country experienced its' severest economic collapse since the Great Depression. Triggered by bankruptcy of the Lehman Brothers investment firm on September 13th, the largest such filing in US history, a Wall Street meltdown of almost unimaginable proportion would further sink the GOP brand which had been in decline for the last several years due to the unpopularity of the Bush Administration.

Politically, the economic implosion gave those Democrats who had supported Hillary Clinton in the primary, but may have given pause to voting for Obama, a reason to come home. Whatever cultural differences that they may have had were trumped by the economic consequences the nation faced. Even McCain's repeated charge linking Obama with Reverend Wright, and also William Ayres, a leader of the 1960s radical group, the Weather Underground, whom he had an association with going back to his years in Chicago, couldn't change the dynamic.

McCain and the Republicans, however, never gave up on the state. In fact, they decided to double down, sensing that their fortunes were fading in traditionally red states such as North Carolina and Virginia. After pulling out of historically blue states such as Michigan, they even poured more resources into the state. The Republicans ultimately spent well over $21 million in Pennsylvania, a few million less than the Democrats, trying to appeal to the state's voters, older and whiter than the national average and perhaps more receptive to the cultural cues they were promoting. Nevertheless, with the economy imperiled, more than enough of those key Reagan Democrats decided that the cultural issues were no longer paramount, and came back to their party.

Obama's 3.25 million votes still stand as the highest ever recorded by any candidate in the Commonwealth's history. With a plurality of 620,000 (55 percent), the newly elected president carried 19 counties. The Democratic surge in the southeast continued unabated, with Obama carrying each of the five counties, including Chester, where he became the first Democrat to do so since Lyndon Johnson in 1964. Overall, he took 58 percent of the two party share of the vote in the region. Even more tellingly, was how well he fared in what was previously "Clinton Country," the areas that his primary rival had done so well in, particularly the northeast. He swept the region, easily winning Lackawanna and Luzerne, two places he had been thrashed in the spring.

The Democrat even held his own in central Pennsylvania, holding McCain to 54 percent, which exactly matches the GOP registration total. The only area in which the Obama campaign underperformed was in the southwest, were he did have difficulty attracting more socially conservative Democrats. He only slightly carried the region with 51 percent, 15 points shy of the Democratic registration total, and except for a few hundred vote plurality in Fayette County, that accounted for the margin he built up in Allegheny, the only other one in the southwest that he carried. Here is where the McCain strategy can be seen and why they decided to devote such resources to the state. Had other areas they targeted similarly produced, he certainly could have been much more competitive.

After the amount of resources the GOP poured into Pennsylvania in 2008 only to come up empty for the fifth straight time, going forward the party would need to reflect on whether this state was truly worth the investment anymore.

2012: OBAMA/ROMNEY

The question of whether Pennsylvania remained a presidential battleground state was answered four years later when the Republican nominee, former Massachusetts Governor Mitt Romney, essentially abandoned the idea of competing in Pennsylvania. The days of the state being a true battleground appeared to have passed. As a comparison, after Labor Day Romney visited the states of Ohio, Florida, and Virginia, 21, 18, and 10 times, respectively in non-fundraising events. In contrast, his visits in Pennsylvania were relegated to a September 28th event, at the Valley Forge Military Academy and College, in Wayne, Delaware County (plus a stop at Philadelphia's Union League for a fundraiser later in the day), and a November 4th rally at Shady Brook Farms, Morrisville, Bucks County, and one final push on the day of the election at a Pittsburgh campaign office on his way to a stop at the Pittsburgh International Airport.

The hugely successful event in Morrisville was one that some within the party would later look to as proof that the Republican candidate should have expended more time and effort into taking Pennsylvania's 20 electoral college votes. Sensing that the polls were closer than what they had expected, the rally itself was scheduled at this last minute and turned out to be one of the highlights of the Romney campaign. Braving cold and blustery conditions, with a temperature near freezing, a widely enthusiastic crowd estimated at over 25,000 came to hear Romney. It was a stirring event, with great visuals that were ready-make for television. Glowing reports on the evening news skyrocketed GOP confidence levels throughout the state. This was backed up by a decision by the Romney campaign to spend over $2 million dollars and GOP allied groups over $9 million in television advertising in the state for the final week.

The response of the Obama campaign was that this was nothing more than an expensive bluff that with all of the advertising time already locked up in the more competitive states, they simply had to spend their money somewhere. It should be noted that the Democrats did deem it was important enough to send their top surrogate, former President Bill Clinton to make a visit to Scranton, the hometown of Vice President Joe Biden on the day before the election.

However, despite the optimism spurred by the Bucks County rally, the Republicans would fall short once again in Pennsylvania, losing their sixth straight contest. While President Obama's overall 300,000 vote victory was roughly half of what he achieved four years earlier, it did enable him to carry the state relatively comfortably by five percentage points. The political structure of the state now clearly appears settled, as despite what GOP supporters viewed as a highly vulnerable incumbent, Obama was still able to win a larger share of the vote than either Al Gore or John Kerry in previous elections. Also, in having a candidate who was viewed (like McCain) as a more moderate Republican, many in the GOP believed that their candidate would have broader appeal in those suburban households where their support has been declining.

Since Bill Clinton's victory in 1992, the deciding factor in presidential elections in this state has been the Philadelphia suburbs. Once a linchpin of the GOP coalition, Obama was able to carry it by 123,000 votes, winning each of the counties, except Chester, which he lost by a mere 500 votes. Delaware and Montgomery counties, which happen to be the most populous of these four suburban counties, also continue to be the most troublesome for the Republicans. In Delaware County, where the GOP still maintains a stranglehold locally which is only now beginning to loosen, Obama took an astonishing 61 percent. While in Montgomery, were the Democrats have now broken through at the local level to take control of the county government, the President's numbers, while dropping slightly from 2008, still registered 57 percent. Philadelphia, now a lost cause for the GOP, even saw Obama's number increase two percentage points since his previous election, climbing to 86 percent. It's not certain how much higher it can actually go, but 90 percent isn't that far off.

In the northeast, the Democrat's numbers dropped two percent overall, to 55 percent. Though its status as the state's political bellwether can now be questioned, this area does offer potential for the GOP, especially if they could improve their position in Lackawanna, Luzerne, and fast-growing Monroe County. Outside of a few counties, such as Erie, Centre and Dauphin counties, the latter two recently going Democrat, central Pennsylvania continues to remain a stalwart for the Republicans. While a large proportion of these 47 counties are sparsely populated, the accumulation of all of these votes should not be underestimated. President Obama's share declined by five points to 41 percent in his reelection, and that translated to an overall advantage of approximately 325,000 votes for Romney. Some of these counties, such as Lancaster and York, are also fast growing counties, which should only add to the GOP share in the future. Others, on the periphery of the west, such as Cambria or Indiana, at one time tilted Democratic, but now continue to move in the opposite direction.

That takes us to the last region, the southwest. When the timeline for this book started in 1950, it was clearly the base of the Democratic Party in Pennsylvania. Now, it represents the best hope for the GOP in their effort to retake control in the Commonwealth. In a sense, it is on the other side of the cultural coin from the southeast suburbs. While issues like abortion rights, gun control, and support for same-sex marriages have contributed to reversing the fortunes of the two major parties in the Philadelphia area, those same issues are driving a wedge through long held advantages that Democrats possessed in the southwest.

Mitt Romney's 51 percent in the southwest may have been a narrow edge, but it is also symbolically notable. With it, he became the first Republican Party candidate to carry this region since Richard Nixon did in his 1972 landslide victory over George McGovern. In fact, outside of Allegheny County, the President took a shellacking throughout the southwest, reaching a nadir of just 38 percent in Westmoreland County. Unfortunately for the GOP, despite their gains here, many of these counties are rather sparsely populated and, in fact, losing population. Even combined, they cannot possibly make up for the votes that the party is losing in the southeast.

That is, except for Allegheny. Still, by far the second largest county in the state, containing the second largest city, Pittsburgh, it holds out the best hope for a GOP revival. While President Obama's numbers did slightly decline here, it was only by one percent, not nearly enough to have any impact. Until the Republicans find a way to increase up their support in the Pittsburgh area so that it can match the realignment taking place throughout the rest of the southwest, their hopes are likely to end in disappointment.

In sum, it's now been 24 years since the Republican Party has carried Pennsylvania at the presidential level. This is a dramatic transformation of a state that went for Herbert Hoover over Franklin Roosevelt back in 1932, and where the GOP had been totally dominant since the end of the Civil War. For longtime Pennsylvania residents, this also means that by the time the next election rolls around in 2016, unless you are older than the age of 46, you would not have voted in an election in which the Republican presidential candidate carried the Commonwealth. As time unfolds, recollections of defeating Michael Dukakis will continue to appear even more as a distance memory.

BIBLIOGRAPHY

Baer, John M. 2012. *On the Front Lines of Pennsylvania Politics.* Charleston, SC. The History Press.

Beers, Paul M. 1980. *The Pennsylvania Sampler.* Harrisburg, PA: Stackpole Books.

Beers, Paul M. 1978. *Pennsylvania Politics Today and Yesterday, The Tolerable Accomodation.* University Park, PA: The Pennsylvania State University Press.

Bissinger, Buzz. 1997. *A Prayer for the City.* New York, NY: Random House.

Bumstead, Brad. 2013. *Keystone Corruption, A Pennsylvania Insider's View of a State Gone Wrong.* Philadelphia, PA: Camino Books.

Carocci, Vincent P. 2005. *A Capitol Journey: Reflections on the Press, Politics, and the Making of Public Policy in Pennsylvania.* University Park, PA: The Pennsylvania State University Press.

Commonwealth of Pennsylvania. *The Pennsylvania Manual,* Volumes 90-116. Harrisburg, PA: Department of General Services.

Ferguson, John H. 1969. "History." In *Toward Tomorrow's Legislature.* Report of Commission on Legislative Modernization. Harrisburg, PA: General Assembly.

Greenawalt, II, Charles E., and G. Terry Madonna. 1992. "The Pennsylvania General Assembly-The House of Ill Repute Revisited." In Eugene W. Hickok, Jr., ed., *The Reform of State Legislatures and the Changing Character of Representation.* Lanham, MD: University Press of America.

Greenstein, Fred I, and Raymond E. Wolfinger. 1959. "The Suburbs and Shifting Party Loyalties," in Public Opinion Quarterly 22: 80-82.

Harrigan, John J. 1989. *Political Change in the Metropolis.* Fourth Edition. Glenview, IL: Scott, Foresman and Company.

Hazlett, Jr., Theodore L. 1969. "The Legislature in Perspective." In *Toward Tomorrow's Legislature.* Report of Commission on Legislative Modernization. Harrisburg, PA: General Assembly.

Kantor, Paul, with Stephen David. 1988. *The Dependent City.* Glenview, IL: Scott, Foresman and Company.

King, Michael R., and Michael E. Cassidy. 1992. The Pennsylvania Legislature. Unpublished manuscript.

Kraus, Scott. *Email Interview.* 23 May 2014.

Lamis, Renee M. 2009. The Realignment of Pennsylvania Politics Since 1960. University Park, PA: The Pennsylvania State University Press.

Mollenkopf, John H. 1983. *The Contested City.* Princeton, NJ: Princeton University Press.

Smith, Reed. 1964. *State Government in Transition: Reforms of the Leader Administration, 1955-59.* Philadelphia, PA: University of Pennsylvania Press.

Speel. Robert W. *Changing Patterns of Voting in the Northern United States.* University Park, PA: The Pennsylvania State University Press.

Sorauf, Frank J. 1963. *Party and Representation.* New York, NY: Atherton Press.

Temple University, University of Pittsburgh, The Pennsylvania State University. 1989. *Atlas of Pennsylvania.* Philadelphia, PA: Temple University Press.

Treadway, Jack. 2005. *Elections in Pennsylvania.* University Park, PA: The Pennsylvania State University Press.

Weber, Michael. 1988. *Don't Call Me Boss David Lawrence, Pittsburgh's Renaissance Mayor.* Pittsburgh, PA: University of Pittsburgh Press.

Wise, Sidney. *The Legislative Process in Pennsylvania.* Second Edition. Harrisburg, PA: Commonwealth of Pennsylvania, 1984.

Wood, Robert C. 1958. *Suburbia: Its People and Their Politics.* Boston, MA: Houghton Mifflin.

Woshinsky, Oliver H. 1995. *Culture and Politics: An Introduction to Mass and Elite Political Behavior.* Englewood, NJ: Prentice-Hall, Inc.

INDEX